THE LIMITS OF
COERCIVE DIPLOMACY
Laos, Cuba, Vietnam

THE LIMITS OF
COERCIVE DIPLOMACY
Laos, Cuba, Vietnam

Alexander L. George *Stanford University*

David K. Hall *Stanford University*

William E. Simons *Colonel, USAF*

LITTLE, BROWN AND COMPANY *Boston*

FIRST PRINTING

Published simultaneously in Canada by
Little, Brown & Company (Canada) Limited

PRINTED IN THE UNITED STATES OF AMERICA

PREFACE

This book emerges from a new research program on "Theory and Practice in International Relations," which is under the direction of Alexander George at Stanford University. The objective of the research program is to examine fundamental problems in international relations in a way that will contribute both to better foreign policy-making and to the development of international relations theory. To achieve both purposes requires us to bridge the gap between the perspectives of the academically oriented investigator and those of the policy-maker. This requires a special research approach which we outline in the Introduction and apply in our study of coercive diplomacy. The strategy of coercive diplomacy, of long-standing interest to both the policy-maker and the academic scholar, has been adequately understood by neither. We hope we have added new illumination to this subject by combining scholarly rigor and policy relevance in our study of it.

While each chapter of the book represents the effort and views of its individual author, we have read each other's drafts and have gained valuable ideas from the interchange. In addition, we want to express appreciation for the help and encouragement we have received from others. The senior author's interest in this topic began while he was a member of the Social Science Department of The RAND Corporation. He wishes to express his appreciation to Gabriel A. Almond, Bernard C. Cohen, and Stanley Hoffmann

v

for their reading of the manuscript and for their encouragement.

Helpful suggestions for clarifying the analytical structure and conclusions of the study, presented in Chapters One and Five, were given by Scott Flanagan, Ole R. Holsti, Robert Jervis, Richard Smoke, Raymond Tanter, and Robert G. Weinland.

The chapter on Laos was read by Michael V. Forrestal, Katherine P. Hall, Roger Hilsman, David Mozingo, James C. Thomson, Jr., Richard Smoke, Charles Stevenson, and Allen S. Whiting. The chapter on Cuba was read by Seyom Brown, Herbert S. Dinerstein, Thomas Ehrlich, Ole R. Holsti, Robert Jervis, Richard Smoke, Hans Speier, and Robert G. Weinland. The chapter on Vietnam was read by Alfred Goldberg, Melvin Gurtov, Hans Heymann, Konrad Kellen, David Mozingo, Frederick Sallagar, and William Stewart.

For financial support in preparing their contributions to this book Alexander George and David Hall express their appreciation to the Committee on International Studies at Stanford University. Colonel William Simons expresses his appreciation to The RAND Corporation for making possible his research and writing of the chapter on Vietnam. We are, of course, solely responsible for the views expressed in this book.

CONTENTS

3

Alexander L. George
THE CUBAN MISSILE CRISIS, 1962   86

I. The decision to try coercive diplomacy. II. Kennedy's view of the stakes. III. Choice of the blockade: its uses and limitations for coercive diplomacy. IV. The president's problem: signal determination without risking war. V. Negotiations: the importance of timing. VI. Implementation of the blockade. VII. From "try-and-see" to ultimatum. VIII. What if? IX. Lessons and conclusions.

4

William E. Simons
THE VIETNAM INTERVENTION, 1964–65   144

I. Background. II. The context for direct United States intervention. III. The nature and intent of direct United States intervention in Vietnam. IV. Conclusions.

5

Alexander L. George
COMPARISONS AND LESSONS   211

I. Laos and Vietnam. II. Preconditions for coercive diplomacy. III. Problems of operationalizing coercive diplomacy. IV. Other examples of American efforts to use force as an instrument of diplomacy. V. The limits of power and will.

INTRODUCTION*

I. THE NEED FOR POLICY-RELEVANT THEORY

The distinguished historian of the Renaissance, Jacob Burckhardt, once remarked that the true use of history is not to make men more clever for the next time but to make them wiser for ever. Following Burckhardt's advice in world politics has proven particularly difficult. Admittedly, it is not easy to learn from history, though almost every statesman and general has professed to have done so. In the first place, people often disagree on the lessons of a particular historical event. Second, even if they agree on the correct lessons, they often misapply these lessons to a new situation that differs from the past one in important respects. Clearly, attempting to draw lessons on an ad hoc basis from a single historical case is dangerous, and a more systematic way of stating lessons from a broad range of historical experience is needed. This is a challenging task for theory.

Developing a policy-relevant theory is one way in which scholarly research can contribute to better foreign policy making. But theory cannot absorb and transmit the "lessons" of history unless it employs a framework that identifies the many variables at play

* This Introduction draws upon an earlier paper by Alexander George presented at a conference on "Research on American Foreign Policy," sponsored by the Graduate School of International Studies and the Social Science Foundation, held in May 1968 at the University of Denver.

to indicate the possibilities for influencing the course of events in different types of situations. Progress in developing this kind of policy-relevant theory has lagged for several reasons. The most significant of these reasons is that this approach requires the investigator to draw upon the perspectives and special methods of both the historian and the political scientist. Such a synthesis is possible, but historians and political scientists have traditionally either disparaged its potential value or exaggerated its difficulty and have set various other barriers in its way.

This book demonstrates how such a synthesis can be achieved. The scope of the theory developed here is deliberately circumscribed and is confined to the use of coercive diplomacy. As noted in Chapter One, coercive diplomacy is one of several alternative strategies for employing force as an instrument of diplomacy.* Certainly, the difficulties of learning from history and the danger of misapplying its lessons are all too painfully evident in recent American efforts to make use of coercive diplomacy. The Cuban missile crisis was hardly over in late October 1962 when some members of the administration, including President Kennedy himself, cautioned against the temptation to generalize from its successful outcome. Commentators and scholars joined in warning that unique features of the Cuban case could not be expected to recur in many future situations. Their observations were frequently perceptive but did not constitute a comprehensive analysis of the conditions that had favored Kennedy's success or an adequate description of the strategy and tactics he had employed to capitalize upon these conditions. Yet, a clear statement along these lines was necessary in order to ensure that the lessons of the Cuban case were not improperly drawn and to safeguard against the danger than the formula that had worked in this case would be misapplied to a rather different new situation in the future.

The task of placing the success achieved in the Cuban missile crisis within a systematic theoretical framework was particularly important since some members of the administration and other observers were drawing a quite different, less sober set of lessons from the crisis. For them, Kennedy's success in forcing Khrushchev

---

* It would certainly be possible to construct a more general theory that would cover the entire domain of force and diplomacy. A broad theory of this kind, however, is likely to remain at a level of generality that would reduce its value for the formulation or evaluation of policy. To achieve greater policy relevance, theory must be differentiated and focussed on well-defined problems, strategies, and classes of international behavior.

to remove the missiles demonstrated the potentialities of a coercive strategy that had been all too seldom employed in defense of American interests throughout the world. The major lesson, as they saw it, was that the Cuban case showed that success in such international crises was largely a matter of national guts; if the president could convey resolution firmly and clearly, the opponent would back down in the face of superior American military capabilities. The failure to comprehend the special characteristics of the Cuban crisis may well have contributed, as some critics have charged, to the errors of policy planning and, even more so, of judgment that accompanied the Johnson administration's decision to use air power as a coercive instrument against North Vietnam in 1965.

This book provides the first systematic description of the ill-defined, elusive strategy of coercive diplomacy that Kennedy managed — but only with great difficulty — to apply successfully in the Cuban missile crisis and that boomeranged when Johnson attempted to use airpower to coerce Hanoi in 1965. Systematic comparison of these two cases and a third — Kennedy's handling of the Laos crisis of 1961 — enables us to formulate a theory regarding the uses and limitations of coercive diplomacy. We find that this strategy is a viable one only when a special set of conditions is present in the situation. But even when these "favoring" conditions are present, policy-makers will encounter difficult problems trying to tailor the strategy of coercive diplomacy to the specific configuration of the case at hand. These problems of "operationalizing" the strategy emerge in clear focus in the historical case studies.

II. THE RELATION OF THEORY TO ACTION

We have spoken of the need for policy-relevant theory and our effort to develop such a theory for coercive diplomacy. The prior questions, however, are whether such a theory is a feasible undertaking, how useful it would be to the policy-maker, and how we would expect him to use it. These are familiar questions in the long-standing discussion of the relation of theory to action. The answers to these questions are by no means self-evident; in fact, they generate considerable controversy. Misconceptions about "theory" often prevent better communication between scholars and policy-makers. Many of these misconceptions can be discovered in the sharply critical review that Richard Goodwin, a former policy adviser in the Kennedy and Johnson administrations, wrote about the book *Arms and Influence* (New Haven: Yale University Press, 1966), written by Thomas Schelling, a leading strategic theorist.*

Goodwin states that Schelling's book "raises troubling questions about the growing body of social-science literature devoted to military theory." Goodwin then asks, somewhat rhetorically, whether what Schelling calls " 'the diplomacy of violence' can be the subject of systematic theory." Goodwin answers this question negatively and marshals many familiar arguments to buttress his conclusion. He reminds us that history is *sui generis* and that to generalize from one historical crisis to another is dangerous and "almost guarantees error." To recognize this is not enough, Goodwin adds, for if the researcher wants to have a theory at all "he cannot escape the necessity of drawing general conclusions from particular episodes."

The task of developing valid generalizations is virtually insuperable, according to Goodwin, because "the variables in a moment of danger are so numerous that they elude analysis. . . . It is this fact that makes it necessary to qualify almost every assertion to the point where its value virtually disappears." In Goodwin's view, theory-building is also stymied because in almost every situation the decision-maker must act without knowing all the relevant facts and with even more uncertainty as to how other political actors perceive them. All these problems lead to a sober warning: "The most profound objection to this kind of strategic theory is not its limited usefulness but its danger, for it can lead us to believe we have an understanding of events and a control over their flow which we do not have."

Goodwin is wrong in concluding that a "systematic theory" is impossible; on the other hand, though overargued, most of his concerns are germane. Let us consider his objections in greater detail.

Goodwin misunderstands the nature of "systematic theory" as something that seeks, or ought to seek, to provide the decision-maker with detailed, high-confidence prescriptions for action in each contingency that may arise. If this is what is meant by a "systematic theory" on the subject of force and diplomacy, then indeed such a theory is not feasible.

* Goodwin's review appears in the *New Yorker*, February 17, 1968.

For Goodwin's rhetorical question as to whether a systematic theory is possible, we must substitute three different questions: (1) What is the relation of theory to action? (2) What kind of theory is most relevant for guiding the decision-maker? (3) How can *this* kind of theory be developed?

The last of these questions is the most relevant since there are a variety of ways to theorize about international relations, some of which are more relevant to policy than others. It is useful in this connection to regard the decision-maker himself as being an ad hoc intuitive theorist — just as he is also an intuitive statistician and an intuitive logician. We need to know more about how the decision-maker uses theory and what kinds of theory he needs for different purposes. We can make several observations regarding the use of theory:

1. A primary requirement for good policy-making is the ability to make discriminating diagnoses of specific situations. The decision-maker is interested in theories that will help him make such diagnoses. Many of the theories offered the decision-maker by political scientists, however, do not cover the major relevant variables critical to policy-making; as a result, these theories have relatively low diagnostic power *when applied to a single case.* This is partly due to the fact that in theory-building political scientists often do not attempt to develop a rich, sufficiently differentiated typology of situations.

2. It is often assumed that policy-makers do not make use of generalizations in diagnosing and prescribing. This view is mistaken. Indeed, one of the major tasks of policy-oriented scholars is to discourage the decision-maker from applying oversimplified or dangerously irrelevant generalizations for purposes of policy-making. It is not only academic researchers — mostly now of an earlier era — with a passion for correlating only two variables who can be charged with engaging in "crude empiricism." The policy-maker, too, is often a crude empiricist. He, too, can make highly dubious use of univariate propositions of the form: if A, then B — for example: "If appeasement, then World War III."

3. The decision-maker does not always operate as a crude empiricist. Rather, he "goes beyond" available generalizations to note, in addition, what is "special" about the case at hand. We need to study and learn more about what a person does when he "goes beyond" available generalizations in order to deal with a

single case. Evidently he is trying to assess other relevant variables — not included in the generalizations — and the possible interactions among these many variables in order to make a judgment about the present case that goes beyond a crude probabilistic treatment of it.

The methodology of historical explanation is relevant and instructive. As Patrick Gardiner has pointed out, the historian does indeed use generalizations in trying to explain a single case, but the fact that he does so often is obscured because the explanatory power of the generalizations he employs is weak and, therefore, he doesn't rely heavily on them. It is for this reason — the weak explanatory power of the generalizations — that Gardiner regards the historian's generalizations as being typically "loose" and "porous." Carl Hempel, like Gardiner, thinks that the historian's generalizations provide at best an "explanation sketch" which has to be "filled out." The process of "filling out" takes the form of dealing with and attempting a detailed reconstruction of the action-sequence or set of intervening events that lie between the two variables in the simple generalization that is available.* Perhaps what the historian does, therefore, can be usefully regarded, in the language of statistics, as an ad hoc effort at multivariate analysis of a single time series.

4. The historian's procedure of "filling out" his explanation of the single case is highly suggestive of what the decision-maker does when he "goes beyond" the available broad generalizations that are only loosely relevant for diagnosing and prescribing for a single case. In doing this, both the historian and the policy-maker employ additional theories and generalizations of a narrower and more particular character — for example, a theoretical model of how a *particular* political opponent behaves, rather than a theory that purports to describe how *all* political actors in world politics tend to behave. Therefore, for purposes of single-clase analysis and for policy-making, general theory must be supplemented with more particular theories. Political scientists interested in developing broad-gauged theory and generalizations are often not sufficiently interested in relating them systematically to lower-level theories and generalizations of narrower scope.

* See Patrick Gardiner, *The Nature of Historical Explanation* (London: Oxford University Press, 1952); and Carl G. Hempel, "The Function of General Laws in History," in H. Feigl and W. Sellars, eds., *Readings in Philosophical Analysis* (New York: Appleton-Century-Crofts, 1949).

5. It is true, as the historian never tires of reminding us, that history does not repeat itself and that each case possesses unique features. The usual rebuttal by the scientifically oriented political scientist is that, nonetheless, one can deal with unique cases by treating them as members of a "class" — the class being defined to encompass only some of the interesting features common to cases that are different in other respects. This approach to the study of historical cases helps, but it will not suffice. It is useful because the policy-maker is indeed interested — or should be — in knowing how the case with which he must deal is similar to past cases. But the policy-maker is also interested — or should be — in how the present case differs from past cases.

6. To develop a policy-oriented theory, therefore, we must take systematic account of at least some of the differences between otherwise similar cases — not all the differences but certainly those that are likely to be particularly relevant to policy. We must supplement the usual conception of theory-building as an enterprise that aims to produce broad-spanning generalizations with more attention to developing a differentiated theory that attempts to account for the *policy-relevant variation among particular cases.* (This approach to theory-building characterizes our analysis of the case studies of coercive diplomacy in this book.) It is useful to recognize that the sophisticated policy-maker tries in his own way to become an expert at ad hoc multivariate analysis. That is, he is interested in all the things he can do to increase the probability of a desired outcome and to reduce and control the probability of a distasteful outcome.

Sophisticated policy-makers are often explicit about their need for information about the critical variables in a situation and go at least halfway to meet the academic theorist. Dean Acheson, for example, advanced a theory of the "missing component" in describing how he adapted the problem-solving approach to policy-making. Acheson believed that many problems can be solved provided the statesman discovers the "missing component," the introduction of which would make a difficult situation manageable. The art of finding the "missing component" lies in mastering a knowledge of all the present and potential elements in a situation and determining what new increment, if added by United States policy, would make a critical difference in making the difficult situation more manageable. Acheson tried to apply his theory of the "missing component" to the perennial question of whether to give economic and military aid to underdeveloped countries. He recommended against it in those instances in which United States aid could not provide the local governments in question with the other necessary elements they lacked; namely, the loyalty of their people and honest and efficient administration.*

What, then, can we conclude regarding the kind of theory that is likely to be particularly useful for policy-making? A "rich" theory — one that tries to encompass many policy-relevant variables — is better than a simpler theory of narrow scope — i.e. one that encompasses fewer variables. A "rich" theory is preferable even though it is likely to have been subjected to fewer rigorous assessments than a simpler theory. There is a tradeoff here between the richness-complexity of theories on the one hand and their level of verification on the other. Because scholars and policy-makers have different interests and priorities, they are likely to resolve this tradeoff question somewhat differently. The policy-maker, who has to deal with any one of a number of different contingencies to which a theory is relevant, gets more help from a "rich" theory even though it enjoys only modest verification than from a simple theory that establishes a linkage between a few variables in many cases.†

A "rich" theory that embraces policy-relevant variables is useful to the policy-maker with two caveats: its contents must be at least plausible, and it must contain indications of the special conditions under which its propositions are likely to be true or false. Such a theory is useful to the policy-maker for reducing the gap between theory and action. But the policy-maker must "go beyond" available theory in any case in order to diagnose and deal with the specific case at hand. (That a simple theory enjoys relatively good verification does not relieve the policy-maker of this necessity.)

---

* David S. McLellan, "Comparative 'Operational Codes' of Recent U.S. Secretaries of State: Dean Acheson," paper delivered to American Political Science Association, September 1969, pp. 18, 28. Professor McLellan's paper will be published in a forthcoming book on comparative operational codes of political leaders, which I am editing.

† A different kind of question may be raised about a certain kind of mathematically oriented theory in which the independent variables are constructs of the mathematical model and, as such, do not explain the *process* by means of which the outcome of the dependent variable is produced. While often useful for prediction, such theories are of limited utility to the policy-maker insofar as they do not deal with those independent variables over which he can exercise some control.

Thus, in any case, the policy-maker must apply available theory in the light of his detailed, though imperfect, knowledge of the case at hand. This is what we mean when we say that in order to diagnose and deal with a specific situation the policy-maker engages in creative problem-solving — he does so, that is, to the extent that he recognizes and attempts to cope with what is novel and different about the present situation. ("Routine" decision-making is, of course, a different matter in that it consists of selecting one of a given number of standardized response patterns from an existing repertoire.) This discussion of "rich" and "simple" theories, of course, does not imply that they are mutually exclusive or that we must settle for one or the other.

Theory-building that attempts to encompass the variables that are of concern to the policy-maker will reduce the gap between theory and action. But it cannot eliminate the gap. No matter how policy-oriented theory becomes, an irreducible gap will remain between what theory offers and what the decision-maker must consider in deciding what action to take. The role of judgment in decision-making is crucial. Some years ago George Ball, then undersecretary of state, offered a useful reminder of its importance in describing the complexity of the problem that had faced policy-makers during the Cuban missile crisis:

> We were presented, therefore, with an equation of compound variables and multiple unknowns. No one has yet devised a computer that will digest such raw data as was available to us and promptly print out a recommended course of action.*

We conclude, therefore, that efforts to produce theory that is more policy-relevant need to be supplemented with analytical studies of the role of judgment and the nature of different kinds of judgment. By careful observation, we may be able to "decompose" complex judgments and diagnose their ingredients and perhaps begin to say something useful by identifying the conditions, procedures, and analytical devices that favor better performance in this respect. This, of course, is another way that scholarly research can contribute to better foreign policy-making. Studies

* George Ball, "Lawyers and Diplomats," address before the New York Lawyers' Association, New York City, December 13, 1962; reprinted in Department of State, *Bulletin*, December 31, 1962, pp. 987–991.

of organizations can identify structures and processes that enable policy-makers to make better use of available knowledge and theory and, going beyond that, to exercise better judgment in making difficult decisions.*

* See, for example, the discussion of organizational "pathologies" in Harold L. Wilensky, *Organizational Intelligence* (New York: Basic Books, 1967); Keith C. Clark and Laurence J. Legere, eds., *The President and the Management of National Security* (New York: Praeger, 1969); Thomas E. Cronin and Sanford D. Greenberg, eds., *The Presidential Advisory System* (New York: Harper & Row, 1969); Raymond A. Bauer and Kenneth J. Gergen, eds., *The Study of Policy Formation* (New York: Free Press, 1968); Austin Ranney, ed., *Political Science and Public Policy* (Chicago: Markham, 1968).

THE LIMITS OF
COERCIVE DIPLOMACY
Laos, Cuba, Vietnam

I

Alexander L. George
THE DEVELOPMENT OF DOCTRINE AND STRATEGY

I. PRESIDENTIAL CONTROL OF FORCE

The Korean War, which broke out in late June 1950, was the first major American experience with limited warfare under modern conditions. Until this time the predominant American view regarding the role of force in international relations had been hostile to the idea of limiting the use of available force once a conflict was joined. Rather, conditioned by World Wars I and II, many Americans viewed war, when it was justified or became necessary, as a moral crusade against an aggressor. There was little room in such an image of war for limiting one's objectives or limiting the means one employed to achieve them. Americans regarded war and peace as two separate and distinct states and, therefore, thinking in terms of Clausewitz's dictum that war was a continuation of policy by other means was not congenial.

This traditional American view of war had other implications and consequences that are of particular relevance to the present discussion of presidential control of force. The image of war as a moral crusade encouraged the belief that when war broke out military factors and military judgment should have great weight,

1

if indeed not dominate, in shaping policies for the conduct of the war.

It is not surprising, therefore, that President Truman should have faced unexpected and novel problems in Korea when he attempted to use force on behalf of limited objectives and to do so in ways that did not risk transforming that conflict into a much bigger war. In this respect the Korean situation differed from the situation when the United States became a combatant in World War II, for little possibility remained at that point in the war of further major escalation. In Korea, the potential for escalation was substantial and was necessarily a dominant policy consideration. Moreover, the danger of escalation affected not only the United States, but allies and neutrals as well. Therefore, in attempting to deal with the Korean conflict the president and his national security advisers were caught in a morass of domestic and international political considerations to a far greater extent than in World War II. Not only strategic decisions affecting the war in Korea but occasionally tactical operations as well were caught up in the conflict between the local military commander's judgment of what was required and Washington's desire to limit the risks of a major enlargement of the war. As a result the necessity emerged for a form of detailed control over military operations from Washington that went considerably beyond the traditional wartime relationship between the civilian heads of government and a theatre commander. The ensuing conflicts culminated dramatically in April 1951 when President Truman relieved General MacArthur of his command. Reviewing quickly some of these events and their consequences might be useful.[1]

At a time when Chinese intervention in the Korean War was still a hypothetical possibility, Truman delegated to MacArthur a degree of control over military operations that proved to be incompatible with the imperfectly understood requirement for detailed presidential control. In early October 1950, the United States, backed by the United Nations, adopted the aim of unifying Korea and authorized MacArthur to pursue the defeated North Korean forces into North Korea. Truman approved new directives to MacArthur that gave him far-reaching discretion:

> Hereafter in the event of open or covert employment anywhere in Korea of major Chinese Communist units, without prior announcement, you should continue the action as long

as, *in your judgment*, action by your forces now under your control offers a reasonable chance of success.[2]

Thus, as Neustadt points out, the definition of a "reasonable chance of success" was delegated to the judgment of MacArthur. "In the weeks to come he would misjudge with tragic consequences, but it cannot be charged that he exceeded his instructions. . . . The discretion given to MacArthur in October contributed directly to disaster in November." [3]

By the end of October and early in November the Chinese Communists had entered North Korea with substantial forces and had engaged United Nations forces in sharp tactical combat. Truman was now confronted with the need to reestablish direct presidential control over the risks of the new situation. But he could do so only by taking back the discretionary power he had earlier delegated to MacArthur for it soon became clear that the General could not be persuaded to see the new development in the war through the more cautious eyes of the administration. Truman's failure to recognize this dilemma and to change MacArthur's directives resulted in a severe maldeployment of MacArthur's forces which, in turn, substantially increased their vulnerability to the Chinese forces when they struck in full force in late November. Thus, in mid-November 1950, taking full advantage of his broad directives, MacArthur undertook the questionable strategy of marching to the Yalu in the face of evidence that large Chinese Communist forces had entered the war. A more prudent course of action was *suggested* to him by Washington but he was free under the existing directive to use his own judgment. On November 25 the Chinese command unleashed its all-out offensive that sent United States forces reeling. A military catastrophe was barely averted by the longest retreat in American military history.

Truman incurred this disaster as a result of following the traditional presidential practice of giving the theatre commander a broad delegation of control over military operations within the framework of directives specifying objectives, missions, and forces. Truman's viewpoint and rationale for doing so was expressed some years later:

> We knew the Chinese had close to a million men on the border and all that. . . . But [MacArthur] was commander in the field. You pick your man, you've got to back him up. That's the only way a military organization can work. I got

> the best advice I could and the man on the spot said this
> was the thing to do. . . . So I agreed. That was my deci-
> sion—no matter what hindsight shows.[4]

Truman's retrospective justification of his error notwithstanding, at the time he had drawn the proper lessons from his failure to exert closer control over MacArthur, and he was prompt in applying those lessons. For the remainder of the Korean War Truman monitored military operations closely and exerted a new measure of control over the strategy and tactics the theatre commander was allowed to employ.

Indeed, the Korean War taught not only Truman but all succeeding administrations as well that the president's responsibility does not stop with establishing the objectives to be pursued in a conflict; he must also *maintain firm control over the level of costs and risks that are acceptable* in pursuing those objectives. To exert control over costs and risks requires that the president be willing to control military strategy and tactics. Moreover, the responsibility for keeping the costs and risks of a military conflict at an acceptable level is exclusively the president's. He must not delegate it to the theatre commander, as Truman did in effect when he left it up to MacArthur to judge how best to react in case the Chinese Communists intervened.

In contrast to the practice in some other armies, United States theatre commanders had always been given considerable freedom to decide on tactical operations in the field. As a result, the traditional viewpoint of the theatre commander was that once he was allocated his forces he should be allowed to use them in those ways which his professional military judgment indicated were likely to be most effective. Accordingly, when civilian heads of government or his military superiors in Washington imposed constraints on his conduct of military operations in the name of political considerations, the theatre military commander was likely to regard them as undue "interference," especially if they made accomplishment of his mission more difficult and costly.

Much has changed since the events and controversies of the Korean War. Traditional practices and attitudes have been considerably modified. Both civilian and military leaders have understood that the president must retain control over all decisions and developments affecting the nature, scope, and termination of limited conflicts. At the same time, however, the president is not all-powerful and seldom imposes a decision arbitrarily. Military leaders have a strong advocate's role in determining policies, and once a diplomatic crisis erupts into warfare their bargaining position within the policy-making arena becomes even stronger. As a result, even though the president retains control over critical decisions of strategy and tactics, he may feel obliged to negotiate and bargain with his military advisers before making these decisions. In any case, the president's retention of close control of military operations does not by itself guarantee either success in limited war or control over its potential for escalation. Critical in this respect are the strategic concepts on behalf of which the president exerts his control of military forces and, hence, the need to understand better the nature of strategies such as coercive diplomacy.

Moreover, the problem remains of understanding the implications of the acknowledged requirement of presidential control for the composition of military forces, military strategy, and crisis management. Since the Kennedy administration gave particular attention to these three problems, we shall turn now to some of the new concepts and doctrines it introduced into defense planning.

II. KENNEDY'S DOCTRINE OF FLEXIBLE, CONTROLLED RESPONSE

Interest in controlled use of force and in what we shall call "coercive diplomacy" was heightened with Kennedy's accession to the presidency. Many of the Kennedy administration's new defense concepts and priorities stemmed from the vigorous criticism which the Eisenhower administration's doctrine of "massive retaliation" had received in preceding years. When John Foster Dulles announced massive retaliation as the administration's policy in January 1954, he seemed to imply that the United States would respond to any low-level aggression with a strategic nuclear attack against the homeland of the aggressor — i.e., Soviet Russia or Communist China. The possibility that the United States might convert any local war into a general war alarmed responsible United States and Allied opinion, and this in turn led Dulles into a series of efforts to clarify his meaning in a more specific and moderate direction. He was not entirely successful in this respect, and indeed could not afford to be. For massive retaliation was primarily a declaratory policy intended to deter various kinds of possible aggressions against members of the free world. In effect, Dulles was using the slogan massive retaliation in an attempt to generalize and apply more widely the threat to expand the war that he had directed at Communist China following the conclusion of the Korean cease-fire in 1953 in order to warn it against resumption of that war.

Dulles believed that a frequent cause of past wars, including both world wars, had been miscalculation by an aggressor power of the conditions under which the war would be fought. Accordingly, Dulles chose the threat of massive retaliation as a means of warning any would-be aggressor that the United States would not necessarily allow him the choice of conditions. Rather, as Dulles put it, the United States would respond "at places and with means of its own choosing."

Massive retaliation, therefore, threatened substantial escalation of any conflict imposed on the United States or its allies. Beyond that, however, the declaratory policy was deliberately vague, presumably, in part at least, to take advantage of the element of uncertainty it attempted to introduce into the aggressor's calculations.

Dulles and other members of the administration made threats of massive retaliation during several crises, particularly in Asian conflicts such as the Dien Bien Phu crisis of 1954 in Indochina. But, in fact, a striking divergence occurred between the slogan of massive retaliation and the Eisenhower administration's actual behavior in dealing with challenges in Third World areas. As one observer has said, when "war threatened over Indochina, Lebanon, the offshore islands of Quemoy and Matsu, and Berlin, the [Eisenhower] Administration either refrained from action or desperately sought the conventional forces with which to manage the situation." [5] As a matter of fact, although adherents of Kennedy's defense doctrine rarely acknowledged it, the prudent practice of the Eisenhower administration in dealing with crises was entirely consonant with what came to be called "flexible, controlled response" by the new administration.

The Kennedy administration's interest in controlled use of force sprang as well from other elements of the critique of massive retaliation advanced by defense intellectuals and by members of the opposition party during the Eisenhower era.[6] Massive retaliation and its cornerstone, United States strategic superiority, they pointed out, had not prevented the occurrence of many limited conflicts. Deterrence had failed and would fail again in the future because the threat of "massive retaliation" (i.e., a strategic nuclear response against the homeland of the aggressor) was simply not a credible response to low-level aggression, particularly when Soviet forces were not involved. Massive retaliation would become even less credible in the future as the strategic superiority on which it rested gradually declined as the Soviet Union acquired larger strategic forces of its own. Sooner or later, United States strategic superiority would be replaced by strategic parity with the Soviet Union. Then a state of mutual deterrence would emerge between the United States and the Soviet Union on the strategic level which, critics of Eisenhower's defense policies predicted, would render United States allies much more vulnerable to Communist encroachments. Moreover, for various reasons the United States could not rely on tactical use of nuclear weapons in local conflicts as a substitute for its declining strategic superiority. The Soviet Union, too, was acquiring nuclear weapons for tactical use; hence the possibility arose of a two-sided tactical use of nuclear weapons, carrying with it the danger of uncontrollable escalation. Therefore, most critics of massive retaliation concluded that to deter and deal with lower-level threats to the security of free world allies, the United States would need much stronger, conventional, limited war forces.

For all these reasons the major thrust of Kennedy's defense policies was the acquisition of a fuller array of military capabilities that would permit the development of a larger, more diversified set of military options along the entire spectrum of violence. This was expected to open the way for many more discriminating and effective uses of limited force on behalf of a variety of foreign policy objectives. This expectation has not been fully realized, however, for reasons that deserve careful analysis.

In his "Special Message on the Defense Budget," submitted to Congress on March 28, 1961, Kennedy asserted that a new doctrine of flexible, controlled response would guide his administration's defense policies. Response to attacks against any part of the free world, he said, would be "suitable, selective" as well as "swift and effective." The president also stated some general guidelines for the design and use of military force: "Our weapons systems must be *usable* in a manner permitting *deliberation* and *discrimination* as to timing, scope and targets *in response to civilian authority*." (Italics added.)

8   ALEXANDER L. GEORGE

Kennedy's statement on this occasion foreshadowed many of the criteria applied later in formulating and evaluating military options for possible use in international crises. Plans for the use of military capabilities that did not meet the complex criteria implied in these general guidelines, as we shall see, would prove to be less acceptable to the president, particularly at the critical opening stages of a crisis. The Kennedy administration was attempting to develop a concept of force that would enable it to be employed as a highly refined instrument of diplomacy. Force and threats of force would unfortunately continue to be necessary even in the dangerous world of nuclear weapons; therefore, the administration gave greater emphasis than ever before to ensuring controlled, discriminating use of force. What gradually emerged from this conception during the Kennedy years was a set of principles for the careful management of military-diplomatic crises. It is to this aspect of the doctrine of flexible, controlled response that we now turn.

III. PRINCIPLES OF CRISIS MANAGEMENT

The task of adapting military capabilities to presidential use in limited, controlled crises can be highlighted by drawing a distinction between gross military capabilities and usable options. There can be a substantial difference between gross military capabilities to attack and destroy military targets — capabilities that may be plentiful and readily available — and usable options which, as the quotation from Kennedy's special message suggested, are military capabilities the president is willing to use in a crisis only if they accomplish his whole purpose, diplomatic as well as military, the way *he* thinks appropriate and necessary. From this standpoint, military capabilities do not necessarily provide usable options for the president; they are, rather, the ingredients from which planners must develop usable options of a more refined, discriminating character, if possible.

Military capabilities must meet several special political-military requirements in order to constitute usable options in controlled crises. More than any preceding crisis, the Cuban missile case forced leading members of the Kennedy administration to determine what their general doctrine of controlled, flexible response meant in terms of specific design criteria for formulating usable options for the president out of the ample gross military capabilities available in the United States arsenal.

From the available accounts of the Cuban missile crisis we can identify as many as seven criteria that were evidently in the minds of Kennedy and his advisers when they were comparing and evaluating various possible military options. Some of these criteria can be detected also in the planning that entered into Kennedy's handling of the intricate Laos situation in 1961 and Johnson's use of air power against North Vietnam in 1965, although they were not all systematically articulated by policy-makers and planners at the time. These criteria or requirements for controlled, measured use of force and effective crisis management are interrelated but are listed separately here:

1. *Presidential control of military options:* The president must authorize each military option in an unfolding sequence of events. Moreover, he or those to whom he delegates his authority — when he feels he can do so — must be able to monitor the developing crisis very closely so that they can modify political and military plans and improvise new, appropriate actions as needed.

2. *Pauses in military operations:* The momentum of events must be slowed down. Military options must be devised and selected that lend themselves to this requirement; military action must be programmed in such ways as to create significant pauses in the momentum of military operations. Time must be provided for the opponent at each point to assess the actions already taken, to receive and reflect upon the signals and proposals addressed to him, and to decide whether he will call a halt or open up negotiations. Furthermore, the opponent must be given an opportunity to do this without being subjected to too much "noise" from other, seemingly contradictory signals and actions which are coming to his attention, whether or not they are intended for him. To this end the president and his advisors must control and eliminate actions and statements that might give confusing signals regarding his demands and offers, and how he proposes to act if the opponent rejects them.

3. *Clear and appropriate demonstrations:* Military options must provide a clear and appropriate demonstration of the president's resolution and of his crisis objectives. Military and other actions taken should together constitute a consistent signal. None of the

actions taken, or not taken, should be capable of being interpreted by the opponent as being at variance with the specific demand the president has made on him. That is, they should not suggest that the president is really seeking objectives more ambitious than those he has proclaimed or that he will really settle for much less.[7]

4. *Military action coordinated with political-diplomatic action:* Military and political-diplomatic actions must be closely coordinated. Military actions should be coupled with — that is, preceded, accompanied, or followed by — those political and diplomatic actions, communications, consultations, and proposals that are an essential part of the overall strategy for persuading the opponent to alter his policy and behavior in the desired direction. In order to satisfy this requirement the president needs military options that, as we have already noted, are discrete, separable, and under his personal control.

5. *Confidence in the effectiveness and discriminating character of military options:* The president also must use military options that will be militarily effective in accomplishing their specific tactical objective. From the president's standpoint, moreover, it is often preferable that tactical objectives be accomplished with relatively small increments of force and with weapon systems that operate against assigned targets accurately and with low collateral damage to surrounding areas. Otherwise the attempt to convey a clear and appropriate demonstration of resolution and of objectives may backfire, either by demonstrating military ineffectiveness or by damaging the wrong targets. It is perhaps unnecessary to add that carrying out military measures that are *both* effective *and* discriminating is difficult and may not always be regarded as essential for crisis management.

6. *Military options that avoid motivating the opponent to escalate:* In addition to satisfying the other criteria noted, the military options needed for crisis management must not confront the opponent with an urgent requirement to escalate the conflict himself in order to avoid or compensate for the military or political damage inflicted upon him. A demonstrative use of force may be self-defeating if it punishes the opponent to the extent that it requires an immediate strong military reaction on his part. Since it is difficult to avoid altogether motivating the opponent to escalate, crisis management also requires the ability to deter him from engaging in the more dangerous forms of escalation.

7. *Avoidance of impression of resort to large-scale warfare:*
Finally, the president requires military options that can be employed without giving the opponent the impression that large-scale warfare is being initiated. For this would indicate to him that the president is abandoning efforts to resolve the dispute by diplomatic means and is relying largely on a military strategy to achieve his objectives.

The importance of these criteria was recognized by Kennedy and Johnson and played an important role in their efforts to manage crises in Laos, Cuba, and Vietnam. These criteria were also relevant in some earlier crises, even though they were not always well understood and their importance not explicitly recognized by policy-makers. This lack of understanding emerges in a striking manner if we examine the ineptness of the Truman administration's handling of the threat of Chinese Communist intervention in the Korean War with the special hindsight that the more recent theory of crisis management affords.

In early November 1950 Truman's National Security Council recognized that, given the now unmistakable intervention of substantial Chinese Communist forces into the war, the task of accomplishing the war aim of unifying Korea by force of arms was no longer feasible without enlarging the conflict. Since the National Security Council opposed this, it recognized the necessity for negotiations with Peking in order to salvage as much as possible of the objective of a unified Korea. Reliance would no longer be placed on military force to accomplish the objective. Rather, more so than before, force and threats of force would have to become part of, and subordinate to, a new diplomatic strategy which had now to be quickly improvised. The war entered a new phase, therefore, in which the requirements of crisis management listed above would become more pertinent and more critical.

Discussions to explore a negotiated settlement were initiated at the United Nations, but for various reasons they were slow in getting under way. Obviously considerable time would be needed for the processes of diplomacy and negotiations to take hold. One of the principle requirements of crisis management in a situation of this kind is that the momentum of events on the battlefield be restrained, if necessary, to enable diplomatic communications to be exchanged and weighed — the second of the criteria listed above. Equally important, military actions must be closely coordinated with the diplomatic strategy being relied upon to secure the objective in question — the fourth criterion; and, further, any military actions taken should be consistent with the emphasis on a diplomatic approach for settling the conflict and should constitute signals to the opponent that are clearly consonant with the president's objectives and his search for a negotiated, compromise settlement — the third criterion. And, most certainly, military actions that confront the opponent with an urgent requirement to escalate the war should be avoided — the sixth criterion.

As it turned out, all of these four criteria for crisis management were in effect violated when Washington proved unable or unwilling to control MacArthur's actions in the interests of the new diplomatic strategy it was beginning to evolve. Negotiations would require time. The possibility that the other side might be interested had to be explored. The Chinese Communist forces broke contact with United States and South Korean forces after the sharp tactical engagements of late October and early November. Days and weeks passed without important battlefield contact being reestablished. Whether the Chinese leaders were merely implementing their guerrilla warfare doctrine of melting away following a military action or whether they were also waiting to see what political effects their military actions would have on United States and United Nations policies is one of the intriguing mysteries of the war. We cannot exclude the possibility that the Chinese were employing military force as an instrument of a political-diplomatic strategy and that they, at least, were adhering to the necessary principles of crisis management. The sharp military engagements they had inflicted on South Korean and American forces in North Korea had conveyed the message intended by the Chinese — namely that they had intervened with substantial forces and would and could fight — and had the desired shock effect on United States military and political leaders. Perhaps the Chinese disengaged their forces, deliberately creating a prolonged pause on the battlefield, in order to give time for their signal to be weighed by United States and United Nations policy-makers, and to see whether the demonstration of the Chinese intervention and willingness to fight would force a fundamental recalculation and modification of American war policy.

As we have noted, such a recalculation of United States policy and a shift in strategy toward a diplomatic solution was indeed set into motion in early November. But within a few weeks Mac-

Arthur was allowed to resume his march toward the Yalu with the proclaimed intention of ending the war.

If the administration thought that the diplomatic track it had set into motion at the United Nations required additional battlefield pressure on the Chinese, then Washington might indeed have authorized MacArthur to undertake appropriate military actions. But in this event, MacArthur's military moves would have had to have been carefully coordinated with and made to serve the new negotiating strategy being developed at home. But this was clearly not the rationale for MacArthur's resumption of the offensive. In fact, MacArthur was employing a different strategy; indeed, his march to the Yalu in mid-November was in pursuit of the original war aim of unifying Korea by force. MacArthur's offensive was not intended by either MacArthur or Washington to support the new strategy, recommended by the National Security Council on November 9, of relying on negotiations with the Chinese to salvage as much of the war objective as possible. The administration was aware of this discrepancy, but it allowed itself in the last analysis to follow an inconsistent course, wavering between the perceived necessity for pursuing a negotiated, compromise solution and the hope that MacArthur's gamble might work after all.

Both MacArthur's gamble and Washington's failure to coordinate his actions with the requirements of the new diplomatic strategy can be traced partly to their inability to perceive the significance of the Chinese Communist withdrawal from battlefield contact. As the days went by during November without any further significant contact with or sign of large-scale Chinese volunteers, apparently MacArthur and Washington both began to feel that the marked apprehension each had experienced in early November had been misplaced. Perhaps the Chinese Communists had now had second thoughts and were withdrawing from North Korea or could be induced to; or perhaps their actions indicated that their objectives in North Korea were quite limited. This miscalculation of Chinese motivation was reinforced in turn by a tendency to seriously underestimate Chinese military capabilities.

Thus, if the Chinese had disengaged in early November in order to give time for their intervention to bring about a possible change in United States war policy, they received an unmistakable answer when MacArthur was allowed to resume his march to the Yalu in mid-November. Under the circumstances, the Chinese could hardly be expected to credit earlier indications that Washington was interested in working out a compromise settlement. Whether or not Washington realized it, it had behaved in such a way as to confirm the Chinese Communist image of its insincerity and duplicity. The Chinese then launched their all-out offensive of November 25, beginning a long and bitter war. Whatever the opportunity had been for avoiding it earlier in November it was now irretrievably lost because of Washington's indeciveness, its wavering and inconsistent attitude toward the alternative military and diplomatic strategies before it, and its gross ineptness at crisis management. Instead of creating the time needed for developing its new diplomatic strategy by halting the momentum of action on the battlefield or, at least, ensuring that military actions would be consistent with its new strategy, the administration wavered in its adherence to the new diplomatic strategy and allowed Mac-Arthur to revert to the earlier military strategy for unifying Korea by force.

As this indicates, Truman's effort to apply novel crisis management principles was severely handicapped by his failure to define his objectives clearly and to relate them to a consistent strategy. But we should note, also, that the seven criteria for crisis management are indeed stringent requirements to impose on the use of military force. It is not easy to adapt military capabilities to meet these exacting criteria unless weapons systems possess flexible characteristics and planners are ingenious in contriving somewhat novel uses of existing forces. As a result, providing the president with many usable options that meet his special requirements for crisis management has often been difficult in past crises. Moreover, options that meet these criteria tend to be quickly used up in a prolonged crisis. A president who is determined to retain control will search for ways of subdividing his options into smaller, discrete steps. He jealously safeguards these options and uses them sparingly, spacing them out over a period of time in order not to reach the point at which the momentum of events and the lack of additional controllable options will defeat his efforts to maintain control of the conflict.

Also, efforts to impose the requirements of careful crisis management on the use of military force often exacerbate the latent tension between competing political and military considerations in limited warfare. Crisis management requires novel concepts of military planning, operations, and control that strain the experience, imagination, and patience of military professionals. The civilian's effort to transform military force into a highly refined, discriminating instrument suitable for effective management of crises eventually breaks down if pushed too far. The refinements of modern military technology can only moderate, not eliminate, the transformation of force into a crude, blunt instrument of coercion. The policy-maker must remember this when deciding whether and to what extent to involve himself and the nation in international crises.

IV. FOUR STRATEGIES FOR THE USE OF FORCE

We have pointed out that Kennedy's doctrine of flexible, controlled response relied upon crisis management and escalation control to make possible the use of limited force to achieve limited objectives. But flexible, controlled response offers no basis for gauging whether and to what extent the national interest is at stake in a particular crisis. In advancing this new doctrine in 1961 Kennedy was not clarifying the national interest or offering guidelines for applying this ambiguous criterion in crisis situations.* Rather, he was reasserting the basic principle, seemingly lost sight of in the preceding administration's rhetorical emphasis on massive retaliation, that force and threats of force should be tailored more closely to what is at stake in a crisis.

Thus, while crisis management is of undoubted importance for the conduct of foreign policy, the prior question of whether the national interest is sufficiently engaged in a particular situation to warrant some form of United States military intervention is always present. To be sure, before deciding upon intervention, policy-makers do attempt to determine the nature and magnitude of expected damage to United States national interests. Presumably they also attempt to judge the level of costs and risks that would be warranted in an effort to limit or prevent that expected damage. Judgments of this kind, however, are typically made in the face of multiple uncertainties, inadequate knowledge

---

* Many writers have discussed the ambiguity of the concept "national interest" and the difficulties of applying this criterion in policy-making or for explaining decisions. James N. Rosenau summarizes this problem and draws sober conclusions in his article, "National Interest," in the *International Encyclopedia of the Social Sciences* (New York: Macmillan, 1968), XI, pp. 34–40.

and information, and under the pressures of the situation. The requirements for a rational, well-calculated decision whether or not to intervene are indeed difficult to meet in practice. Not surprisingly, such decisions have a strong subjective element and may be influenced by doctrines and general beliefs that fill the vacuum left by the inability to make more refined calculations.

Belief in the virtues of flexible, controlled response and in the feasibility of crisis management possibly exercised a beguiling effect on attitudes toward intervention in the Kennedy and Johnson administrations. These beliefs — when coupled with the ample conventional military capabilities obtained by the Kennedy administration — may have encouraged initial involvements in conflicts that were not based on a sober calculation of whether what was at stake from the national standpoint really warranted accepting the risks of further involvement, should the initial attempt to deal with such conflicts by means of limited force and careful crisis management break down.

If "flexible, controlled response" and "crisis management" did not provide sufficient guidelines for answering the all-important question of whether the national interest was sufficiently at stake in a particular situation to warrant any form of American intervention, neither did these doctrines constitute a well-defined or complete strategy. Elements of strategy were implicit, to be sure, in their emphasis on the necessity for tailoring the use of force for achieving limited objectives and in the notion, however vague, that force was to be employed with constraint for coercive purposes. But these considerations do not add up to a theory of coercion, nor do they describe the strategy by means of which force and threats of force may be employed coercively. We must turn, therefore, to a brief discussion of alternative strategies — of which coercive diplomacy is one — for using force as an instrument of foreign policy. Traditionally force and threats of force have been used in several ways in order to influence the calculations and behavior of opponents in world politics. We can identify at least four general strategies.

1. The Quick, Decisive Military Strategy

The first of these approaches, traditionally favored by military strategists, attempts to alter an opponent's will by a quick, decisive use of force against him. This strategy calls for ample force to be applied promptly in an effort to destroy a significant portion of the opponent's military capability to contest what is at stake in the conflict. Accordingly, this strategy largely dispenses with threats, diplomacy, or subtle modes of persuasion to alter the opponent's policy. It relies, rather, on military force to provide a "war winning" strategy.

The quick, decisive strategy, however, can be and has been employed to achieve limited political objectives; it is not coterminous, that is, with unlimited war aims, total war, or unconditional surrender.* Nonetheless, if negotiations and bargaining do occur together with the employment of this strategy, they take place after the effort to apply force in the quick, decisive mode has been made, whether or not it achieved its military objectives.

On behalf of this strategy the familiar argument has been advanced that if ample force is used quickly and in a militarily efficient manner, i.e. unhobbled by too many political constraints, it offers the possibility of terminating the conflict before it spreads or develops into a prolonged war of attrition. For this reason, among others, this strategy is generally preferred by military leaders and, on occasion, by political leaders as well.

The strategy of quick, decisive use of force has been employed successfully, at least in the military sense of the word, on many occasions. Examples are by no means confined to Hitler's successful uses of blitzkrieg but include, more recently, the crushing of the Hungarian revolution in 1956 by massive Soviet forces and the Israeli war against Egypt and its Arab allies in 1967. But the "quick, decisive" strategy has also failed or back-fired — for example, the all-out North Korean effort to overrun South Korea in 1950 and the abortive Anglo-French-Israeli attack on Egypt in 1956.†

At the same time, on numerous occasions the political leaders of a country have been reluctant or unwilling to resort to the quick, decisive military option. If, nonetheless, they believe that

* Thus, in one significant variation of this strategy, force is employed to achieve a quick fait accompli seizure of territory before the opponent, or a protecting power on his behalf, can react effectively. The territory seized may be held permanently or used for bargaining purposes to secure concessions on other issues.

† Mention should also be made of an interesting variant of the quick, decisive strategy in which large forces are employed not to attack the military capabilities of the opponent but, by threatening them directly, to induce compliance or passivity. Examples of this kind of preemptive use of the quick, decisive strategy include the large-scale deployment of American forces into Lebanon in 1958 and into the Dominican Republic in 1965, and, of course, the sudden massive intervention of Soviet forces into Czechoslovakia in 1968.

the stake in a conflict is important enough to warrant resort to force or the risk of war, they will consider some alternative strategy.

2. Coercive Diplomacy

One such alternative strategy is what we shall refer to here as coercive diplomacy. This strategy has a number of variants; they are similar, however, because, in contrast to the traditional military strategy we have just discussed, the coercive strategy focusses upon affecting the enemy's will rather than upon negating his capabilities. It does not rely on ample or quick use of force to achieve political objectives. Rather, if threats alone do not suffice and force is actually used, it is employed in a more limited, selective manner than in the quick, decisive strategy. That is, force is used in an exemplary, demonstrative manner, in discrete and controlled increments, to induce the opponent to revise his calculations and agree to a mutually acceptable termination of the conflict. In this strategy force plays a modest, and often an inconspicuous, role. And, again unlike the traditional military strategy, force and threats of force may become part of a carrot and stick approach to the opponent. Hence, force is subordinated to what is essentially not a military strategy at all but rather a political-diplomatic strategy for resolving or reconciling a conflict of interests with the opponent. This is why coercive diplomacy is an apt way of describing the strategy.

The strategy of the coercive diplomacy, then, calls for using just enough force of an appropriate kind — if indeed one passes beyond threats of force — to demonstrate resolution to protect well-defined interests and also to demonstrate the credibility of one's determination to use more force if necessary. To this end, the employment of force is coupled with — i.e. preceded, accompanied, or followed by — appropriate communications to the opponent. The coercive strategy, therefore, has a signalling, bargaining, negotiating character that is built into the conceptualization and conduct of military operations, a feature that is absent in the traditional military strategy.

Coercive diplomacy seeks to make force a much more flexible, refined, psychological instrument of policy; in contrast, the quick, decisive strategy uses force as a blunt, crude instrument of policy. Coercive diplomacy seeks to persuade the opponent to do something, or to stop doing something, instead of bludgeoning him into doing it, or physically preventing him from doing it.

For several reasons a state would prefer to employ coercion rather than a purely military approach for achieving a resolution of limited conflicts with other states. The coercive strategy offers the possibility of achieving one's objectives economically, with little bloodshed, for fewer psychological and political costs, and often with much less risk of escalation. As a result, a crisis resolved by means of coercive diplomacy is also less likely to contaminate future relations between the two sides than the quick, decisive strategy. If the coercive strategy can be made to work successfully, it is a less costly, less risky way of achieving one's objectives than the traditional military strategy. This strategy, however, is viable only under special conditions and, moreover, is quite difficult to implement successfully.

3. Strategy of Attrition

A third way in which force may be used as an instrument of foreign policy is one which both of the strategies already discussed seek to avoid. This is the alternative of prolonged warfare under a set of conditions or limitations on military operations that give neither side a clear advantage. Some conflicts may degenerate into wars of severe mutual attrition with physical and psychological exhaustion of one or both sides the only avenue to eventual termination. As in the case of the Korean War, a recent historical example of this kind of limited war, the outcome may be inconclusive and frustrating, particularly in comparison to the costs incurred.

Both the quick, decisive military strategy and coercive diplomacy promise a more economical and effective alternative to the strategy of attrition. But the failure of either of these two preferred strategies may result in reluctant acceptance of the third approach, its costs and frustrations notwithstanding. This is a risk which the leaders of a country must soberly weigh before embarking on either of the two preferred strategies.

Under special conditions we can regard the strategy of attrition as a preferred strategy. We have in mind, of course, the form of attrition strategy employed in guerrilla warfare. A highly motivated but relatively weak adversary can adopt a guerrilla form of attrition strategy in an effort to wear out an opponent who is much stronger militarily but not so highly motivated to continue the war if his losses become excessive, compared to the stakes. Typically, the attrition strategy is the preferred strategy for the weaker side in part because it lacks the capabilities needed for the other strategies. Also, a stronger power with enough motivation may also choose to pursue an attrition strategy against a weak adversary when alternative strategies are not feasible. A possible example of this is the Nigerian war against Biafra.

4. Test of Capabilities Within
Very Restrictive Ground Rules

The leaders of a country may resort to another strategy when they are confronted with a low-level challenge to which they cannot or do not wish to respond by means of either the quick, decisive or the coercive strategy. Caught in this predicament the defending power may decide, however reluctantly, to accept a test of capabilities within the narrow framework of limitations and ground rules implied by the carefully chosen opening action of its opponent. Even though these initial ground rules are clearly disadvantageous, the defending power accepts the challenge without, for the time being, escalating the conflict.

An example of this occurred in 1948 when the United States attempted to cope with the Soviet blockade of ground access to West Berlin by means of a hastily organized airlift even though its estimated maximum capability was expected to fall far short of the minimum needs of the West Berlin population. Thus the Allied airlift was initially intended merely to buy some time for negotiations which, however, failed to resolve the dispute. In time, hard work, skill at improvisation, and use of increasingly larger resources eventually transformed the airlift into an effective weapon for breaking the ground blockade. The defending power thus succeeded in reversing the expected outcome of the test of capabilities without having to escalate the conflict, thereby transferring back to its opponent the onerous decision whether to engage in a risky escalation or to accept defeat.

Essentially the same strategy was employed by the United States — again successfully — in the Quemoy crisis of 1958 against the Chinese Communist artillery blockade. With indirect, limited United States naval assistance, the Chinese Nationalist Navy was finally able to re-supply the garrison on Quemoy. The next move was up to the opponent, who decided to curtail and abandon the artillery shelling rather than to escalate its tactics.

This strategy is clearly more conservative than either the quick, decisive military option or coercive diplomacy. However, accepting a test of capabilities under the invidious ground rules defined by the opponent does not exclude resort to one of the other two strategies later on, should it become necessary to do so in order to avoid defeat.*

What is clear in both the Berlin blockade crisis and the Quemoy case is that United States leaders decided not to embark on a policy of limited escalation backed by threats of additional escalation in order to force the opponent to call off his blockade actions. To have done so would have been to choose the strategy of coercive diplomacy. In that event, neither of these two crises would have been a test of capabilities under well-defined and stable ground rules but would have been converted into a test of resolution. The coercive strategy emphasizes a test of the opponent's resolution via threats of escalation rather than a test of his capabilities within an established situation. We turn, now, to a more detailed consideration of the theory of coercive diplomacy.

V. THE STRATEGY OF COERCIVE DIPLOMACY

The theory of coercive diplomacy is not esoteric or difficult to understand. Indeed, it is readily comprehensible in common sense terms. However, it must be defined as fully and explicitly as possible since, unfortunately, it has been seriously oversimplified in recent times. The essentials of this strategy and some of the problems of applying it have long been known, although the coercive diplomacy of an earlier era, so far as I have been able to establish, was not articulated systematically. Rather, it was part of the conventional wisdom of those who engaged in statecraft and diplomacy, implicit in what they did and occasionally discussed in memoirs rather than explicated in scholarly works.

In the modern era theorizing about these matters has taken on an ahistorical, abstract character. Those who have attempted to construct a theory of coercion have drawn primarily upon game

---

* On the other hand, accepting for a period of time the ground rules defined by the opponent makes it more difficult to escalate later on since then one has to accept the onus of violating a stable pattern of limitations.

theory and bargaining theory. They have used historical experience with coercive diplomacy sparingly, employing it as a source of ad hoc illustrations rather than as material for further development of the theory. As a result, modern theorists have had to rediscover many things that were known to decision-makers of an earlier era. This is unfortunate, for properly analyzed, historical cases of the kind presented later can contribute usefully to the further development of the theory in two respects. First, they enable us to identify in greater detail the key variables of the strategy of coercive diplomacy and to formulate it in more comprehensive terms. Second, study of historical cases enables us to contrast the theory of coercive diplomacy with its practice. As a result, we can understand better the difficulties policy-makers are likely to encounter when they attempt to employ the strategy of coercive diplomacy in a variety of concrete situations.

The distinction between theory and practice is a critical one for evaluating the uses and limitations of the strategy of coercive diplomacy. We shall draw lessons from this distinction in the three case studies to be presented and we shall attempt to pull these lessons together in Chapter Five. Here we shall confine ourselves to stating the theory of coercive diplomacy in richer detail and more systematically than has heretofore been the case, providing the analytical framework with which we shall approach our three case studies in the next chapters.

Two variables that have not always been clearly identified in theory determine what is necessary to successfully coerce an opponent: first, what is demanded of the opponent and, second, how strongly disinclined the opponent is to comply. These two variables are not independent and must not be treated by the coercing power as if they were. Rather, the strength of the opponent's motivation not to comply is highly dependent on what is demanded of him. In order to determine how difficult the task of coercive diplomacy will be in any specific situation the coercing power must take into account the strength of the opponent's disinclination to yield. But this cannot be calculated without reference to what precisely the coercing power is demanding or plans to demand of its opponent, and how the opponent perceives the demand.

Two types of demands can be made on the opponent. The opponent may be asked to *stop* what he is doing; or he may be asked to *undo* what he has been doing or to reverse what he has already accomplished.[8] This distinction applies to many, though not all, types of behavior to which the defending power may decide to respond by means of coercive diplomacy. The distinction is of considerable importance for the theory and practice of coercive diplomacy in view of the fact that the first type of demand asks appreciably less of the opponent than the second type. To ask the opponent to stop the encroachment in which he is engaged constitutes a more modest objective for the strategy of coercive diplomacy than to ask him to undo what he has already done. Because it asks less of the opponent, the first type of demand is easier to comply with and easier to enforce. The opponent's disinclination to yield is maximized, on the other hand, by a demand that he undo whatever his action has already accomplished — for example, to give up territory he has occupied. Stronger threats and greater pressure may be needed, therefore, to enforce the second type of demand.

This distinction has been found useful in our case studies. In Laos, as we shall see, Kennedy demanded merely that the opposing forces halt their forward progress against vital Royal Lao territory. He was also interested, it is true, in obtaining a reversal of some of the gains already made by the Pathet Lao, but, and this is critical, he left this question to be taken up later via negotiations at the conference table. His coercive diplomacy in this case focussed exclusively on the more modest and easier objective of getting the opponent to halt his forward progress and agree to negotiations. In the Cuban missile crisis, on the other hand, Kennedy made both types of demands on Khrushchev. The blockade, an example of the first type of demand, was designed to halt Soviet moves in progress, i.e. the shipment of additional missiles and bombers to Cuba. In addition, Kennedy also demanded that Khrushchev undo the fait accompli he had already accomplished by removing the missiles already in Cuba. The same distinction, while logically applicable in the Vietnam case, was blurred somewhat because of the nature of the situation and the way in which Johnson chose to formulate his demands on Hanoi.

We can argue that the first type of demand is similar to deterrence, insofar as it is a matter of persuading the opponent not to do something he has not yet done. Thus, we might say, Kennedy's demand in the Laos case was perhaps as much an example of deterrence strategy as it was an example of coercive diplomacy. It seems preferable, however, to limit the concept of deterrence strategy to its original and more familiar meaning, namely the effort to dissuade an opponent from doing something he has not yet started to do. What emerges, then, is a continuum in which deterrence may be attempted before the opponent has initiated an action, and coercive diplomacy employed afterwards either to persuade him merely to halt or to undo his action. This is depicted in Figure 1.

So far we have depicted only the defensive uses of coercive diplomacy in which it is employed to persuade an opponent to stop doing something he is already doing that is distasteful or harmful to the defender, or to undo what he has already accomplished. In contrast to this defensive use of the strategy, coercion may also be employed offensively to get the opponent to do something he has not done and does not want to do — to make him pay a price, give up territory — in order to avoid the threatened sanctions. An analogy here is the robber who persuades his victim to turn over his money peacefully. The term "diplomatic blackmail" is often applied to this offensive use of the strategy. This study considers only defensive uses of coercive diplomacy.

What we have been emphasizing, essentially, is that the task of coercion is determined or set by the magnitude of the opponent's motivation not to comply and that this, in turn, is a function of his perception of what is demanded of him. Thus, asking very little of an opponent makes it easier for him to permit

FIGURE 1

Deterrence	Coercive Diplomacy	
	Type A	Type B
persuade opponent not to initiate an action	persuade opponent to stop short of his goal	persuade opponent to undo his action

(increasing difficulty from standpoint of the "defender," in terms of pressure on "aggressor" necessary to achieve the desired effect) himself to be coerced. Conversely, demanding a great deal of an opponent — and even asking him merely to stop may be asking a great deal — makes the task of coercing him all the more difficult.* In this event, it may be difficult for the coercing power to threaten sanctions sufficiently potent and sufficiently credible to overcome the opponent's strong disinclination to comply with what is demanded of him.

This leads to another major proposition in the theory of coercive diplomacy. The feasibility of this strategy in any particular case may depend on whether one relies solely on negative sanctions or whether one combines threats with positive inducements in order to reduce the opponent's disinclination to comply with what is demanded of him. This point is of considerable practical as well as theoretical significance. Some theorists and practitioners subscribe to an oversimplified, crude notion of coercive strategy that relies exclusively on threats. Their version of coercive diplomacy makes no provision for use of the carrot as well as the stick. Or, to put it somewhat differently, their theory envisages that one offers an opponent only face-saving gestures on trivial or peripheral matters. This theory overlooks the possibility that coercive diplomacy in any given situation may be facilitated by, if indeed it does not require, genuine concessions to an opponent as part of a quid pro quo that secures one's essential demands. Coercive diplomacy, therefore, needs to be distinguished from pure coercion; it includes the possibility of bargains, negotiations, and compromises as well as coercive threats.

What the stick cannot achieve by itself, unless it is a very formidable one, can possibly be achieved by combining a carrot with the stick. Thus, a proper reading either of Kennedy's modest success in Laos or of his more spectacular success in coercing the Soviets to withdraw the missiles from Cuba would call attention not only to the threats Kennedy made but also to the willingness he conveyed to give the opponent a substantial quid pro quo. Thus, the inducement offered the opponent for this purpose must be viewed as credible by him. Finding a way of making the quid pro quo offered the opponent plausible and binding, of com-

---

* Demanding "a great deal" of the opponent can mean either "a great deal" in material or real terms or "a great deal" in psychological or symbolic terms. What is critical here, as we have emphasized, is the opponent's perception of what is demanded of him, which may be at variance with what the coercing power thinks it is demanding.

mitting oneself to it in a way that removes the suspicion that it will not be honored after the crisis is over, is very important.[9]

Earlier we pointed out that in devising a coercive strategy the defending power must calculate the strength of the opponent's motivation to resist what is demanded of him. We emphasized that the opponent's motivation is a variable that is dependent upon his perception of the nature and magnitude of what is demanded of him. The coercing power's own motivation is also an important factor that must enter into the calculus of a coercive strategy. Moreover, the coercing power's motivation, too, is a variable that is affected by the nature and magnitude of the demand it chooses to make on the opponent.

The choice of the demand to be made on the opponent, therefore, affects the strength of motivation of both sides. This takes on special importance because the relative motivation of the two sides in a conflict can exert critical leverage on the outcome.[10] There is often an important strategic dimension, therefore, to the choice of the objective on behalf of which coercive diplomacy will be employed. The chances that coercive diplomacy will be successful will be appreciably greater if the objective selected — and the demand made — by the coercing power reflects only the most important of its interests that are at stake,* for this is more likely to create an asymmetry of motivation favoring the coercing power. Thus, for example, if Kennedy had chosen as his objective in the Cuban missile crisis the removal of all Soviet military and political influence from Cuba, the Soviet motivation to resist would have been appreciably greater than it was. Instead, Kennedy limited his objective — and his demand on the Soviets — to the removal of offensive missiles. Such a limited, focussed objective not only concentrated and maximized motivation on the United States side; it also delimited what was at stake for the Soviets and helped to create an asymmetry of motivation favoring the United States. This facilitated the president's effort to exert unrelenting, eventually successful pressure on behalf of his demand on Khrushchev.

Let us turn now to the central task of a coercive strategy: how to create in the opponent the expectation of unacceptable costs

---

* The credibility of the threatened force, too, as David Hall points out, will be greater in the opponent's eyes under these circumstances.

of sufficient magnitude to erode his motivation to continue what he is doing. Success may depend upon whether the initial military action directed towards the opponent stands by itself or is part of a credible threat to escalate the conflict further, if necessary, and to do so within a short period of time. Even without this additional threat, a quite limited military action or even a mere alert or deployment of one's forces may suffice to alter the opponent's expectations and his policy. But against a determined opponent or one who feels he is on the verge of an important success, even a stronger coercive threat may not be effective.

This leads us to introduce an important distinction in the theory of coercive diplomacy between weaker and stronger variants of the strategy. Oversimplifying to make the point, we can distinguish between two basic variants of coercive strategy:

1. The try-and-see approach, the weak variant, and
2. The tacit-ultimatum, the strong variant.

These two variants represent the endpoints of a continuum; intermediate variants are also possible.

In the try-and-see approach, the defending power in an attempt to persuade its opponent to call off or curtail its encroachment takes only one step at a time. It deliberately postpones the decision to take additional action until it becomes clear whether the steps already taken will have a sufficient coercive impact on the opponent. When employing a try-and-see approach, the coercing power may make a more or less specific demand on the opponent to stop his encroachment or to pull back altogether; but it does not create a sense of urgency for his compliance with the demand. In contrast, in the tacit-ultimatum variant of the strategy, at the same time the defending power takes its initial actions it communicates to the opponent that other, more damaging steps will follow in short order if he does not comply with the demand made on him.

"Tacit-ultimatum" [11] is an appropriate designation for the strong variant of coercive diplomacy, for it utilizes all three elements of a classical ultimatum:

1. a *specific demand* on the opponent;
2. a *time limit* (explicit or implicit) for compliance;

3. a *threat of punishment* for non-compliance that is *sufficiently strong and credible.**

To the extent that one or more of these three elements of an ultimatum are not conveyed by the power that is attempting to coerce, the coercive impact of what it says and does on the opponent is weakened. Nonetheless, coercive diplomacy may succeed in the absence of a full-fledged ultimatum, and a weaker variant of the strategy, resembling the try-and-see approach, may suffice in some circumstances. Still another possibility, as we shall see, is that the coercing power may start with the try-and-see approach and resort at some point to an ultimatum.

Even a relatively small increment of force can have a disproportionately large coercive impact if it is part of the tacit-ultimatum rather than the try-and-see approach. The coercive effect of what little is actually done can be magnified substantially by linking it with a credible threat of additional action. This is the essence of any form of intimidation.

Intimidation, of course, does not always require a formal, explicit ultimatum. Coercive diplomacy may succeed without it in some situations. The defending power may not need to state a specific time limit or define the threat of punishment for non-compliance to reinforce its demand on the opponent. Either or both may be sufficiently implicit in the structure of a situation and, in particular, in the way that situation is developing. Thus, a sense of urgency may spring from the way events unfold to lead one or both sides to believe that the crisis is approaching a critical threshold. That the opponent is continuing his activity and thereby threatening to create a fait accompli may imbue the defending power with an increasing sense of urgency to act or to accept the consequences. In this kind of developing situation the defender may not need to articulate a full-fledged ultimatum. A demand that the opponent stop or undo what he is doing may generate sufficient pressure, especially if the defender also makes visible preparations to employ the sanctions at his disposal. As a result, the opponent may believe that the situation will now head

---

* What is threatened by way of punishment for non-compliance need not be spelled out. But, in any case, the credibility of the threat is generally enhanced by, or may require, an alert or deployment of appropriate military forces.

towards a clearly identifiable climax unless he halts or slows down the activity to which the defending power is objecting. The time limit for compliance with the defender's demand may spring from the structure of the situation itself, from the actions and postures being taken by one or both sides that point them towards a possible collision within a short period of time unless one or both alter their behavior.[12]

Certain similarities exist between what has been described here and the game of chicken. Some writers have drawn upon the model of this game to illuminate a class of real-life crisis situations.[13] But the model ignores both the importance and intricacy of crisis management in many international crises. It also overlooks the flexibility inherent in the strategy of coercive diplomacy that makes it possible to adapt to a variety of situations. The game of chicken, in brief, encompasses only the crudest form and extreme methods of intimidation; it shrinks the role of diplomacy in this strategy to the vanishing point and ignores the possibility (and, oftentimes, the necessity) of combining a carrot with the stick. The analogy of the game of chicken, therefore, is imperfect as either a description or an explanation of the behavior of the two sides in the historical crises we examine here. Moreover the analogy with the game of chicken would be positively dangerous if used as a basis for offering advice on how a defending power may employ coercive diplomacy to halt the opponent's encroachment. This is not to deny that elements of an externally imposed time limit, or sense of urgency, were present in both the Laos crisis of 1961 and the Cuban missile case. In both crises, the structure of the developing situation that was set into motion by the actions of the opponent generated a sense of urgency for the defender which he then managed to transmit back to the advancing opponent. In neither case, however, did Kennedy rely exclusively on the structure of the situation itself to transmit a sense of urgency and the threat of credible punishment for non-compliance. Particularly in the Cuban crisis, Kennedy eventually felt himself obliged to reinforce the message implicit in the structure of the situation by delivering a verbal ultimatum which contained a time limit and a threat of punishment for non-compliance.

As the preceding discussion has indicated, coercive diplomacy may operate on two levels of communication; in addition to what is said, significant non-verbal communication may emerge from the structure of the developing situation. Therefore, analysis of coercive diplomacy cannot be restricted to the verbal communications that the defending power transmits to the opponent. Coercive persuasion depends not merely on whether the defending power includes all three components of a classical ultimatum in its verbal messages to the opponent. The structure of the situation, as it develops and is expected to develop, must also be taken into account. The defending power can shape the opponent's expectations in this respect by means other than, or in addition to, a verbal ultimatum. The actions it takes — for example, deploying and alerting its military forces, making political and diplomatic preparations of the kind needed to back its demand and enforce it, if necessary — can reinforce and make credible the verbal communications employed to coerce the opponent.

Actions, then, may reinforce strong words and make them more credible. But, as we have suggested, actions may also compensate for weak words; that is, something less than a classical explicit ultimatum may be strengthened by the actions the defender is taking. Still another aspect of the relationship between words and actions should be described. Contrary to the conventional wisdom on these matters, actions do not always speak louder than words. Actions may be perceived by the opponent as equivocal, as not excluding the possibility that the coercing power is bluffing and is not prepared to act if its demand is not accepted. Words, then, may be needed in some situations to clarify the meaning of the actions taken and to reinforce the credibility of the threat implied by the preparatory actions. If, then, actions may be needed in some situations to reinforce strong words, in other situations strong words, explicit ultimata, may be needed to reinforce and to define the meaning and credibility of the threatening actions the defender is taking as part of his attempt to make coercive diplomacy work.

We conclude, therefore, that while the relationship between words and actions — the two levels of communication — is likely to be very important in the strategy of coercive diplomacy, there is no single way of stating what that relationship must be to ensure the success of this strategy. Accordingly, such situations are replete with opportunities for miscommunication and miscalculation. This, then, is another aspect of coercive diplomacy that makes it an elusive, problematical strategy to employ effectively as an instrument of foreign policy.

This chapter has stated a theory of coercive diplomacy that identifies critical variables and depicts their relationships. Any theory is necessarily somewhat general and abstract, and this theory is particularly so because coercion is highly context-dependent. Such a text-book model of coercive diplomacy does not enable us to say very much about the feasibility of strategy in particular cases. Nor does it clarify what it will take in a particular situation on the part of the defending power to persuade an opponent to cease, curtail, or undo altogether its encroachment.

It is necessary to emphasize the limited utility of a theory of this kind because of the tendency to assume that a strategy can be operationalized in practice more easily and effectively than in fact is the case. A theory rarely identifies all the difficulties a strategy may encounter in concrete situations. Or, if it identifies some of these practical difficulties, the theory rarely goes beyond general observations to the effect that overcoming these potential pitfalls is a matter of skill or art that varies with the practitioner. Of course, no theory can provide blueprints to ensure skillful implementation of a strategy such as coercive diplomacy in the variety of complex situations in which it may be tried. The most that can be done is to call attention to the specific problems — all of them difficult ones — of operationalizing the strategy of coercive diplomacy in practice. For this purpose we turn now to our historical case studies.

Before proceeding, the reader should be aware that we shall be undertaking two separate, though related, tasks in our analysis of these cases. We want to describe as best we can, given the limitations of available historical data, the policies and strategies the president formulated and implemented in each case. But we also want to explicate what he did and conceptualize it in strategic terms. In all three cases — which, indeed, were chosen for this purpose — we find that the president's ad hoc, improvised conduct of the crisis constitutes an example of a general strategy which we call coercive diplomacy. This is by no means to say that coercive diplomacy was a well-defined strategy at the time it was used. It was not. Both in the Laos crisis of 1961 and again in the Cuban missile crisis the following year, President Kennedy improvised a coercive policy. In neither case, that is, did he implement a pre-existing strategy — coercive diplomacy or whatever else it might have been called. It is true, as pointed out at the beginning of this chapter, that the Cuban missile crisis did encourage later efforts to articulate theories and strategies of coercion. But, despite this, Johnson's effort to use airpower in early 1965 to coerce Hanoi was only partly influenced by such theories. To a considerable extent, Johnson's policy in this case was also an ad hoc improvisation. Nonetheless, in each of our case studies, and particularly in the concluding chapter, we shall examine the president's improvised policies from the standpoint of the strategy of coercive diplomacy which we have explicated. This we will do because it enables us to make a more incisive and didactic analysis of the difficulties of tailoring this strategy to a particular situation. Unless the reader keeps this in mind, however, he may conclude that we are erroneously implying that the administration was attempting to apply a well-defined strategy to the situation at hand and was experiencing the difficulties of implementation we allude to in exactly the terms in which we have described them. Since our purpose is to learn from history and to draw the lessons of several different cases into a comprehensive and systematic framework, we have added an explicit theoretical interest to the way in which a historian would attempt to describe and explain these three crises.

NOTES

[1] No wholly satisfactory scholarly analysis of American policy-making vis-à-vis the threat of Chinese Communist intervention in the Korean War exists. The explanation for the American miscalculation of Chinese intentions and, particularly, for the failure to take steps to reduce the risks of that miscalculation in November 1950 remains somewhat clouded and, certainly, controversial. See, for example, Richard E. Neustadt, *Presidential Power* (New York: Wiley, 1960), pp. 123–151; Martin Lichterman, "To the Yalu and Back," in Harold Stein, ed., *American Civil-Military Decisions: A Book of Case Studies* (University, Ala.: University of Alabama Press, 1963); Trumbull Higgins, *Korea and the Fall of MacArthur* (London: Oxford University Press, 1960); Allen S. Whiting, *China Crosses the Yalu*, (New York: Macmillan, 1960); David S. McLellan, "Dean Acheson and the Korean War," *Political Science Quarterly*, LXXXIII (March 1968) pp. 16–39; Walter Zelman, "Chinese Intervention in the Korean War," Security Studies Paper, UCLA, 1968; Dean Acheson, *Present at the Creation* (New York: Norton, 1969); J. Lawton Collins, *War in Peacetime: The History and Lessons of Korea* (Boston: Houghton Mifflin Co., 1969); John W. Spanier, *The Truman-MacArthur Controversy and the Korean War* (Cambridge, Mass.: Harvard University Press, 1959); David Rees, *Korea: The Limited War* (New York: St. Martin's Press, 1964); Roy Appleman, *United States Army in the Korean War* (Washington, D.C.:

Office of Chief of Military History, Dept. of Army, 1961). I have utilized
these and other sources in a study of this case that will appear in a forthcoming volume on the theory and practice of deterrence in recent American
foreign policy.

2 Harry S Truman, *Memoirs: Years of Trial and Hope*, II (Garden City:
Doubleday, 1956), p. 362. Italics added.

3 Neustadt, *Presidential Power*, p. 138; see also Lichterman, "To the Yalu
and Back," pp. 594, 611.

4 Interview with Richard Neustadt, in Neustadt, *Presidential Power*, p. 128.

5 William W. Kaufmann, *The McNamara Strategy* (New York: Harper
& Row, 1964), p. 27.

6 For statements and summaries of the critique of massive retaliation, see,
for example, William W. Kaufmann, "The Requirements of Deterrence," in
Military Policy and National Security, ed. W. Kaufmann (Princeton: Princeton University Press, 1956); Bernard Brodie, *Strategy in the Missile Age*
(Princeton: Princeton University Press, 1959), pp. 248–263.

7 Cf. Thomas Schelling's related remarks on what he calls the "connected-
ness" of military options, that is, features that help communicate the intended
threat more effectively and also help to show the limits of what one is demanding in order to avoid unnecessary spiralling of the conflict. (*Arms and
Influence* [New Haven: Yale University Press, 1966], pp. 87–88.)

The concept of "signalling," essential to the requirements of crisis management, is the subject of a forthcoming major analytical study by Robert Jervis,
The Logic of Images in International Relations (Princeton: Princeton University Press, 1970).

8 Both types of demands, it may be noted, satisfy Thomas Schelling's
definition of "compellance" and indeed are discussed by him without being
explicitly differentiated. (*Arms and Influence*, pp. 72, 77.) I am indebted to
David Hall for pointing out the value of distinguishing between them and for
the major points made in the discussion here.

9 I am indebted to David Hall for calling attention to the fact that the
requirements of credibility and potency apply to the carrot as well as the
stick.

10 The importance of relative motivation has been emphasized recently by
several writers, for example by Stephen Maxwell "Rationality in Deterrence,"
Adelphi Paper No. 50, Institute of Strategic Studies, London; and Jervis's
The Logic of Images.

11 Although many have attempted to define the Latin word "ultimatum,"
past definitions have been noted for either their narrowness or their overly
general assertions about the nature of ultimata. Definitional shortcomings,
however, have not prevented ultimata from being incorporated into the
strategy of coercive diplomacy and into the rules of war and international
law. The Hague Convention III (1907), for example, intending to prevent
"surprise" and "equivocation" in the beginning of war, provided in Article I
that the Contracting Powers "recognize that hostilities between them are
not to commence without a previous unequivocal warning, which shall take
the form either of a declaration of war, giving reasons, or of an ultimatum
with a conditional declaration of war." Yet, now under the United Nations
Charter such threats of war are legal only in self-defense or in collective defense of the Charter, which, under other circumstances, prohibits not only
acts of force but also threats of force. See H. Lauterpacht, ed., *Oppenheim's
International Law, A Treatise* (7th ed.) (London: Longmans, Green and
Co.,) Vol. II, *Disputes, War, and Neutrality* (London: Longmans, Green
and Co., 1952), pp. 133 and 295–297; Sir Ernest Satow, *A Guide to Diplo-*

matic Practice (4th ed.) (London: Longmans, Green and Co., 1957), pp. 105–107; James Brown Scott (ed.), *Proceedings of the Hague Peace Conference of 1907*, Vol. III (New York: Oxford University Press, 1921), p. 43; Norman Hill, "Was There an Ultimatum Before Pearl Harbor?" in *The American Journal of International Law*, Vol. XLII (1948), pp. 355–367; *Dictionnaire Diplomatique, Académie Diplomatique Internationale*, Vol. II (Paris: Associates, Academie Diplomatique Internationale, 1933), pp. 999–1000; and Hans Asbeck, *Das Ultimatum im modernen Volkerrecht* (Berlin: Walter Rothchild, 1933). In preparing this footnote I have drawn on the valuable paper on the nature and uses of ultimata since the middle of the nineteenth century written for my seminar by Paul Gordon Lauren, a graduate student in the History Department, Stanford University.

[12] Discussions with Robert Jervis and Robert Weinland have helped me to clarify the importance of the structure of the situation in which coercive diplomacy takes place.

[13] See, for example, Herman Kahn, *On Escalation* (New York: Praeger, 1965); Anatol Rapoport, *Fights, Games, and Debates* (Ann Arbor: University of Michigan Press, 1960); and Karl W. Deutsch. *The Analysis of International Relations* (Englewood Cliffs, N.J.: Prentice-Hall, 1968).

BIBLIOGRAPHY

Beaufre, Andre, *Deterrence and Strategy*, trans. R. H. Barry (New York: Praeger, 1966).

Brodie, Bernard, *Strategy in the Missile Age* (Princeton: Princeton University Press, 1959).

Brown, Seyom, *The Faces of Power* (New York: Columbia University Press, 1968).

Bloomfield, Lincoln P., and Amelia C. Leiss, *Controlling Small Wars* (New York: Knopf, 1970).

Deutsch, Karl W., *The Analysis of International Relations* (Englewood Cliffs, N.J.: Prentice-Hall, 1968), chap. 11, "How Conflicts Arise Among States."

Enthoven, Alain C., "American Deterrent Policy," in *Problems of National Security*, ed. Henry A. Kissinger (New York: Praeger, 1965).

Halperin, Morton, *Limited War in the Nuclear Age* (New York: Wiley, 1963).

Hermann, Charles F., *Crisis in Foreign Policy* (Indianapolis: Bobbs-Merrill, 1969).

Hoffmann, Stanley, *The State of War* (New York: Praeger, 1965).

Jervis, Robert, *The Logic of Images in International Relations* (Princeton: Princeton University Press, 1970).

Kahn, Herman, *On Escalation* (New York: Praeger, 1965).

Kaufmann, William W., *The McNamara Strategy* (New York: Harper & Row, 1964).

———, ed., *Military Policy and National Security* (Princeton: Princeton University Press, 1956).

Kissinger, Henry, *The Necessity for Choice* (New York: Harper & Row, 1961).

———, *Nuclear Weapons and Foreign Policy* (New York: Harper & Row, 1957).

Knorr, Klaus, *On the Uses of Military Power in the Nuclear Age* (Princeton: Princeton University Press, 1966).

Lieberman, E. James, "Threat and Assurance in the Conduct of Conflict," in Roger Fisher, ed., *International Conflict and Behavioral Science* (New York: Basic Books, 1964).

Maxwell, Stephen, "Rationality in Deterrence," Adelphi Paper No. 50, Institute of Strategic Studies, London.

McDougal, Myres S. and Florentino Feliciano, *Law and Minimum World Public Order: Legal Regulations of International Coercion* (New Haven: Yale University Press, 1961).

Milburn, Thomas W., "What Constitutes Effective U.S. Deterrence," in Dale J. Hekuis, C. G. McClintock, and A. L. Burns, eds., *International Stability* (New York: Wiley, 1964).

Osgood, Robert E., *Limited War: The Challenge to American Strategy* (Chicago: University of Chicago Press, 1957).

Pfeffer, Richard M., ed., *No More Vietnams* (New York: Harper & Row, 1968).

Rapoport, Anatol, *Fights, Games, and Debates* (Ann Arbor: University of Michigan Press, 1960).

———, *Strategy and Conscience* (New York: Harper & Row, 1964).

Rosenau, James N., "National Interest," in *International Encyclopedia of the Social Sciences*, XI (New York: Macmillan, 1968), pp. 34–40.

Quester, George H. *Deterrence Before Hiroshima* (New York: Wiley, 1966).

Schelling, Thomas C., *Arms and Influence* (New Haven: Yale University Press, 1966).

———, *The Strategy of Conflict* (Cambridge, Mass.: Harvard University Press, 1960).

Shure, G. H.; Meeker, R. J.; Moore, W. H., Jr.; Kelley, H. H.; "Computer Studies of Bargaining Behavior: The Role of Threat in Bargaining," SP-2196, System Development Corporation, Santa Monica, California, 1966.

Snyder, Glenn, *Deterrence and Defense* (Princeton: Princeton University Press, 1961).

Speier, Hans, *Force and Folly* (Cambridge, Mass.: M.I.T. Press, 1968).

Taylor, Maxwell, *Responsibility and Response* (New York: Harper & Row, 1967).

———, *The Uncertain Trumpet* (New York: Harper & Row, 1959).

Young, Oran R. *The Politics of Force* (Princeton: Princeton University Press, 1968).

2

David K. Hall
THE LAOS CRISIS, 1960-61

Biographers of the Kennedy administration portray the Laotian crisis of 1960–1961 as the most worrisome and time-consuming problem confronting the president during his first few months in office. During the waning days of his presidency, Eisenhower had confided to Kennedy that the most difficult and dangerous situation he was passing on was the crisis in Laos.[1] That the Russians also perceived Laos as a dangerous confrontation of Soviet-American interests is apparent. G. M. Pushkin, the Soviet Deputy Foreign Minister at the time, told Arthur Schlesinger that aside from World War II, the Soviet airlift of arms and ammunition to the Pathet Lao during 1960–1961 was the highest priority supply operation since the Russian Revolution.[2] Yet less than five months after the inauguration of John F. Kennedy, a moderately effective cease-fire had been arranged in Laos, and the probability of Russian-American confrontation in that small nation had been reduced considerably. Laos, 1960–61, is one of only a handful of instances in recent history where two great powers actively engaged in a Third World country have so quickly and peacefully resolved, or at least "tabled," their differing interests in that nation. For this reason, the case of Laos can be particularly important in increasing our understanding of the decisions which facilitate such desirable outcomes and the conditions which favor such successes.

I. THE HISTORICAL SETTING

To appreciate the significance of the 1960–61 Laotian crisis for United States interests in Southeast Asia, it is necessary to review the relations of that small nation with the United States between 1954 and 1960. The Indochina War terminated in July 1954 with the negotiation of the Geneva accords. With respect to Laos, the accords called for complete withdrawal of the Viet Minh to North Vietnam and the regroupment of the indigenous Communist force, the Pathet Lao, in the two northernmost provinces of the country while it negotiated an agreement with the new independent government concerning its integration into the Royal Lao Army.[3] All foreign nations except France were proscribed from establishing or maintaining military bases on Laotian territory, while France was entrusted with the training of the Royal Lao Army. An International Commission for Supervision and Control in Laos (ICC) composed of members from India (chairman), Canada, and Poland was created to guarantee the fulfillment of these agreements. The Geneva accords did not, however, affect prior aid agreements negotiated between the United States and Laotian governments, so the United States was able legally to continue these economic and military programs.

With the end of the Indochina War and the departure of the French army, the Eisenhower administration hurried to forge an effective alliance of Southeast Asian governments against the further encroachment of communism. On September 6, 1954, the Southeast Asia Treaty Organization (SEATO) was founded with the prime intention of deterring any Korean-type invasion of Southeast Asia. The charter members of the organization were the United States, Great Britain, France, Thailand, Pakistan, the Philippines, Australia, and New Zealand, and with the consent of the Laotian, Cambodian, and South Vietnamese governments, a protocol was attached to the security pact unilaterally extending its military and economic provisions to these three nations.

As a part of the Dulles plan for Southeast Asian defense, the State Department provided the funds necessary to increase the

Royal Lao Army from its wartime strength of 15,000 in 1954 to 25,000, despite persistent Defense Department recommendations that the Lao army be reduced to the level needed for only routine internal policing.[4] Between 1955 and 1960, $300 million of United States aid in the form of budgetary support and technical and military assistance flowed into Laos. This equaled $150 for every inhabitant — an amount double the annual per capita income of Laos and more American aid per capita than granted any other country during the same period.[5]

Attempting to protect this sizable investment, the State Department and the CIA covertly supported those Lao politicians who promoted close national ties with the United States. Additionally, secret agents worked to undermine all indigenous politicians and movements neutralist or leftist in appearance.[6] A constant victim of such American intrigue was Prince Souvanna Phouma.

In November 1957 while serving as Laotian prime minister, Souvanna signed an agreement with the Pathet Lao establishing procedures for the reunification of the country. The political arm of the Pathet Lao, the Neo Lao Hak Xat (NLHX), was recognized as a legal political party, two Communist leaders were seated in the national cabinet, the Pathet Lao were to be integrated into the Royal Lao Army, and special elections were to be held in four months. Of twenty-one National Assembly seats contested in the special elections, the Neo Lao Hak Xat and an allied party captured thirteen. Souvanna viewed the elections as marking a successful reintegration of Lao political elements into a national community and a fulfillment of the obligations which Laos had assumed at Geneva in 1954. Therefore, in July 1958 he asked that the ICC discontinue its activities in Laos, and this request was acted on favorably by the three-member commission.[7]

Some United States officials and Lao leaders were unwilling to accept the election results or the neutralist foreign policy which Souvanna intended to pursue. The United States government had aided the Laotian government since 1954 on the assumption that the Pathet Lao would eventually be deprived of any significant voice within the reintegrated national community. Instead, the Communists' electoral success was an ominous sign of increasing Pathet Lao power and the failure of American economic and administrative assistance. In the face of growing congressional criticism of the loosely administered and politically unsuccessful aid program in Laos, the Eisenhower administration decided to hold up the monthly American aid payment to the Lao government on the pretext of corruption. The strong anti-Communist elements in Laos took advantage of this opportunity to foment a parliamentary crisis and succeeded in ousting Souvanna from office on a vote of no confidence.[8]

In an effort to prevent further Communist gains and to secure resumption of United States assistance, the new government removed the two Pathet Lao ministers appointed by Souvanna, sought legal means of dismembering the NLHX, and made it clear that it regarded the Pathet Lao as agents of the North Vietnamese. The Pathet Lao, with Viet Minh assistance, began to drive government forces and officials out of the two northeastern provinces. The Lao government, in turn, claimed that elements of the North Vietnamese army had invaded the northern provinces of Laos and appealed for assistance from both the United States and United Nations. The United States responded by increasing the size of its furtive military training mission, the Programs Evaluation Office (PEO), by one hundred advisers and boosting military aid by 30 per cent.[9] The United Nations investigated the charges but was unable to document the movement of regular troops from the Democratic Republic of Vietnam into Laos.

Growing fear of civil war, counsel from United Nations Secretary General Hammarskjold in favor of future Laotian neutrality, and disappointment at the failure of the United States to take decisive action against the alleged invaders led to a moderation in the Laotian government's policy toward the Pathet Lao. Strict anti-communism was reestablished in December 1959 following a military coup by General Phoumi Nosavan, only to be reversed once again in August 1960 when Phoumi was removed from power by Captain Kong Le, commander of the Second Paratroop Battalion. Kong Le viewed the Laotian government's departure from neutrality as the source of the growing civil strife and corruption, and he called on the king to appoint Souvanna Phouma as prime minister. In August 1960, Souvanna formed a new government, and the ousted Phoumi departed for southern Laos.[10]

Souvanna once again opened negotiations with the Pathet Lao and permitted the Soviet Union to establish an embassy in Laos. The decisions precipitated another crisis in Washington. A deal was concluded with the new prime minister whereby he would continue to receive American financial support but would agree to allow Phoumi to receive deliveries of United States military assistance. Souvanna was told that Phoumi promised not to use this aid against Kong Le, and thus bring down the new government, but would only use it against the Pathet Lao.[11]

Phoumi never intended to live up to this agreement. Immediately following his ouster, he began soliciting support for a countercoup from his cousin, the benevolent dictator of Thailand, Marshal Sarit, and from United States agencies sympathetic to his cause. Soon Thailand had imposed an unofficial blockade on goods going to the Laotian capital, Vientiane. In a test of American support for his government, Souvanna asked for rice and oil to relieve the shortages created by the Thai blockade, but by this time the State and Defense departments had agreed that the prime minister had to be removed. When Washington refused to deliver the supplies, Souvanna turned to the Soviet Union, which instituted an airlift of rice and oil from Hanoi on December 3.[12]

At the same time, General Phoumi's forces in southern Laos started north along the Mekong River toward Vientiane. Realizing that Phoumi was massing for an attack on the capital, Souvanna called on the United States to honor its pledge to prevent the general from using American aid to overthrow the government. Receiving no satisfaction, Souvanna again turned to the Soviet Union, which this time began arms and ammunition shipments to Vientiane on December 11 in exchange for an alliance between Kong Le's neutralist troops and the Pathet Lao. Russian aid proved to be too late, and Souvanna's supporters were driven north from the capital on December 16, and the prime minister fled to Cambodia. A new government consisting of Prince Boun Oum as prime minister and General Phoumi as deputy prime minister and minister of defense was approved by the Lao National Assembly, but the Soviet Union and other Communist states continued to recognize Souvanna Phouma as the legal ruler of Laos. The United States and other Western countries quickly granted recognition to the new Laotian government.[13]

Despite his capture of Vientiane, General Phoumi was slow to pursue Kong Le's forces. Each passing day decreased Phoumi's chances of overtaking his opponent who was receiving arms, ammunition, and food parachuted from Soviet planes. American intelligence estimated that 184 Soviet cargo missions were flown into Laos between December 15 and January 2. In addition, Vietnamese and Lao advisers and officers were constantly ferried in small planes between Hanoi and northern Laos. Kong Le retreated north toward the all-weather landing field at the strategic Plain of Jars and, on December 31, in combined attack with the Pathet Lao, he seized the airfield and surrounding villages from the surprised Phoumists and French advisers guarding the Plain. Quickly the area was transformed into a fortress-like staging point, with forty-five tons of Soviet supplies arriving daily from Hanoi.[14]

With the military initiative shifting to the neutralist-Communist forces, the Eisenhower administration sought to spur Phoumi into renewed action. Six AT-6 aircraft equipped to carry machine guns, rockets, and bombs were sent to Laos in early January, and the original three hundred infantrymen of the Programs Evaluation Office were replaced by four hundred Special Forces personnel from United States guerrilla training schools.[15] Additionally, the United States Seventh Fleet was redeployed to bring it within striking range of Laos, and an extraordinary session of the SEATO Council was convened in Bangkok.[16] But the new American support did little to invigorate the Royal Lao forces and only succeeded in prompting a strong protest from the Soviet Union. Thus, the United States and the Communist bloc supported opposite sides in an increasingly explosive Asian civil war as John F. Kennedy assumed office as president.

II. IMAGE OF THE OPPOSITION

The crisis facing the new administration was complicated because the threat to the American position came from more than one source. Although the Soviet Union served as the major purveyor of arms and ammunition to the neutralist-Pathet Lao forces, North Vietnam and Communist China were also important actors. Viet Minh advisers had served as cadres within the Pathet Lao forces since 1951, and with the establishment of a central supply area on the Plain of Jars, the North Vietnamese began delivering supplies to the rebels in truck convoys originating in North Vietnam. In January 1961, a number of regular North Vietnamese units were identified by the United States government as having entered northern Laos.* Communist China was not actively in-

* A well-documented study of the relationship between the North Vietnamese and Pathet Lao concludes that "the Lao revolutionary movement

volved in the fighting, but it publicly commended and encouraged Hanoi's efforts. Furthermore, any American decision regarding involvement in Laos had to be made with the Korean War in mind, for history had shown that the Chinese were not willing to sit idly by while the United States Army occupied a neighboring state.[17]

The Kennedy administration's perception of these three actors' objectives and risk calculations is somewhat uncertain since we have only one detailed account of these facts, that of Roger Hilsman.[18] However, one point is rather clear: during its first few months in office, the Kennedy administration was ambivalent in its evaluation of Russian behavior and intentions throughout the world and in Laos in particular. In his dealings with the Soviet Union, Kennedy had hoped to straddle the "realist" and "idealist" positions through adoption of, to use use Schlesinger's words, "a policy of reasoned firmness accompanied by a determination to explore all possibilities of reasonable accommodation." [19] But the new president found the establishment of a consistent and optimal balance between firmness and accommodation extremely difficult as the Russians turned seemingly contradictory faces toward the new administration. In his New Year's Day address, Khrushchev hailed Kennedy's election as a repudiation of the Eisenhower Cold War policy. The Soviet premier announced that the U.S.S.R. would drop its demand for a review of the U-2 incident by the United Nations and ordered the release of two United States RB-47 reconnaissance pilots shot down over the North Sea. But at the same time, Khrushchev's January 6 speech was taken by Kennedy as an authoritative pronouncement of Soviet intentions to expand operational support for Communist insurgencies and "wars of national liberation." The president instructed all members of the new administration to read the speech, discussed it with his

owes its existence to the direct initiative, guidance, and support of the Viet Minh movement and its leaders, and . . . it has remained heavily dependent on Vietnamese assistance and direction." Paul Langer and Joseph Zasloff, *Revolution in Laos: The North Vietnamese and the Pathet Lao* (Santa Monica: The RAND Corporation, 1969), p. v. At the same time, it must be emphasized that the level of North Vietnamese involvement in Laos has often been exaggerated by the Laotian government, as for example during July 1959, January 1961, and May 1962, so as to induce increased American support. See Arthur Dommen, *Conflict in Laos* (New York: Praeger, 1964), pp. 119–124; *Time*, January 13, 1961, p. 20; and Bernard Fall, *The New Republic*, June 18, 1962, pp. 19–20.

staff, and quoted excerpts from it to the National Security Council.[20]

The Russians' behavior in Laos seemed particularly inconsistent to the new administration. In the words of James Reston, Kennedy and his advisers wondered "why Moscow — which is far from Southeast Asia — rather than Communist China — which has a common frontier with Laos — has led the Communist intervention." One explanation popular within the Kennedy administration was that "Moscow feared that a Peiping intervention in Laos might lead to a major war." [21] According to this viewpoint, the Russians were trying primarily to control and moderate the tempo of the Laotian crisis through exclusion of the reckless Chinese rather than exploit a political opportunity presented them by American bungling. However, as the fighting dragged on and hopes of a quick diplomatic settlement faded, this interpretation of Russian motives was increasingly questioned. It was no longer clear whether the Soviet Union was stalling on the diplomatic front so that it might further explain its position to Peking and Hanoi or whether it was delaying so that the Pathet Lao and Viet Minh might pursue their war of national liberation under direct Russian sponsorship.

This analysis reflected the Kennedy administration's cautious reappraisal of the notion of a monolithic Communist bloc, and its attempt to use the discernible differences among the Communists to explain their behavior with respect to Laos. According to Hilsman, the administration believed the Soviet Union, Communist China, and North Vietnam were in basic agreement on the desirability of making Laos a Communist satellite, but it thought there were important differences in the three nations' willingness to assume costs and risks on behalf of this goal. It believed the Soviet Union to have only modest interest in Southeast Asia and much greater commitments in Europe, the Middle East, and Africa. It did not expect the Soviet Union to be willing to pay a high price for the immediate communization of Laos and thought the Soviet Union interested in keeping the risk of war with the United States as low as possible — particularly over such a non-vital nation as Laos.[22] This expectation, in turn, suggested the supposition that the Soviet Union had intervened in Laos only to forestall a greater risk such as the intrusion of Chinese forces and expansion of the war beyond the borders of Laos.

The Kennedy administration's analysis of Soviet motivation rejected the notion of Russian-Chinese collaboration, but it was a conservative interpretation of the developing Sino-Soviet split which failed to encompass the notion of actual competition and antagonism between the two Communist powers.* It did not see that Russia directly feared the expansion of Communist China's power into Southeast Asia but only that it feared the possibility of China's provocation of an East-West confrontation which could endanger Soviet plans and interests. However, subsequent research has indicated that the former of the two is the more accurate interpretation of the Soviet Union's motivation. As Dommen has expressed it, "The Soviet Union was acting out of the imperative need to retain the allegiance of North Vietnam in the developing quarrel with China." [23] Oliver Clubb has drawn a similar conclusion: "Had the Soviet Union remained aloof while Laos was being drawn forcibly into the Western camp, the hand of the pro-Chinese element in Hanoi would have been strengthened." [24] The Soviet Union began its campaign to lure North Vietnam away from China in August 1960 by extending large credits for Vietnamese industrial expansion,[25] but the Kennedy administration was probably not aware of this competition for Vietnamese favor. The American image of the Communist bloc, while less than monolithic, still failed to comprehend the full magnitude of its fragmentation.

Washington saw the Viet Minh as the most motivated of the three opponents, having held the domination of Laos as a primary goal for fifteen years. But there were two costs which Washington believed Hanoi was unwilling to pay in behalf of this goal. First, Hanoi could not allow the capture of Laos to interfere with the even more immediate aim of communizing South Vietnam. Second, Laos could not be purchased at the expense of political subordination to Peking. The provocation of a large-scale American intervention in Laos might result in either or both of these occurrences, so Washington assumed Hanoi to be particularly interested in controlling the risk of such an event. According to Hilsman, the administration believed the Chinese Communists

---

* In his first visit with de Gaulle on May 31, 1961, Kennedy downgraded the immediate impact of Russian-Chinese differences, saying that the affair reminded him of Caesar and Pompey, who did not discover their dislike for each other until after they had vanquished their common enemy. Hugh Sidey, *John F. Kennedy, President* (New York: Atheneum, 1963), p. 181.

feared the costs of American intervention and were acutely interested in avoiding war with the United States but also had a higher
estimate than the Russians of the losses which the United States
would tolerate before launching on a war policy.[26] The failure of
China's Great Leap Forward, which McNamara has written was
"clearly evident by 1960–61," was undoubtedly an important reason for American expectations of Chinese restraint.[27] But this appears to have been only part of the Kennedy administration's
view of the Communist Chinese, for a more ominous set of calculations underlay much discussion of the crisis. Arguments in support of deploying American troops in Laos were often rebutted on
the grounds that China would not permit American occupation of
a bordering buffer state and would feel compelled to intervene as
it had under similar circumstances during the Korean War. This
argument was particularly popular within the military for refuting
the feasibility of limited intervention, but with some civilian advisers utilizing it to oppose intervention in any form, Kennedy was
bound to give it full consideration. In conversation with Nixon in
April, the president commented, "I just don't think we ought to
get involved in Laos, particularly where we might find ourselves
fighting millions of Chinese troops in the jungles." [28]

III. ASSESSING THE POSSIBLE DAMAGE

From the viewpoint of Kennedy and his advisers, important national interests were endangered by the Communist thrust in
Laos. Laos itself was of little intrinsic value, but as a nation pro-
tected under the SEATO protocol and bordering non-Communist
Thailand, South Vietnam, Cambodia, and Burma, it had substantial psychological and strategic importance for the American position in Southeast Asia and future United States relations with
other members of SEATO. American policy in Laos was particularly crucial to continued cooperation with Thailand, the most
important Asian member of SEATO.* The Thai government had
long felt that its relationship with Laos was "of a special character," that its neighbor to the northeast must serve as Thailand's

* As Fred Greene notes, "The SEATO system itself is very Thai-oriented;
its headquarters are in Bangkok, and many of the ablest Thai officers participate actively in planning and other staff work. Moreover, Thailand takes part
in frequent SEATO combat exercises." U.S. Policy and the Security of Asia
(New York: McGraw-Hill, 1968), p. 116.

buffer against Communist power in Asia. Should Laos fall to the Communists, the Mekong River border between the two countries would offer unlimited opportunities for infiltration into Thailand. As a result, throughout 1960–61, the Thai government made it unmistakably clear to Washington that United States support for an anti-Communist Laotian regime, even to the point of military intervention, was the touchstone by which it chose to judge the worth of its continued affiliation with SEATO and alignment with the West.[29] Such Thai pressures as the commencement of discussions with the Soviet Union regarding trade expansion and cultural exchanges appear to have been important in bringing the Eisenhower administration to support the military overthrow of Souvanna in December 1960. Similarly, as the Pathet Lao position improved during the first months of 1961, Thailand began to question publicly the value of collective security and increased its pressure on the Kennedy administration for United States intervention.

Of comparable consequence in weighing the importance of Laos was the apparent interrelationship between that nation and the developing crisis in South Vietnam. As Kennedy entered office, he was briefed on Communist efforts to establish control over Laotian territory bordering on South Vietnam and was informed by the CIA that the Communists' road improvement program from Laos into South Vietnam "was obviously preparatory to stepped-up military activity." [30] To this was soon added General Edward Lansdale's special report to the president on the already precarious and deteriorating state of the South Vietnamese government and the increasingly successful operations of the Viet Cong.[31] Under these circumstances a decision to abandon the American commitment in Laos appeared equivalent to demoralizing an already embattled Vietnamese government and permitting unimpeded Communist infiltration into South Vietnam.

Thus, conditions in Southeast Asia did seem to suggest the truth of the "domino theory," i.e. the loss of Laos would result in the increased probability — perhaps even inevitability — of the loss of neighboring Thailand and South Vietnam and the need to increase defense expenditures in these proximal nations so as to counteract their heightened vulnerability. This highly interrelated image of Southeast Asian politics found a receptive audience in the new president. As early as March 1954, Kennedy had professed that partition of Indochina and withdrawal of the French would merely be "the first step toward the seizure of complete control in that area by Communist forces." [32] Later, in his March 23, 1961, news conference on Laos, the president would assert that "the security of all Southeast Asia will be endangered if Laos loses its neutral independence." *

Perhaps as important, Kennedy's opinion was never seriously challenged by members of the outgoing administration or his own chief advisers. In his final pre-inaugural meeting with Eisenhower, Kennedy was told by the former general that if the Communists gained Laos, they would bring "unbelievable pressure" against Thailand, Cambodia, and South Vietnam.[33] Sorensen recalls:

> In general, the Joint Chiefs (and most other advisers) accepted without reservation the "falling domino" theory—the premise that an absence of American military intervention would lose Laos, which would move Thailand toward the Communist orbit, which would jeopardize SEATO, which in five or six years would lose all Southeast Asia, and so on down a trail of disaster.[34]

But even given this attitude, Kennedy might have had greater freedom in interpreting Laos's value to American national interest had it not been for the extraordinary degree of United States involvement in that small nation prior to 1961. Whatever wishful thinking there might have been in the Eisenhower-Dulles attempt to transform Laos into a strong and loyal ally, a "bastion of freedom," the effort had been made and by the time Kennedy assumed office the prestige of the United States, particularly in Asia, was closely associated with the future of Laos. Kennedy was a politician extremely sensitive to matters of appearance and prestige, and on March 20 he told Arthur Schlesinger and Walter

* "The Situation in Laos," *Department of State Bulletin*, April 17, 1961, p. 544. Kennedy would reaffirm his belief in the "domino theory" in his attitude toward Vietnam. When asked if he had "any reason to doubt this so-called 'domino theory' that if South Vietnam falls, the rest of Southeast Asia will go behind it" in a televised interview with Huntley and Brinkley on September 9, 1963, Kennedy responded: "No, I believe it. I believe it . . . China is so large, looms so high just beyond the frontiers, that if South Vietnam went, it would not only give an improved geographic position for a guerrilla assault on Malaya, but would also give the impression that the wave of the future in Southeast Asia was China and the Communists. So I believe it." *Public Papers of the Presidents of the United States: John F. Kennedy, 1963* (Washington, D.C.: United States Government Printing Office, 1964), p. 659.

Lippmann that "we cannot and will not accept any visible humiliation over Laos." [35] Thus, while complaining from time to time about the United States' "overcommitment" in Southeast Asia, the president would in the same breath confess that he felt compelled to operate within this framework of inherited obligations.[36]

Finally, Kennedy's view of the importance of Laos was subtly but significantly influenced by his interpretation of the international system and the ground rules within which Soviet-American relations were to be conducted during his presidency. The world through Kennedy's eyes was a precariously balanced bipolar system which could be easily destabilized by additions to one side or the other. Consequently, political and social change had to take place without involving the prestige or commitments of the United States or Russia, "without transferring power from one bloc to the other," and "without making either side feel threatened and constrained to resist change by force." [37] Laos was a case where these guidelines were being ignored: the crisis was perceived as a threat to American prestige and commitments in Southeast Asia and a menace to the existing balance of power in that region. To Kennedy this made abandonment of Laos impossible and the situation extremely dangerous.

IV. CONSTRAINTS ON PRESIDENTIAL ACTION

While all these factors pressed toward a firm American stand in Laos, Kennedy and his advisers learned quickly of the multiple human and environmental constraints within which they had to operate. A primary frustration was the overall weakness of American conventional forces. The previous administration's reliance upon air power and nuclear deterrence had been so great that by the end of 1960 there were only eleven army divisions ready for combat. Schlesinger recalls how "Kennedy was appalled to discover a few weeks after the inauguration that, if he sent 10,000 men to Southeast Asia, he would deplete the strategic reserve and have virtually nothing left for emergencies elsewhere." [38] But Laos was only one of several international trouble spots inherited by the president wherein the United States might conceivably be forced to exercise military power. The Congo crisis was at its peak, the Berlin conflict was simmering and likely to erupt once more, South Vietnam might soon require military support, and Cuba constituted a persistent irritant. Kennedy had to ration his available forces among these global responsibilities, and this alone made a heavy deployment of American troops in or around Laos, if only as a bluff, extremely risky.

But while lack of conventional preparedness and the volatile international situation militated against any massive show of force in Laos, the use of more delicate — and what Kennedy and some of his civilian advisers considered to be more valuable — levels of military force would meet resistance from the president's top military advisers. While generally in support of some military response in Laos, the Joint Chiefs of Staff (JCS) were quick to point up the immense problems which any American contingent would face there. Northern and eastern Laos was a mountainous terrain covered with dense rain forest, and the tropical climate of the region spawned seasonal floods and quagmires and debilitating parasites and diseases. It was a landlocked nation with few roads, no railroads, no telephone system, no national radio system, and no airfields capable of accommodating jets.[39] Moreover, JCS force-level recommendations took into account the risks of provocation and escalation entailed in deploying American soldiers so close to the Chinese and North Vietnamese borders. To deter counter-intervention by either or both of these Communist countries, the Joint Chiefs advised that any United States entry into Laos be accompanied by the threat to bomb such key cities as Canton and Hanoi. Considering all of these factors, the Joint Chiefs approved intervention in Laos with no less than 60,000 soldiers, supporting air cover, and, if necessary, nuclear weapons.[40] In late April, after the Pathet Lao and their Viet Minh supporters had demonstrated a surprising level of strength, the JCS would revise its minimum force level upward to 140,000 soldiers.[41]

If accounts by Schlesinger and Hilsman are accurate,[42] several of Kennedy's foreign policy advisers were impatient with this standard military approach emphasizing preparedness for all possible contingencies, and the president himself was disturbed by the Joint Chiefs implied request for a blank check permitting escalation to whatever level field commanders thought necessary. Some civilian advisers argued for a more limited troop commitment requiring less disruption of United States forces around the world and aimed rather exclusively at the psychological task of enhancing the American commitment in the eyes of both the Communists and allied forces. But as Schlesinger notes, the Joint Chiefs' warnings and opposition to limited intervention did have a power-

ful constraining influence.[43] And later that year Kennedy told
Arthur Krock that "United States troops should not be involved
on the Asian mainland, especially in a country with the difficult
terrain of Laos." [44]

A further constraint on American policy was the lack of una-
nimity within the Southeast Asia Treaty Organization. Thailand,
the member nation most directly threatened, Pakistan, and the
Philippines were in favor of military intervention, although only
the former two were willing to make promises of substantial military support.[45] From New Zealand and Australia would come
token support at best. The true strength of the organization lay
with its North Atlantic members, but France and Great Britain
privately refused to offer assistance and instead urged the United
States to support a neutralist Laos with a coalition government
that included the Pathet Lao. France was resolutely unwilling to
embark upon another Indochina War, while Great Britain, although somewhat more sympathetic to the American position, had
itself been burned before in a ten-year jungle campaign against
guerrillas in Malaya.[46] With France and Great Britain cool toward
intervention, the deterrent value of SEATO intervention was
unquestionably diluted, any American attempt to glorify its intrusion as a multi-national police action was only imperfectly possible,
and the preponderance of any military costs was destined to fall
squarely on the United States government.

As a successful domestic politician, Kennedy was acutely sensitive
to public opinion, but with respect to foreign policy the president sensed — as he told Chalmers Roberts early in 1961 — contradictory attitudes in American society: both an extensive desire to
stand up to the Communists and a strong reluctance to become
involved in any military action. This meant that Kennedy could
expect little clear-cut guidance for foreign policy from the general
public, but it also required that — as a president narrowly elected
and deeply conscious of old Republican charges of "Democratic
wars" — he move very cautiously so as not to deviate from that
treacherous political path between these contradictory American
attitudes.[47] As a result, the general public's reaction as anticipated
by Kennedy would serve as an additional constraint on decisive
United States action during the Laos crisis. Unfortunately, such a
cautious attempt to maintain maximum public support was capable of degenerating into prolonged ambivalence and indecision,
and during certain stages of the crisis, Kennedy drifted dangerously

close to this state of mind. At one point he said to Schlesinger, "If I decided to do nothing, I could be an exceedingly popular President." Hilsman has mildly criticized the president for holding such an attitude during the crisis.[48]

Yet, Kennedy's public support during the crisis was never in doubt. His popularity, as measured by the monthly Gallup Poll, was higher during April 1961 — the month during which the Laotian crisis peaked and he was required to make his most difficult decisions — than at any other time in his administration. The 83 per cent approval which he received from the general public in April was a figure 4 per cent higher than Eisenhower ever received during his eight years in office.[49]

Kennedy was fortunate in that the first few months of his administration were marked by the rather traditional nonpartisan atmosphere which accompanies the inauguration of a new national leader. He was "given a chance" to formulate his Laos policy in comparative isolation from political attack, and except for a few minor exceptions, actually received strong Republican support throughout the crisis. In late April, when American losses in Laos were becoming increasingly apparent, some opposition surfaced in both Congress and the press against any attempts at negotiation with the Communists and the formation of a coalition government in Laos. But when Kennedy privately consulted with leaders of both political parties on the possibility of committing United States troops to Laos, he found them to be solidly opposed to such action.[50]

V. THE "QUIET DIPLOMACY" PHASE

As Kennedy assumed official responsibility for United States policy in Laos, several proposals for dampening the crisis were already in existence. On December 15, India had addressed a special message to the co-chairmen of the 1954 Geneva Conference, Great Britain and the Soviet Union, calling on them to reconvene the International Control Commission in Laos. Anxious to avoid involvement in a major conflict, Britain placed Nehru's proposal on the December agenda of the NATO council, but the United States rejected it as counter to its full commitment to the Boun Oum government. While the Communist bloc publicly supported reconvening the ICC, it proposed that a new and enlarged Geneva Conference first be called. The proposal to reconvene the Geneva

Conference had previously been made by the Soviet Union on September 14, renewed by Prince Sihanouk of Cambodia on December 19, and been endorsed by Peking in a note to the conference co-chairmen on December 28.[51] The United States had remained unresponsive to this proposal as well.

During its first week in office, the Kennedy administration took two actions which indicated an important change in the American objective from the previous administration. The first of these actions came on January 22 in the form of a United States-backed plan handed to the Soviets by the British ambassador which called for the resumption of the ICC to supervise a cease-fire.[52] In agreeing to Nehru's original suggestion, the United States indicated that at least for the moment its immediate objective had been reduced to a simple discontinuation of hostilities at the status quo. While this proposal did not preclude the possibility of eventual United States intervention on behalf of this goal, it did suggest a significant change from the Eisenhower conviction, expressed on January 2 at a White House briefing, that "if we ever have to resort to force [in Laos], there's just one thing to do: clear up the problem completely." [53] As Eisenhower left office he was convinced that force should be used in Laos only with the intent of undoing all Communist gains. Whatever Kennedy's ultimate objective, for the present he was suggesting that the Communists be granted their territorial gains on condition that they stop fighting.

The Kennedy administration's approach to the Laotian problem was further revealed at the president's first press conference on January 25 when he stated that "the United States is anxious that there be established in Laos a peaceful country — an independent country not dominated by either side." [54] The statement strongly implied reduction of the American political objective from the establishment of a pro-Western government, as consistently pursued during the Eisenhower administration, to a truly neutralist government as privately recommended by the French and British.

In all probability, these first decisions regarding Laos did not require a great deal of soul-searching by Kennedy. As already noted, the United States was ill-prepared to intervene in Laos, and the hoped-for results of the British diplomatic initiative did not seem unfavorable to the American-backed regime. The Royal Lao Army, while not quick to pursue the enemy northward, nevertheless did control the vital Mekong River basin and many important outposts in the northern and eastern mountains. A cease-fire would

insure continuance of this situation. The earlier a semblance of
neutrality was restored, the earlier Russian and Vietnamese aid
would be discontinued. This would guarantee that the American-
backed troops, who outnumbered their neutralist and Pathet Lao
opponents approximately five to one,[55] would maintain their apparent superiority. And even should the Communists fail to accept
an immediate cease-fire, Kennedy had little worry. The chairman
of the Joint Chiefs of Staff, Lyman Lemnitzer, had assured the
president that Phoumi Nosavan's troops were launching a major
offensive which would recapture the Plain of Jars.[56]

After his initial flurry of diplomatic activity, Kennedy paused
for further developments in Laos and Moscow, and the events
which unfolded were not to his liking. The Soviets rebuffed the
American call for activation of the ICC and instead reiterated
their proposal that an enlarged Geneva Conference on Indochina
be reconvened to settle the conflict.[57] An unrelenting stream of
Russian supplies poured into Laos, and the Royal Lao Army proceeded north so slowly that it was late February before it came
within striking distance of the Pathet Lao.[58] Finally, Phoumi's
ineffectiveness and Moscow's obstinacy motivated an American
alternative to the earlier ICC proposal. On February 19, the king
of Laos read a statement drafted in the State Department declaring a policy of Laotian non-alignment and asking Burma, Cambodia, and Malaya to serve as supervisors and guarantors of his
nation's independence and neutrality.[59]

The new initiative was immediately denounced by Moscow,
Peking, and Hanoi, and the three neutralist nations which were
to comprise the international commission declined to participate
as well. Perhaps more significantly, the American offer was generally interpreted by diplomats as a sign of weakness. The *New York
Times* described it as "amounting to a decision not to be drawn
into a Laotian jungle war" which was "based on the reluctance of
Britain, France and other United States allies to go along with a
hard line and doubts as to the practicability of waging a campaign
in land-locked Laos." [60] Such an American posture hardly gave the
Communists any incentive to decrease their support for the Pathet
Lao and only tended to confirm Chinese allegations that the
United States was a "paper tiger."

Perhaps not coincidentally, the neutralist and Pathet Lao forces
soon commenced their major offensive. During the first days of
March, they struck west from the Plain of Jars toward the highway

which linked the administrative capital, Vientiane, with the royal capital, Luang Prabang. After a few minor clashes with Phoumi's advancing troops, they sent the Royal army in disorderly retreat south toward Vientiane. On March 9, the neutralist-Pathet Lao troops captured the vital road junction between Luang Prabang and Vientiane, thus threatening the safety of the nation's two major cities.[61]

This turn of events now presented Kennedy with the possibility of a complete loss of Laos, and according to Sorensen, it was during these first days of March that the president commenced a review of his alternatives and a reappraisal of American policy.[62] Kennedy decided that he had to choose one of four options. First, he could do nothing and allow what appeared to be an increasingly Pathet Lao-Vietnamese-dominated force to overrun the country. He quickly concluded that American national interest precluded this decision as it would risk the destruction of United States prestige in Asia and its Asian allies' faith in the American commitment. It might precipitate a "domino effect," which Kennedy thought would eventually necessitate a more costly stand against communism somewhere else in Southeast Asia.

Second, he could send whatever troops were necessary to insure victory by the pro-American government. But the United States was unlikely to receive even minimal support from its European allies for such an endeavor. Furthermore, such a policy would contain all the risks of a Korean-type conflict, perhaps including confrontation with China, in a country whose government was unpopular, whose army lacked the will to fight, whose terrain was treacherous, and whose internal transportation and communications structure was totally inadequate for modern warfare.

Third, he could settle for a partition of the country as in Korea and Vietnam. But these two earlier divisions had revealed the problems of defending such artificial frontiers, and the result might be a prolonged stationing of many American troops in Laos. Furthermore, he would face criticism at home for his appeasement of Communist aggression.

Fourth, and Kennedy's ultimate choice, he could continue to seek negotiations with the Communists toward the restoration of an independent and neutral government. Through this offer he could maintain the United States objective at its reduced level and ameliorate the expected damage to United States interests by nonmilitary means. This alternative would mean, Kennedy hoped, the denial of Laos to the Soviet Union, Communist China, or North Vietnam and would allow for a gradual disengagement from that country which would be less damaging to American prestige than a blatant military defeat. This would not threaten the vital interest of either the Soviet Union or the United States and might be a stable solution acceptable to both the North Vietnamese and the Chinese.

Even in January neutralization had not been an inexpensive policy to pursue. It had required a willingness to negotiate at the same table with Red China, which the United States did not even recognize. It had necessitated a willingness to withdraw the American military mission and throw support behind Souvanna Phouma, whom many State Department, CIA, and Pentagon officials still regarded as a Communist. It had meant an acceptance of Communist participation in a coalition government, something which many analysts viewed as tantamount to accepting eventual Communist control.

But Kennedy's March reaffirmation of a neutralization policy required a willingness to accept additional damage to American interest. He might have to wait patiently for the development of a political solution despite continuous military victories by the Pathet Lao. He might have to accept growing estrangement from Thailand and South Vietnam. It would mean all the dangers of negotiating with the Communists, who could exploit their opponents with "talk and fight" procedures, as the Korean peace talks had demonstrated.

According to Sorensen, this last point particularly bothered Kennedy. He recalled the weakness of the French bargaining position at the 1954 Geneva Conference which opened on the day Dien Bien Phu fell to the Viet Minh. In his determination not to let this happen to the United States, he decided to attach to the American offer of neutralization the uncompromisable stipulation that talks could not begin *until* a cease-fire had gone into effect. Should these "terms of compliance" prove unacceptable to the Communists, Kennedy was reluctantly willing to intervene militarily.

Given the Kennedy administration's perception of the opposition, it was logical that it would consider the Soviet Union as pivotal to any hopes for neutralization. Of course, desertion of the Pathet Lao at a time when military success was beginning to run with the Communists would not be typical Soviet behavior.

Furthermore, what started as a limited and reversible response to low-level American intervention in Laos could soon reach the status of a permanent commitment, thus seriously complicating the termination of Soviet aid. But if Russian involvement in Laos was an attempt to control the tempo of the crisis, then given the proper circumstances the Kremlin might be seriously interested in a viable neutralization of Laos as a device to take the pressure off it to intervene. Assuming this to be true, the general requirements of a coercive diplomatic strategy were apparent, and Kennedy was in a position to develop a plan aimed at securing agreement to a cease-fire.

First, the United States commitment to prevent the Communists from overrunning Laos had to be communicated convincingly to Moscow, Hanoi, and Peking so that each would appreciate the dire consequences of forcing a military confrontation with the United States. Second, the American offer of a neutralized Laos had to be reaffirmed so that Moscow could be certain neither the United States nor Red China would dominate Southeast Asia. This would be compatible with longer-range Communist goals since all three Communist governments could appease themselves with the thought that political conditions could be exploited to bring all of Laos eventually within the Communist orbit.

Basically, then, the strategy was to reaffirm the reduced United States objective of a neutralized Laos, and hence what was demanded of the opposition, but to *increase* the pressure on its behalf.[63] However, to make the offer of a neutralized Laos appear genuine, the administration recognized that the steps taken to establish the authenticity of its commitment to the defense of Laos could not be so substantial or heavy handed as to prompt fears of an American occupation of that country. Both the Pathet Lao and Hanoi would not agree to a cease-fire if such an event appeared probable, and China would be forced to consider an assault on the United States position. The military threat had to be employed delicately, with enough strength to make the American commitment credible yet not so much as to make the promise of neutralization appear fraudulent.[64] Neither the carrot nor the stick could dominate strategy. Following all of this, of course, would be the task of getting the various Lao political factions to agree on the composition of a coalition government, but as Brown has commented, "at the time this was viewed as a subordinate problem to that of bringing the intentions of the superpowers to-gether on the neutralization outcome." [65]

On March 9, the same day that Laos's main highway fell to the Communists, Kennedy met with his chief policy advisers on the deteriorating situation. As Sorensen recalls, "preparations were initiated for a seventeen-part, step-by-step plan of increasing military action, moving from military advisers to a token unit to all-out force." [66] For the present, a program of more and better supplies and improved troop training and deployment was approved.[67] On the same day in Siberia, American Ambassador Llewellyn Thompson was meeting with Khrushchev. Thompson conveyed Kennedy's desire for neutralization of Laos and his utmost resolve to prevent a Communist takeover. Specifically, the American ambassador informed Khrushchev of the willingness of the United States to withdraw completely its military mission from Laos, to channel all aid through an international body acceptable to both sides, and to declare publicly and in writing acceptance of a truly neutral Laos provided the Communists were willing to reciprocate. Messages of a similar nature were to be carried to the Red Chinese through the ambassadorial channel in Warsaw and to the North Vietnamese through Moscow's channels of communication.[68] In addition, Thompson attempted to use Khrushchev's professed desire for improved Soviet-American relations to United States advantage by telling the Soviet premier that he could not have both a lessening of the Cold War and advances in Laos. He also inquired whether Khrushchev was prepared to underwrite Communist China's concurrence to a Soviet-American settlement of the crisis.[69]

The Soviet Union failed to respond to the new American offer, and meanwhile the Laotian government's military position continued to worsen daily. Kennedy temporized before deciding that Rusk should speak with Soviet Foreign Minister Andrei Gromyko, who was visiting the United Nations in New York, to make one last diplomatic appeal for a neutralized Laos.[70] On March 18, Rusk held a five-hour meeting with Gromyko during which he emphasized the now standard American position: the United States sincerely desired Laos to be independent and neutral, and the United States was resolved not to let Communist forces overrun Laos. He also reiterated the threat that improved Soviet-American relations hinged on settling the Laos crisis.[71] Gromyko covered the same weary ground as well, insisting that it was the legitimate government of Laos which was receiving aid and opposing the United States proposal for a commission of three neutral nations. It was obvious that he had come primarily to get an indication of the Kennedy administration's resolve.[72]

VI. FROM "TRY-AND-SEE" TO "TACIT ULTIMATUM"

According to Sidey, "minutes after Rusk finished with Gromyko, he was on the phone to the White House. Kennedy, listening to the report of the Rusk-Gromyko talk, made up his mind that quiet diplomacy would, for the time being, have to be abandoned." [73] It was becoming increasingly clear to Kennedy that while the Communists might still be willing to settle for neutralization, the urgency, potency, and credibility of American threats remained insufficient to achieve such a solution. The president's approach to this point had been one of "try-and-see." In an attempt to avoid deeper American involvement and provocation of the Communists, he had taken one small diplomatic step at a time. As each successive step had proved insufficient, Kennedy had reluctantly proceeded with another. Through diplomatic channels, he had been able to make his demand on the Communists clear, but he had yet to reinforce the credibility and potency of his veiled threats or to convey even an implicit time limit for compliance with his demand. Now the president felt compelled to adopt such stronger tactics, to confront the Communists with a more systematic and potent package of political and military threats.

Kennedy called a special National Security Council meeting for March 20 to discuss the need for increased pressure on the Communists. The council reviewed the military and diplomatic situation but delayed final decisions until Rusk returned the next day from California. At the National Security Council meeting of March 21, plans for a new approach were made definite. All the preliminary steps necessary to the movement of American troops into the Mekong Valley of Thailand were ordered.[74] As Hilsman reports:

> A task force on Okinawa that had been especially formed and trained for fighting in Southeast Asia was put on alert. A Marine force in Japan was readied. The Seventh Fleet steamed at forced draft to the Gulf of Siam. A five-hundred

man unit was dispatched to set up a helicopter repair base at Udorn, the airfield in Thailand nearest Laos, and an advance flight of helicopters arrived shortly thereafter. Stockpiles of supplies and equipment were sent to bases near the Laos border.[75]

This action represented a compromise between the somewhat contradictory recommendations of Kennedy's military and civilian advisers. By preparing for a possible limited deployment of troops into Laos, the president partially accepted the advice of his civilian appointees. At the same time, by leaving himself one more escalatory signal — the actual movement of troops into Thailand — prior to intervention in Laos he mitigated the more immediate fears of the Joint Chiefs of Staff.

At the same March 21 meeting, a press conference was scheduled for March 23, and the president's advisers set to work on the statement he would present at that time. On the evening of March 23, Kennedy appeared on national television to deliver his short address, answer questions pertaining to the crisis, and hopefully convey to the Communists his mounting concern and resolution. Kennedy's presentation contained a subtle blend of the elements in a classical ultimatum. His demand was once again made clear: "If there is to be a peaceful solution, there must be a cessation of the present armed attacks by externally supported Communists." [76] Action to enhance the perceived potency of his threats had commenced the previous day with troop preparations and movements, but the televised address increased the credibility of these acts. Troop movements were noncommittal, and Eisenhower had taken similar, although less extensive, measures in early January. The press conference had more elements of a binding public commitment: not only was it scheduled at 6:00 P.M., maximum-audience time in the United States; it was also the first such news conference to be broadcast live around the world by Voice of America.[77] Kennedy's prepared statement made no mention of a time limit for compliance, but in response to a question concerning this point he commented, "I think the matter, of course, becomes increasingly serious as the days go by." [78] While Kennedy's speech stopped short of an explicit ultimatum, it can be considered a tacit one.

While increasing his pressure on the Communists, Kennedy both enhanced the credibility of his original positive inducement and increased the attractiveness of the presently offered settlement by making yet another major diplomatic concession. On the same day as the news conference, a British-American proposal was handed to the Soviet Union which called for an immediate cease-fire, and the reconvening of an enlarged Geneva Conference to work out a permanent settlement. Thus, for the first time had the United States conceded to the Communist demand for a fourteen-nation conference on Laos but only on Kennedy's terms, i.e., after a verified cease-fire. Many officials had hoped to avoid such a conference since it would give the Soviet Union and Communist China substantial influence over the composition of the new Laotian regime and provide Communist China with an international platform from which it would undoubtedly condemn American operations in Southeast Asia in strident terms.[79] The American peace proposal was also conciliatory in that it did not demand that the Soviet Union suspend its arms airlift to the Pathet Lao-Viet Minh forces as a precondition to the international conference. The president's continuing concern for crisis management also manifested itself, this time in his final, personal revision of the press conference statement which had been prepared for him by Charles Bohlen and McGeorge Bundy. According to Joseph Alsop, Kennedy felt their draft was "too crisp and clear, and might therefore sound bellicose. It would suffice for the Kremlin, he believed, to send the ships and troops quietly on their way, and to make a quiet but earnest statement of warning." [80]

Despite his stern words, Kennedy refused to make public the nature of the Communist provocation which would trigger a decision to intervene. There appear to have been at least two reasons for his not having done so. First, while Kennedy remained willing, if necessary, to accept further losses in Laos in order to avoid intervention, he could hardly admit this publicly because of the "soft on communism" attacks which would be levelled against him.* Second, by leaving the limits of his patience somewhat

* The length to which the Kennedy administration went in order to protect itself from such attacks is suggested by Bernard Fall's statement that "the three maps shown by President Kennedy at his press conference . . . which purported to show the progressively worsening situation in Laos, were so grossly inaccurate in their optimism as to be completely meaningless. At a time when most of the Laotian uplands were more or less under Communist control, the map purporting to show the 'present' situation gave the Communists credit for holding only parts of three provinces and one small isolated spot around Kam Khuet." (*Anatomy of a Crisis*, pp. 246–247.) I have concluded that the inaccuracy was a deliberate attempt to head off public

ambiguous, Kennedy hoped the Communists would interpret his sense of urgency and willingness to intervene as higher than they actually were.

The president's true intentions can be inferred from conversation at a March 20 luncheon reported by Schlesinger. At that time Kennedy expressed the opinion that it was indispensable to prevent "an immediate Communist takeover." The pro-American forces had to hold Vientiane in order to have a basis for negotiation with the opposition. Kennedy was almost fatalistic about the eventual outcome in Laos, willing to concede it to the Pathet Lao but for domestic and international reasons unable to afford a blatant and humiliating military defeat. He felt he had to defend a bargaining position which would allow for slow American disengagement and the extraction of some concessions from the Communists.[81]

Of course, Kennedy's belief as to what would constitute provocation necessitating American intervention was not communicated directly to the Communists, but it does appear that some official agency attempted to inform the Pathet Lao of the exact limits of American patience. A *New York Times* correspondent covering the SEATO military advisers conference in Bangkok wrote on March 23 that "the critical area is the plain along the Mekong, including Vientiane and Luang Prabang." The United States and its allies were thought to be inclined to fix the river basin as the area in which Pathet Lao encroachment would be met with intervention, but "the treaty group would refrain from announcing any such final line of resistance, since to do so might be construed as an invitation to the Communists to envelop less critical areas of Laos." [82] With leaks such as this to the press, a formal announcement of this position would hardly seem necessary. It is important to note, however, that this "final line of resistance" encompassed much territory which Kennedy was apparently willing to give up. This more extensive area conforms rather well with what the State Department considered vital,

criticism and not a result of the intelligence community's failure to know the true extent of Communist gains. This may help explain why Hilsman, then director of the State Department's Bureau of Intelligence and Research, has correctly reported the extent of Communist control as of March 23 but incorrectly described this as having been depicted on Kennedy's third map (p. 91). For pictures of the three maps used in the news conference, see *New York Times*, March 24, 1961, p. 8.

indicating perhaps that the release of this opinion to the press came on the initiative of that agency.

The March 23 news conference and military preparations had almost immediate impact on the Soviet Union. The next day at a luncheon in New York, Foreign Minister Gromyko asked United Nations Ambassador Adlai Stevenson if he could arrange an appointment for him with Kennedy. He had a message to deliver from Premier Khrushchev. Gromyko went on to express his country's desire for a neutralized Laos and hope that such a solution could be reached peacefully. Stevenson called Washington, and an appointment was quickly set for March 27.[83] At the same time, however, Russian attempts to undermine the Kennedy administration's resolve were also proceeding. According to Joseph Alsop, the Soviet Union "planted 'authoritative' warnings, sent through satellite sources . . . that a cease-fire was unthinkable and that President Kennedy could have a war if he wanted one. These reached the American policy makers . . . almost concurrently with the news that Soviet Foreign Minister Andrei Gromyko wished to be received by the President." [84]

Kennedy's new approach was not exhausted with the completion of his press conference; rather, it was followed by a highly coordinated set of diplomatic moves designed to keep the political pressure on the Communist bloc and in particular the Soviet Union. First, Kennedy tried to increase Khrushchev's perceived costs of military support for the Pathet Lao by presenting him with the possibility of alienating neutral India should Soviet intervention continue. On March 24, roving Ambassador Averell Harriman handed Nehru a personal letter from the president which called on the Indian prime minister to assume a leading role in arranging a cease-fire in Laos.[85] Kennedy's note reemphasized the intention of the United States to withdraw completely from that nation provided neutrality should be restored but warned that SEATO would be forced to intervene if this did not develop. Pleased with the neutralist policy of the United States, and concerned that it might be provoked into escalating the war, Nehru sent an urgent personal note to Khrushchev that very day asking the premier to help end the fighting.[86] He also instructed the Indian ambassador to Moscow, Krishna Menon, to inform the Soviets of the urgency of a truce and the reactivation of the International Control Commission.[87]

On March 25, details were quickly worked out for Kennedy to

fly to Florida to meet with British Prime Minister MacMillan, who was in Bermuda at the time.[88] On March 26, MacMillan reluctantly agreed to commit some units of a Commonwealth brigade in Malaya should limited intervention in Laos become necessary. It is probable that the Soviet Union was not left in ignorance of this decision by Great Britain. Meanwhile, on March 23, Secretary of State Rusk had departed for the SEATO foreign ministers conference in Bangkok. Rusk was not as successful as Kennedy, for the French refused to bind themselves to any military intervention. But while the March 28 SEATO resolution published at the conference's conclusion referred to "appropriate retaliatory action if diplomatic efforts fail to restore peace," a private and blunter United States warning to the Soviet Union was reported by several sources to have been attached to the document leaving no doubt that "appropriate action" included American military intervention.[89]

March 27 brought Kennedy better understanding of how much his new approach had budged the Russians. In his talk with Gromyko, Kennedy received assurances of Soviet interest in a neutral Laos, but the meeting failed to produce any agreement as to how this could be achieved. The Soviet leader's change had been primarily one in attitude. Schlesinger recalls, "Chip Bohlen told me that night that Gromyko was 'serious' this time, as he had not been in his talk with Rusk nine days earlier." [90] A shift in Soviet policy was hinted at in a *Pravda* editorial of the same day. The editorial commenced by complaining that the Kennedy warning "actually means presenting an ultimatum to the Laotian people," an important clue as to how the president's remarks had been perceived by the Kremlin. It then went on to state:

> It is quite evident that the realistic way to the solution of
> the Laos problem lies not in aggravating the situation in the
> area of Laos, not in preparing military intervention, but in
> peace talks and in the calling of an international conference
> and the renewal of the work of the ICC.[91]

It was becoming obvious that Khrushchev was caught in the middle. On the one hand, he was faced with the increasingly hostile demand of the United States for an immediate cease-fire. On the other, he was confronted with Peking's strenuous opposition to any cease-fire prior to an international conference and its eagerness to exploit any sign of weakness in Moscow's revolutionary dedication. On December 28, 1960, Peking had called for reactivation of the ICC in Laos but only on condition that it deal with "the legal government of Laos" — that of Prime Minister Souvanna Phouma — and did not have "any contact with the illegal Boun Oum-Nosavan government fostered by United States armed intervention." [92] Of course, this was unacceptable to the United States, and it soon became clear that, in fact, Peking opposed reactivation of the ICC. According to Brian Crozier,

> It is known that the Chinese fiercely opposed the reactivation of the Commission in the weeks that followed the recapture of Vientiane by the right-wing forces, that is, while the "neutralist" and Pathet Lao forces were preparing, with Communist help, the counteroffensive which they launched at the beginning of March. [93]

When the Pathet Lao March offensive proved a brilliant success, the Chinese press and radio became increasingly aggressive, urging the Laotians to "step up their struggle and further develop the great victory recently achieved." [94] It was clear in late March that Peking was sticking with the policy previously enunciated in February by Premier Chou En-Lai:

> The Chinese Government is, in general, not against reactivating the International Commission for Supervision and Control in Laos, but it is against reactivating it in the present conditions in Laos. . . . It is necessary first to convene an international conference of the countries concerned, which will make new provisions on the tasks and functions of the Commission in light of the new situation. [95]

With the United States and China demanding diametrically opposite phasing of the cease-fire and the international conference, Khrushchev's policy began to reflect an attempt to anger neither Washington nor Peking. On April 1, he responded to an earlier British proposal for the activation of the ICC followed by an international conference with the suggestion that Great Britain and the Soviet Union should issue an appeal for a cease-fire in Laos simultaneously with the commencement of a new international conference. [96] Then two days later, the Soviet Union conceded almost totally to the United States demand. It agreed in private talks with Britain that an end to the fighting in Laos must precede negotiations on the future of that nation, but it failed to consent to ICC verification of the cease-fire prior to the international conference.[97] Prospects for a negotiated settlement of the crisis were improving, but Kennedy remained adamant as to the "terms of compliance" he demanded from the Russians.

On April 4, evidence increased that the Soviet Union fully appreciated and was willing to accept what was demanded of it by the United States provided it could obtain modest support for this from its Asian allies. On that day, the Soviets beamed a program to Southeast Asia in Vietnamese only — declaring that while the Soviet Union did not consider a cease-fire in Laos as a precondition to an international conference, it would "help to create a favorable atmosphere for negotiations." Dommen notes that "this was tantamount to a direct appeal to North Vietnam, and to an admission that the Soviets recognized that only the North Vietnamese had the power to control the ground fighting in Laos and thus to call a cease-fire." [98] At this time it was also becoming clear to Western diplomats, and in particular to British representatives involved in continuous negotiations with Russian diplomats in London, that the Chinese Communists were deeply involved in Soviet policy in Laos and had been exercising considerable influence over Soviet responses to British-American proposals.[99] Therefore, the Russian radio program also represented an important breakdown in what had been, in light of recent Sino-Soviet differences, surprisingly close cooperation between the Soviet Union and Communist China. The Russians were apparently attempting to circumvent Chinese resistance to a verified preconference cease-fire by means of a covert appeal to Hanoi and the Viet Minh. At the same time, the Soviet Union could not afford to jeopardize its campaign for Hanoi's favor and risk loss of power over events in Laos by quickly terminating its support for the war, so the airlift to the Pathet Lao continued unabated.

Now that the Soviet Union had furtively appealed for a cease-fire and the United States had increased its diplomatic and military pressure, there was little more that Kennedy and Khrushchev believed could be done immediately. They paused to observe the effect of their efforts on events in Laos. Out of deference to the limits of American patience and perhaps the "final line of resistance" suggested by the SEATO military advisers, the Pathet Lao during the first weeks of April carefully avoided attacking towns and cities in the Mekong Valley. Instead, they relentlessly extended and consolidated their control over the hills and mountains in northern and eastern Laos.[100] It soon became apparent that the Soviet and American cease-fire appeals were having no measurable effect.

The failure of the Pathet Lao to respond to the president's diplomatic-military signaling and the Soviet Union's continued refusal to appeal publicly for a verified cease-fire prior to an international conference were sobering developments to many Washington officials who during the last days of March were privately expressing confidence in the eventual success of the United States tougher action. Worry mounted that the Russians might be purposefully stalling on the diplomatic front while on the battlefield the Pathet Lao and the Viet Minh resorted to a "creeping" tactic which steadily eroded the Laotian government's defenses but avoided large offensives that might unite SEATO and trigger a Western intervention.[101]

The inadequacy of American action was also suggested by the increasingly obvious relationship between the Communist drive in Laos and Viet Cong gains in South Vietnam. On April 14 *Time* reported that during the preceding week the Communists in Laos had devoted almost as much effort to sending supplies and reinforcements into South Vietnam via the Ho Chi Minh trail in eastern Laos as they had to expanding their territorial holdings. The Viet Cong reign of terror against the Diem regime was reaching a peak of 500 killings a month as the Communists attempted to terrorize the rural Vietnamese into voting against Diem in the April 9 elections. Furthermore, as a result of Communist gains in Laos, the Thai government was becoming increasingly alarmed that the United States might agree to either a coalition government which included strong Pathet Lao representation or a partition of Laos. Thailand felt that the only way to halt the Pathet Lao-Viet Minh offensive and to achieve the non-Communist coalition government in Laos which it considered vital to its security was to station SEATO troops along the Mekong River in Laos. During the second week in April, as the Communists pushed close to the Mekong in central Laos, Prime Minister Sarit sent a personal letter to Kennedy expressing the Thai government's position.[102]

It was against this background of Russian delay and Pathet

Lao success that the Bay of Pigs occurred. By April 18 it had become obvious in Washington that the invasion had been a disaster.[103] Kennedy became worried that his decision not to back up the invaders with troops might be interpreted as a sign of his irresolution everywhere, including Laos, and further erode the credibility of United States military action in defense of its interests. That same day, he ordered the four hundred "civilian" advisers in Laos attached to the Programs Evaluation Office to put on their military uniforms and accompany the Royal Lao Army to the front line combat zones. Although this change in orders meant relatively minor alterations in the advisers' actual duties, the State Department's announcement of this escalation had ominous implications for Communist policy-makers in distant capitals. It implied that the United States was now bold enough to admit its intervention, that United States casualties would soon jump and American honor be more deeply engaged, and that Washington might be taking the first step in a series leading toward greater American participation. These possibilities enhanced the urgency of the situation.

The new move does appear to have had significant effect. On April 20 the North Vietnamese government called upon the Soviet Union and Great Britain to help prevent the United States from sending its advisers with the Royal army.[104] The next day, the New China News Agency accused the United States of expanding the war, and on April 23 Chinese Premier Chou En-lai stated that announcement of the military assistance advisory group was a "serious step taken by the United States in preparation for direct participation in the civil war in Laos." [105] Then on April 24, the Soviet Union and Great Britain announced that as the original co-chairmen of the 1954 Geneva Conference, they were reactivating the ICC and dispatching it to Laos to verify a ceasefire. They also announced that invitations were being sent to thirteen nations to convene at Geneva on May 12 for consideration of the Laos problem.[106] Peking and Hanoi quickly acknowledged their acceptance of the British-Russian plan.

Communist fear of further United States escalation was not the only factor which had helped move the crisis closer to a political settlement. During the week prior to April 24, Souvanna Phouma and Pathet Lao leader Souphanouvong had both visited Moscow, Peking, and Hanoi in efforts to iron out remaining differences over principles of the cease-fire, and these consultations undoubtedly played some part in bringing about unanimous Communist consent to the American terms of compliance.* Still, whatever the importance of these consultations, it is reasonably clear that the American military action had enhanced the Communists' incentive to resolve their differences and was viewed by the Communists as an unjustified intrusion on behind-the-scene bargaining. The Chinese *People's Daily* complained that

> when the Co-Chairmen of the Geneva Conference were negotiating on the convocation of an enlarged Geneva Conference and a ceasefire in Laos, the U.S. government hastily announced the establishment of a so-called "military assistance advisory group" in Laos to enable the civilian-dressed U.S. officers who have all the time been in Laos, to put on their uniforms and personally direct the operations of the rebel forces.[107]

In the Soviet paper *Trud,* the official commentator deplored that

> when the governments of the Soviet Union and Great Britain . . . had virtually agreed to appeal to the contending sides in Laos for a cease-fire, Washington adopted a decision directed at expanding U.S. participation in the hostilities on the rebels' side.[108]

But even though agreement on the phasing of the cease-fire and conference had now been reached, the level of violence in Laos was in fact increasing. As Schlesinger recalls, "according to reports reaching Washington, April 26, the Pathet Lao were attacking in force, as if to overrun the country before the cease-fire could take effect." [109] The accelerated Communist offensive brought the United States to the brink of intervention. On April 27 Kennedy convened the first in a series of National Security Council meetings to consider action necessary to strengthen the deteriorating American position in Laos and bordering countries. The interim Southeast Asia task force which the president had established in February now recommended a limited commitment of one or two American combat divisions to the Mekong Valley in Laos and Thailand and additional military assistance, including

---

* I am indebted to Charles Stevenson of Harvard University for suggesting these conferences as a possible explanation for Communist concessions at this time.

combat troops, for South Vietnam.* These deployments would hopefully rejuvenate the hapless Laotian army and deter the advancing Pathet Lao-Viet Minh force, provide badly needed technical assistance to the South Vietnamese army, and help repair seriously damaged relations between Thailand and the United States. The task force proposal was strongly supported by Walt Rostow, chief White House assistant covering Southeast Asian problems, and by Harriman, who was in Laos conducting an emergency inspection.[110]

At the same April 27 meeting the Joint Chiefs of Staff presented their own revised plan for intervention in Laos. While now divided among themselves on the desirability of intervening, they basically agreed on a plan which called for 100,000 to 150,000 soldiers to be deployed in Thailand, South Vietnam, and the non-Communist portions of southern Laos. If this did not bring a cease-fire, the Joint Chiefs recommended an air attack on Pathet Lao positions and the use of tactical nuclear weapons on the ground. Any counter-invasion by North Vietnam or Communist China would be met by United States bombing of the invaders' homeland. The Joint Chiefs' strong opposition to the limited intervention plan proposed by Kennedy's civilian advisers resulted in a long, heated meeting which Rostow later described as the worst White House conference he attended during the entire Kennedy administration.[111]

With the Communist offensive continuing, the National Security Council met again on April 29 and May 1. While these meetings brought a reaffirmation of the importance of Southeast Asia to United States security, Kennedy devoted most of his en-

---

* This interim task force, which met through April 1961, consisted of Deputy Secretary of Defense Roswell Gilpatrik (chairman), Secretary of State Dean Rusk, CIA director Allen Dulles, USIA director Edward Murrow, and subordinate personnel from other agencies.

Sidey has described a "Plan Five" which called for troops from the United States, Thailand, the Philippines, Pakistan, and Great Britain to move into positions in the Mekong Valley to release Laotian army units for duty in the forward battle areas. This proposed operation is also synonymous with what some government officials at the time were referring to as Track One. Whatever the nomenclature, this apparently was the portion of the task force recommendation pertaining to Laos, and Murphy reports that it was favored not only by task force chairman Gilpatrick but by Secretary of Defense McNamara as well. See Sidey, *Kennedy*, p. 84, and Charles Murphy, "Cuba: The Record Set Straight," *Fortune* (September 1961), pp. 94–95.

ergy to challenging the soundness of both the Joint Chiefs' and the task force's recommendations which he had now had the opportunity to study carefully. Having asked each of the chiefs to submit his views on intervention in writing, the president was surprised to discover that each military adviser held quite different opinions as to which allies would assist, the Communists' likely response, and the probability of success. What written plans were provided Kennedy considered to be too sketchy. He also rejected his task force's proposal; he found it to rest upon too many unverified assumptions and to be lacking in cost and time estimates.[112] As an alternative to his advisers' recommendations, Kennedy once again placed a division of Marines at Okinawa on alert, ready to move into Thailand should the Communists advance dangerously close to Vientiane. Meanwhile, he would continue to rely upon increased diplomatic pressure on the Soviet Union in hopes that the cease-fire would become effective before the rest of Laos was lost. It was clear that the president had decided to make a military stand against the Communists somewhere other than Laos.

Once again Kennedy had consulted his top advisers, and once again he had decided against intervening in Laos. An event which strongly influenced the president's decision was the recent Bay of Pigs debacle. While Kennedy's immediate response to the Bay of Pigs had been to order the American advisers in Laos to put on their uniforms and accompany the Lao army to the front lines, this was not an integral part of a strategy of increased resistance but rather a temporary face-saving gesture.* The president was now unsure whether it would be strategically and politically wise to invade Laos after having just declined such action in Cuba. As he said to Nixon on April 20, "I don't see how we can make any move in Laos, which is 5000 miles away, if we don't make a move in Cuba, which is only 90 miles away." [113] Furthermore, as many of Kennedy's confidants have reported, his confidence in the military-intelligence community had been badly shaken. He entered the last days of April "far more skeptical of the experts,

---

* However, while the "surfacing" of American advisers in Laos was interpreted by Kennedy and his advisers as a weak response to Communist provocation, this does not negate the possibility that this move was interpreted quite differently by Communist leaders on the battlefield and in distant capitals. See pp. 67–68.

their reputations, their recommendations, their promises, premises and facts." [114] His highly critical approach to the intervention plans laid before him was reflective of this attitude.

Kennedy did not reject out of hand everything now suggested by the military-intelligence community. He merely used what aspects of its advice he could to buttress his own inclination against intervention. On April 28 the president solicited the views of General MacArthur on the crisis. While the battle-scarred veteran of the Korean War rather predictably opposed the commitment of American soldiers in Asia, Sorensen reports that "the President never forgot this advice." [115] By contrast, General Lemnitzer travelled to Laos in early May and once on the spot cabled Kennedy his support for the task force's more limited intervention plan. When Schlesinger saw Kennedy on May 3, the president waved Lemnitzer's cables in the air and said, "If it hadn't been for Cuba . . . I might have taken this advice seriously." [116]

Equally important in shaping Kennedy's decision was the ineptitude of the Laotian army. While resisting the temptation to criticize publicly the performance of the Laotians, privately the president asked why the United States should be expected to fight for the Boun Oum government when the Laotian army was unwilling to do the same. If the United States were to make a military stand somewhere in Southeast Asia, much better he felt to make it in a country like Thailand or South Vietnam where the indigenous armed forces seemed willing to defend themselves. The president's attitude in this regard was seconded by most congressional leaders with whom he privately discussed the situation in late April.[117]

Finally, the president had a much more modest conception of what constituted unacceptable Pathet Lao provocation than did most of his advisers. While Sidey reports that "Kennedy in the weeks of April concluded that he might have to commit fighting troops in Laos if the Communists swept on dangerously toward Vientiane, the only city which the president felt could not fall," this was, in fact, a mere reaffirmation of the position he had expressed to Schlesinger on March 20.[118] By comparison, the State Department believed that all of the Mekong basin in Laos had to be defended in order to deny the Communists infiltration routes into Thailand and Cambodia and prevent demoralization of the United States' Asian allies.[119]

Kennedy undertook to make the best of his tentative decision not to intervene through moves designed to limit expected international and domestic repercussions. During the first week in May he approved a program to double the amount of military aid for South Vietnam and triple the number of men assigned to the American military advisory group in that country.[120] On May 9 Vice President Johnson left on a tour of Asia during which he reassured the governments of Thailand, South Vietnam, the Philippines, Nationalist China, and Pakistan of continued American defense and support. In Saigon, Johnson and Diem reached agreement on the details of the military assistance program approved by Kennedy.[121] In Bangkok, the vice president offered Prime Minister Sarit greater military and economic assistance to strengthen Thailand's resistance against Communist subversion.[122] Thus Johnson's trip served not only to enhance faith in the American commitment but also to implement military and economic steps which would impede the "domino effect."

At the domestic level, Kennedy began to establish a rationale for non-intervention. At a dinner in Chicago on April 28, the president stated: "We have committed ourselves to the defense of dozens of countries stretched around the globe . . . but we can only defend the freedom of those who are determined to be free themselves." [123] The Kennedy administration's claim that it would not stand by while Laos was overrun by the Communists was now being modified by the proviso that to receive American support a government must demonstrate a readiness to defend itself. On May 7 a similar argument was used by congressional leaders from both political parties, as senators Mansfield, Bridges, Morse, Javits, and Aiken publicly voiced their opposition to the use of American troops in Laos.[124]

To the great relief of the Kennedy administration, word arrived in Washington on May 3 that representatives of the Pathet Lao and Laotian government had reached agreement on the terms of a cease-fire. The level of fighting diminished to sporadic clashes and shellings along the cease-fire line, and the onset of the monsoon season put a damper on further large-scale action. With the International Control Commission's announcement on May 11 of "a general and obvious discontinuance of hostilities," the path was clear for the reconvening of the Geneva Conference on May 16. However, the Pathet Lao continued to refuse the ICC permission to travel into areas where cease-fire violations were reported, and United States Ambassador Harriman presented a list of thirty violations to the delegates in Geneva and threatened an American withdrawal from the talks if an effective truce were not established.[125]

When Kennedy arrived in Vienna June 3 for talks with Khrushchev, one of his prime objectives was to elicit from the Soviet premier strong support for an effective cease-fire in Laos. During their first day of discussions, Kennedy exacted from Khrushchev a promise to put renewed pressure on the Pathet Lao to cooperate with the ICC.[126] When their talks resumed the morning of June 4, Kennedy again returned to the topic of Laos. He suggested that both the United States and Soviet Union needed to decrease their commitment in Laos. Khrushchev agreed, but he questioned the willingness of the United States to do so in light of Kennedy's decisions to put the American military advisers in uniform and prepare Marines for a possible landing. It was clear that the premier had been carefully monitoring United States military action over the past three months. The two leaders concluded their discussion of Laos by agreeing to make the cease-fire a priority concern.*

Khrushchev apparently abided by his agreement, despite the influence in North Vietnam and China it might have cost him. Over the next months, the Pathet Lao attacks decreased and the cease-fire became effective.[127] The next major violation was a Communist attack on the provincial town of Nam Tha in May 1962 which came largely as a result of the provocative massing of Royal Lao troops at that garrison by General Phoumi. Responding to spurious reports of Pathet Lao and Viet Minh advances toward the Thai border, Washington initiated a large-scale movement of United States troops, planes, and ships to Thailand.[128] But as during the previous spring, the American decision was marked by Kennedy's hesitancy to accept his advisers' recommendations for strong action. Hilsman and Harriman proposed dispatching the Marines to Thailand to halt the supposed Communist drive. According to Schlesinger, "Kennedy was at first reluctant, fearing that once the Marines were installed in Thailand it would be dif-

---

* Schlesinger, *A Thousand Days*, pp. 342–343. During this discussion, Khrushchev wryly observed that the West was better than the Communists in making refined military threats such as those employed by Kennedy. This comment suggests that Khrushchev was aware Kennedy had successfully, however subtly, coerced the Communist side during the Laos crisis.

ficult to find an occasion to withdraw them, but decided to go ahead." [129] The atmosphere at the Geneva Conference soon improved, and on July 23, 1962, after almost fifteen months of negotiation, the Declaration and Protocol on the Neutrality of Laos was signed by the parties in attendance.

While the declaration established a troika government in Vientiane and called for the withdrawal of all foreign troops, it also in principle ratified the de facto partition of the country.[130] The Communists continued to hold the mountains while the Royal Lao government held the Mekong lowlands. The original Kennedy objective had been a negotiated neutral coalition which would preclude loss of, intervention in, or partition of Laos. Instead, the result was a tacitly accepted partition arrived at through negotiations and presided over by a tenuous coalition government. This left the Ho Chi Minh trails and South Vietnam accessible to the Communists and thus negated one of the original American purposes for supporting neutralization of Laos. At the same time, however, it denied the Communists the Mekong River basin in Laos and thus blocked direct access to Thailand — much more than Kennedy's minimal objective of spring 1961. Both Washington and Hanoi were willing to settle for the half of Laos which was felt to be most vital to its immediate national interest.

VII. LESSONS AND CONCLUSIONS

A week after he had taken office, John Kennedy had lowered the military and political objectives of the United States to the establishment of a cease-fire and the creation of a neutral Laos. In doing so he implicitly acknowledged a cardinal principle of coercive diplomacy, namely that both the opposition's as well as one's own level of motivation are highly dependent upon the nature of the objectives sought. Kennedy's decision amounted to a substantial reduction of the goal pursued by the Eisenhower administration, but the compromise which Kennedy was willing to settle for was in fact consonant with the limited military means that the previous administration had been willing to employ. Eisenhower had committed the United States to defeating the Pathet Lao, but during the last days of his tenure he showed considerably less than the level of motivation necessary to undo the gains which the Communists achieved beginning in late December. It is doubtful that Eisenhower would have reacted differently even had it not been the waning moments of his presidency; during a comparable crisis in 1954 he had declined to send United States forces to Indochina. The Communists were clearly more motivated to prevent a pro-Western military victory in Laos than Eisenhower or Kennedy were motivated to achieve one. By reducing the American military objective to the denial of the Mekong basin — or perhaps only Vientiane — to the Pathet Lao, Kennedy eroded the opposition's motivation to resist his demand, enhanced his own level of motivation, and thus established a goal with respect to which there was no clear motivational asymmetry favoring the opposition. Of course, this reduced objective was compatible with Hanoi's immediate aim of communizing South Vietnam since it left eastern Laos in the hands of the Viet Minh, but the Pathet Lao's ambition extended to all of Laos.

As we have observed, however, Kennedy's decision to reduce the United States military objective in Laos did not bring about the cease-fire which he requested. Prior to his shift toward a "tacit-ultimatum" approach in late March, only Kennedy's positive inducement of a promised neutralization served as incentive for the Communists to comply, and this incentive proved to be insufficient. On the other hand, during the month of January the Eisenhower administration had attempted to intimidate the Communists with many of the same military preparations which Kennedy would eventually employ but without clearly specifying the nature of its demand and without any firm offer of positive diplomatic inducement. It was not until late March, then, that the United States confronted the Communists with both substantial diplomatic inducements and a strong variant of coercive diplomacy simultaneously. That this combination proved reasonably effective where Eisenhower and Kennedy's previous efforts had failed suggests the truth of the proposition that what neither the "carrot" nor the "stick" can achieve alone may be obtainable by combining the two.

As stated in Chapter One, the "tacit-ultimatum" approach to coercion entails (1) a specific demand on the opponent, (2) an implicit or explicit time limit for compliance, and (3) a strong and credible threat of punishment for non-compliance. Of particular interest in the Laos crisis are the second and third elements. Kennedy's initial threat of punishment as expressed through military movements and international consultation proved sufficiently strong and credible to erode the Soviet Union's motivation, but it failed to influence significantly the Pathet Lao and North Vietnamese. Only with the assignment of United States advisers to the combat zones does it appear that Kennedy's threat became sufficiently convincing to these forces. This case illustrates, therefore, that when an attempt is made to coerce a multi-national opposition, a threat sufficiently strong and credible for one member of the opposition may be insufficient for the other. Also noteworthy is that the case successfully illustrates a significant potentiality of the tacit-ultimatum approach to coercion. Thus, even a relatively minor change in military posture, such as the official assignment of a few hundred advisers to the front lines in this case, may have disproportionate impact if it is viewed by the opponent as being part of a strong tacit-ultimatum rather than a weak "try-and-see" approach.

The coercive impact of the United States military action during late March was probably diminished by Kennedy's failure to convey an explicit time limit for compliance, but to have established an explicit deadline might have seriously hindered the development of a negotiated settlement. An important requirement of crisis management is that military and diplomatic initiatives be followed by pauses sufficient to allow the decision-makers on the other side to receive and assess the signals and proposals addressed to them and to formulate and initiate a response. Given the uncertainties and intricacies of Russian-Chinese-Vietnamese relations, a hard and fast deadline for compliance might have been less rational and less effective than Kennedy's groping adaptation to new developments as they arose. Furthermore, to establish a time limit would have entailed increased risk of an eventual "put-up-or-shut-up" phase leaving the president few acceptable alternatives. This itself might have negated the intent of Kennedy's coercive strategy, which was to achieve a political objective with minimal — if any — use of force. The Laos case thus highlights that the requirements of rational crisis management and those of maximum coercive impact may at times conflict and necessitate the policy-maker to devise an acceptable trade-off or compromise between the two.

The problem of achieving an acceptable trade-off between the requirements of crisis management and those of maximum coercive impact was a daily preoccupation for Kennedy, and only he could decide how best to resolve the contradictions between these two considerations. Kennedy's differences of opinion with the

Joint Chiefs tended to center about this problem. Whereas the military suggested the deployment of no less than 60,000 United States troops to provide maximum intimidation of the Viet Minh, Chinese, and Pathet Lao, the president feared that such a large movement might be interpreted by the Communists as a prelude to undoing, not stopping, the Pathet Lao drive and thus as contradictory to his avowed offer of neutralization. It was also for this reason, among others, that Kennedy chose the announcement of a military assistance advisory group instead of the more ambitious proposals recommended to him during the harrowing days of late April. Such a move, in and of itself, could not give the impression that large-scale warfare was being initiated.

It was in the field of crisis management, too, that many of the Kennedy administration's diplomatic communications, consultations, and proposals played an important role. In the president's news conferences; in each British-American proposal; in consultations with Khrushchev, Gromyko, and Nehru; in meetings with the Red Chinese at Warsaw; and in communications to Hanoi, one point was consistently and repetitiously driven home: the United States seeks only neutralization of Laos. It was this type of diplomatic redundancy which was useful in precluding Communist misinterpretation of and overreaction to Kennedy's increasing military pressure. This is not to say, however, that United States diplomatic action served only in a crisis management capacity for, in fact, it was instrumental in creating the sense of urgency necessary to gain compliance from the Communists. This very ability to carry out the crisis management objective of specifying the limited demand for which pressure was being increased while at the same time enhancing that coercive pressure made the Kennedy administration's diplomatic campaign an effective but unprovocative instrument of coercive diplomacy.

Despite Kennedy's apparent success at coercive diplomacy, we must be cautious in interpreting the results for at least two reasons. First, Kennedy's victory was only a modest one. It did not approach the order of that achieved, for instance, during the Cuban missile crisis nor was it something about which the new administration cared to brag publicly. In a most difficult political and military situation, the United States government had been forced to concede much and salvage what it could. Despite criticism from some elements of Congress and the press, the president was forced to agree to a negotiated settlement and a neutralist coalition government. Despite knowledge of Viet Minh movement into South Vietnam through Laos, Kennedy was compelled to forego any attempt to seal the Ho Chi Minh trails by force. Only a president willing to tolerate partial success and public criticism can exercise coercive diplomacy at these prices.

Second, only a special set of conditions surrounding the crisis made possible even this moderate success. While Kennedy was able to alter the balance between the opposition's and his own level of motivation by reducing and clarifying the United States objective in Laos, this proved to be an important contribution to achieving an acceptable outcome only because Moscow, Peking, and Hanoi in fact assigned a low priority to the immediate communization of all Laos. Moreover, the Communists were generally fearful of escalation. Given North Vietnam's greater involvement and interest in South Vietnam, it was unwilling to risk war with the United States in Laos. The Soviet Union had no interests in Southeast Asia worth a confrontation with the United States, and Communist China refrained from any action other than vague and highly conditional threats of intervention — perhaps because of its economic weakness following the Great Leap Forward. Fortunately for Kennedy, too, the Soviet Union, Communist China, North Vietnam, and the Pathet Lao all had reasons to favor some form of neutralization over previous United States policy. The clarity with which the United States was able to communicate this new political objective and its specific terms of compliance, an effective and verified cease-fire, was clearly influential in the achievement of a negotiated settlement. But again, the diplomatic machinery established by the 1954 Geneva Conference, the International Control Commission and the Soviet-British co-chairmanship of the Conference, made formulation, communication, and negotiation of these objectives much easier.

While the factors enumerated above enhanced the probability that Kennedy's strategy would succeed, the intriguing question remains as to what Kennedy would have done had he been unable to arrange a cease-fire. Evidently even the president's closest advisers did not know and were never to know — perhaps because Kennedy did not know himself — the answer to this question. Sorensen writes that Kennedy's posture "combined bluff with real determination in proportions he made known to *no one*." [131] Further complicating any speculation, and perhaps one of the more impressive aspects of Kennedy's management of the United States policy during the crisis, was the president's ability to keep his future options open. Prior to the achievement of a cease-fire, Kennedy had prepared the way for negotiation, intervention, or further retreat, and his final choice would presumably have depended upon the manner in which his bluff was called, the Laotian government's response, and the existing global situation.

Kennedy had taken extreme care to avoid any behavior which would obligate him to intervene. When pressed by his advisers at least to introduce troops into Thailand, he instead initiated the preparations necessary for such a commitment. When faced with the need for an additional show of force, he utilized the American advisers already present in Laos rather than send troops to Thailand, Laos, or South Vietnam. He skillfully avoided a rhetorical oversell to the American public or Congress. His March 23 news conference produced no atmosphere of war, no belligerent threats, and no national debate over the pros and cons of United States intervention. The failure of the State Department's maps to depict the true extent of Pathet Lao gains, if deliberate, can be interpreted as additional precaution against arousing undue public and congressional pressure toward intervention. During the last days of the crisis, misgivings about intervening to save an ineffectual government and army were being transformed into a public rationale for deciding not to augment United States forces in Laos.

On the other hand, Kennedy tried — rather unsuccessfully — to prepare the way for possible multilateral intervention. He received firm commitments from Thailand and Pakistan but only highly conditional offers of support from Great Britain and the Philippines. While this fell far short of broad international support, it nevertheless represents one of the few attempts at multi-lateralism prior to actual intervention in recent United States foreign policy. Kennedy also had the foresight to approach Nehru about the crisis, and should the president have ordered troops into Laos, it would have been received by the Indian prime minister as an American response to Soviet provocation.

Finally, whatever military action might have been undertaken, it would have been limited in size and geared strictly toward activation of the diplomatic agenda. Kennedy gave little thought to the immediate withdrawal of enemy troops or the achievement of a military victory, his only demand being the establishment of a cease-fire. The objective which he proposed to achieve by threatening military force was highly limited in nature.

80   DAVID K. HALL

NOTES

1 Theodore Sorensen, *Kennedy* (New York: Bantam Books, 1965), p. 722.
2 Arthur Schlesinger, Jr., *A Thousand Days* (New York: Fawcett World Library, 1965), p. 309.
3 Arthur Dommen, *Conflict in Laos* (New York: Praeger, 1964), p. 55. Reliable historical accounts of postwar Laos in addition to Dommen's excellent book are Bernard Fall's posthumous volume, *Anatomy of a Crisis* (Garden City, N.Y.: Doubleday, 1969), Hugh Toye, *Laos* (London: Oxford University Press, 1968), and Roger Smith, "Laos," in George Kahin, ed., *Governments and Politics of Southeast Asia* (2nd ed.), (Ithaca: Cornell University Press, 1964), pp. 525–592.
4 Dommen, *Conflict in Laos*, pp. 98–99.
5 Schlesinger, *A Thousand Days*, p. 303.
6 Roger Hilsman, *To Move a Nation* (New York: Dell Publishing Co., 1964), pp. 114–117.
7 *Ibid.*, pp. 116–117.
8 Toye, *Laos*, pp. 118–119.
9 *Ibid.*, pp. 119–129.
10 *Ibid.*, pp. 132–145.
11 Hilsman, *To Move a Nation*, pp. 124–125.
12 Dommen, *Conflict in Laos*, pp. 154–155, 164.
13 *Ibid.*, pp. 164–175.
14 *Ibid.*, pp. 177–179.
15 *Ibid.*, pp. 183–184.
16 For a more complete account of the Eisenhower administration's military preparations, consult: Dwight D. Eisenhower, *Waging Peace: 1956–1961* (Garden City, N.Y.: Doubleday, 1965), pp. 609–611; "Bankrupts Slam the Door," *The Current Digest of the Soviet Press*, Vol. XIII, No. 1 (February 1, 1961), p. 27; and Joseph Alsop, *New York Herald Tribune*, March 24, 1961, p. 24.
17 Dommen, *Conflict in Laos*, pp. 185, 193.
18 Hilsman, *To Move a Nation*, pp. 132–133.
19 Schlesinger, *A Thousand Days*, p. 281.
20 *Ibid.*, p. 282.
21 *New York Times*, March 22, 1961, p. 40. Additional documentation of this attitude within the Kennedy administration can be found in: Schlesinger, *A Thousand Days*, p. 309; *Wall Street Journal*, March 23, 1961, p. 12, and April 18, 1961, p. 2.
22 Hilsman, *To Move a Nation*, p. 132.
23 Dommen, *Conflict in Laos*, p. 179. This does not mean, however, that the Russians were unconcerned over the possibility of a spiraling American-Chinese confrontation. They were concerned, as suggested by a Russian diplomat's warning early in the Kennedy administration: "If the war goes on, the Americans will send in a division, the Chinese will answer with ten divisions, and we'll all be in trouble." *Time*, February 3, 1961, p. 27.
24 Oliver Clubb, Jr., *The United States and the Sino-Soviet Bloc in Southeast Asia* (Washington, D.C.: The Brookings Institution, 1962), p. 29.
25 Dommen, *Conflict in Laos*, p. 181.
26 Hilsman, *To Move a Nation*, pp. 132–133.
27 Robert McNamara, *The Essence of Security* (New York: Harper & Row, 1968), p. 18.
28 Richard Nixon, "Cuba, Castro and John F. Kennedy," *Reader's Digest*, November 1964, p. 291. For additional passing allusions to this more threaten-

ing image of the Chinese Communists, see Sorensen, *Kennedy*, pp. 723, 727–728, 732; Schlesinger, *A Thousand Days*, pp. 310, 316; and Hilsman, *To Move a Nation*, pp. 128–130.

[29] The best statement of the Thai government's attitude during this period is Donald Nuechterlein, *Thailand and the Struggle for Southeast Asia* (Ithaca: Cornell University Press, 1965), pp. 156–220.

[30] Eugene Eidenberg, "The Presidency: Americanizing the War in Vietnam" in Allan Sindler, ed., *American Political Institutions and Public Policy* (Boston: Little, Brown and Co., 1969), p. 80.

[31] Schlesinger, *A Thousand Days*, pp. 498–499.

[32] *Congressional Record*, Senate, March 9, 1954, p. 2904.

[33] Schlesinger, *A Thousand Days*, p. 156.

[34] Sorensen, *Kennedy*, pp. 726–727.

[35] Schlesinger, *A Thousand Days*, p. 310.

[36] *Ibid.*, pp. 310, 497.

[37] *Ibid.*, pp. 338, 341.

[38] *Ibid.*, p. 295.

[39] Hanson Baldwin, *New York Times*, January 6, 1961, p. 2, and *Life*, March 31, 1961, pp. 22–23; Sorensen, *Kennedy*, p. 727.

[40] Schlesinger, *A Thousand Days*, p. 310; *Wall Street Journal*, March 23, 1961, p. 12.

[41] *Ibid.*, pp. 315–316.

[42] *Ibid.*, pp. 310, 315–316; Hilsman, *To Move a Nation*, pp. 128–130.

[43] Schlesinger, *A Thousand Days*, p. 316.

[44] Arthur Krock, *Memoirs* (New York: Funk & Wagnalls, 1968), p. 358.

[45] Nuechterlein, *Thailand*, p. 191. Rather surprisingly, Pakistani President Ayub Khan promised Kennedy 5,000 of his best troops should the U.S. intervene. Hugh Sidey, *John F. Kennedy, President* (New York: Atheneum, 1963), pp. 84–85.

[46] C. L. Sulzberger, *New York Times*, January 4, 1961, p. 32.

[47] *The Washington Post*, November 30, 1963, p. 30.

[48] Schlesinger, *A Thousand Days*, p. 310; Hilsman, *To Move a Nation*, p. 134.

[49] Hazel Erskine, "The Polls: Kennedy as President," *Public Opinion Quarterly* (Summer, 1964), pp. 334–335.

[50] Hilsman, *To Move a Nation*, p. 134.

[51] D. R. SarDesai, *Indian Foreign Policy in Cambodia, Laos, and Vietnam, 1947–1964* (Berkeley: University of California Press, 1968), pp. 226–227.

[52] *New York Times*, January 22, 1961, p. 1.

[53] Eisenhower, *Waging Peace*, p. 661.

[54] Press Conference, January 25, 1961, *Public Papers of the Presidents of the United States: John F. Kennedy, 1961* (Washington, D.C.: United States Government Printing Office, 1962), p. 16.

[55] *New York Times*, March 24, 1961, p. 6.

[56] Schlesinger, *A Thousand Days*, p. 308.

[57] *New York Times*, January 24, 1961, p. 12.

[58] Hilsman, *To Move a Nation*, p. 127.

[59] Schlesinger, *A Thousand Days*, p. 309.

[60] *New York Times*, February 20, 1961, p. 13.

[61] Dommen, *Conflict in Laos*, p. 725.

[62] The paragraphs below which describe Kennedy's delineation and evaluation of his policy options summarize Sorensen's account. See Sorensen, *Kennedy*, pp. 722–724.

82   DAVID K. HALL

63 This strategy is referred to in slightly different vocabulary by Sorensen, *Kennedy*, pp. 724–725; Schlesinger, *A Thousand Days*, p. 311; and Hilsman, *To Move a Nation*, p. 131.
64 Hilsman, *To Move a Nation*, p. 131.
65 Seyom Brown, *The Faces of Power* (New York: Columbia University Press, 1968), p. 230.
66 Sorensen, *Kennedy*, p. 725.
67 Sidey, *Kennedy*, p. 76.
68 *Time*, March 17, 1961, p. 20. Sorensen, *Kennedy*, pp. 724–725; Dommen, *Conflict in Laos*, pp. 191–192.
69 Chalmers Roberts, *Washington Post*, March 18, 1961, p. 18, *Time*, March 17, 1961, p. 20.
70 Sidey, *Kennedy*, p. 77.
71 Murrey Marder, *Washington Post*, March 19, 1961, p. 1.
72 *New York Times*, March 19, 1961, p. 1, and March 20, 1961, p. 10.
73 Sidey, *Kennedy*, p. 77.
74 Sorensen, *Kennedy*, p. 725.
75 Hilsman, *To Move a Nation*, p. 131.
76 "The Situation in Laos," *Department of State Bulletin*, April 17, 1961, p. 543.
77 *New York Herald Tribune*, March 26, 1961, II, p. 4.
78 Press Conference, March 23, 1961, *Public Papers*, p. 215.
79 *New York Times*, March 24, 1961, p. 1; *Washington Post*, March 4, 1961, p. 1; *Wall Street Journal*, March 23, 1961, pp. 1, 12, and March 27, 1961, p. 5.
80 *New York Herald Tribune*, March 27, 1961, p. 26.
81 Schlesinger, *A Thousand Days*, p. 310.
82 *New York Times*, March 24, 1961, p. 6.
83 Sidey, *Kennedy*, pp. 80–81.
84 *New York Herald Tribune*, March 29, 1961, p. 22.
85 *New York Times*, March 25, 1961, p. 1.
86 *Ibid.*, March 27, 1961, p. 2.
87 *Ibid.*, March 26, 1961, p. 1.
88 *Ibid.*, p. 2.
89 *Ibid.*, March 30, 1961, p. 1; Frank Darling, *Thailand and the United States* (Washington, D.C.: Public Affairs Press, 1965), p. 205.
90 Schlesinger, *A Thousand Days*, p. 312.
91 *New York Times*, March 28, 1961, p. 1.
92 Brian Crozier, "Peking and the Laotian Crisis: An Interim Appraisal," *China Quarterly*, VII (July–September, 1961), p. 130.
93 *Ibid.*, p. 131.
94 P. J. Honey, *Communism in North Vietnam* (Cambridge, Mass.: The M.I.T. Press, 1965), p. 94.
95 *Peking Review*, February 19, 1961, p. 18.
96 *New York Times*, April 2, 1961, p. 1.
97 *New York Herald Tribune*, April 4, 1961, p. 11.
98 Dommen, *Conflict in Laos*, p. 194.
99 *New York Times*, April 7, 1961, pp. 1, 4.
100 Dommen, *Conflict in Laos*, p. 200.
101 *Wall Street Journal*, March 28, 1961, p. 2; March 31, 1961, p. 2; April 7, 1961, p. 8; April 10, 1961, p. 1; April 18, 1961, p. 2.
102 *Time*, April 14, 1961, p. 31; *New York Herald Tribune*, May 3, 1961, p. 10; Nuechterlein, *Thailand*, pp. 197–200.
103 Schlesinger, *A Thousand Days*, pp. 257–258.

[104] U.S. Consulate General Hong Kong, *Survey of China Mainland Press*, No. 2485 (April 28, 1961), p. 44.

[105] *Ibid.*, p. 37.

[106] *New York Times*, April 25, 1961, p. 1.

[107] U.S. Consulate General, *Survey*, No. 2490 (May 5, 1961), p. 33.

[108] "What Is Washington Trying for in Laos?" *The Current Digest of the Soviet Press*, Vol. XIII, No. 17 (May 24, 1961), p. 24.

[109] Schlesinger, *A Thousand Days*, p. 315.

[110] Sorensen, *Kennedy*, pp. 727, 736; Schlesinger, *A Thousand Days*, pp. 315–316; and Hilsman, *To Move a Nation*, p. 133–134.

[111] *Ibid.*; Schlesinger, *A Thousand Days*, p. 315.

[112] Sorensen, *Kennedy*, pp. 726–728, 736; Schlesinger, *A Thousand Days*, p. 315.

[113] Nixon, "Cuba, Castro and John F. Kennedy," p. 291.

[114] Sorensen, *Kennedy*, p. 726. Documentation of this loss of confidence by other friends of the president includes: Krock, *Memoirs*, p. 371; Robert Kennedy, *Thirteen Days* (New York: The New American Library, 1968), pp. 117–119; and Schlesinger, *A Thousand Days*, pp. 271–272, 276–277.

[115] Sorensen, *Kennedy*, p. 723.

[116] Schlesinger, *A Thousand Days*, p. 316.

[117] Sidey, *Kennedy*, pp. 76–77; Sorensen, *Kennedy*, p. 726.

[118] Sidey, *Kennedy*, p. 84.

[119] Hilsman, *To Move a Nation*, p. 134; *New York Herald Tribune*, April 29, 1961, p. 2.

[120] Sorensen, *Kennedy*, p. 736; *New York Herald Tribune*, May 3, 1961, pp. 1, 10; *Time*, May 12, 1961, p. 17.

[121] *New York Herald Tribune*, May 13, 1961, pp. 1, 2; *Time*, May 19, 1961, p. 20.

[122] Nuechterlein, *Thailand*, pp. 211–212.

[123] Address in Chicago at a Dinner of the Democratic Party of Cook County, April 28, 1961, *Public Papers*, p. 340.

[124] *New York Herald Tribune*, May 8, 1961, p. 2.

[125] Dommen, *Conflict in Laos*, pp. 205–209; Schlesinger, *A Thousand Days*, p. 317; and Hilsman, *To Move a Nation*, p. 135.

[126] Schlesinger, *A Thousand Days*, p. 340.

[127] Hilsman, *To Move a Nation*, p. 136.

[128] For detailed accounts of the Nam Tha incident, consult: Bernard Fall, "Laos: Who Broke the Ceasefire?" *The New Republic*, June 18, 1962, pp. 17–20; Denis Warner, *The Last Confucian* (New York: Macmillan, 1963), pp. 217–219; and Hilsman, *To Move a Nation*, pp. 140–151.

[129] Schlesinger, *A Thousand Days*, p. 477.

[130] Dommen, *Conflict in Laos*, pp. 232–235.

[131] Sorensen, *Kennedy*, p. 728.

BIBLIOGRAPHY

Alsop, Joseph, *New York Herald Tribune*, March 24, 1961.
———, *New York Herald Tribune*, March 27, 1961.
———, *New York Herald Tribune*, March 29, 1961.
Baldwin, Hanson, *Life*, March 31, 1961.
———, *New York Times*, January 6, 1961.
"Bankrupts Slam the Door," *The Current Digest of the Soviet Press*, Vol. XIII, No. 1 (February 1, 1961).

Clubb, Oliver, Jr., *The United States and the Sino-Soviet Bloc in Southeast Asia* (Washington, D.C.: The Brookings Institute, 1962).

Congressional Record, Senate, March 9, 1954.

Crozier, Brian, "Peking and the Laotian Crisis: An Interim Appraisal," *China Quarterly*, VII (July–September, 1961).

Darling, Frank, *Thailand and the United States* (Washington, D.C.: Public Affairs Press, 1965).

Dommen, Arthur, *Conflict in Laos* (New York: Praeger, 1964).

Eidenberg, Eugene, "The Presidency: Americanizing the War in Vietnam," in Allan Sindler, ed., *American Political Institutions and Public Policy* (Boston: Little, Brown and Co., 1969).

Eisenhower, Dwight, *Waging Peace: 1956–1961* (Garden City, N.Y.: Doubleday, 1965).

Erskine, Hazel, "The Polls: Kennedy as President," *Public Opinion Quarterly* (Summer 1964).

Fall, Bernard, *Anatomy of a Crisis* (Garden City, N.Y.: Doubleday, 1969).

———, "Laos: Who Broke the Ceasefire?" *The New Republic*, June 18, 1962.

———, "Reappraisal in Laos," *Current History* (January 1962).

———, "The Laos Tangle," *International Journal* (Spring 1961).

Fifield, Russell, *Southeast Asia in United States Diplomacy* (New York: Praeger, 1963).

Greene, Fred, *U.S. Policy and the Security of Asia* (New York: McGraw-Hill, 1968).

Hilsman, Roger, *To Move a Nation* (New York: Dell Publishing Co., 1964).

Honey, P. J., *Communism in North Vietnam* (Cambridge: The M.I.T. Press, 1965).

Kennedy, Robert, *Thirteen Days* (New York: The New American Library, 1969).

Krock, Arthur, *Memoirs* (New York: Funk & Wagnalls, 1968).

Lall, Arthur, *How Communist China Negotiates* (New York: Columbia University Press, 1968).

McNamara, Robert, *The Essence of Security* (New York: Harper & Row, 1968).

Marder, Murrey, *Washington Post*, March 19, 1961.

Modelski, George, ed., *SEATO: Six Studies* (Melbourne: F. W. Cheshire, 1962).

Murphy, Charles, "Cuba: The Record Set Straight," *Fortune* (September 1961), pp. 92–96.

New York Herald Tribune, 1961.

New York Times, 1961.

Nixon, Richard, "Cuba, Castro and John F. Kennedy," *Reader's Digest* (November 1964).

Nuechterlein, Donald, *Thailand and the Struggle for Southeast Asia* (Ithaca: Cornell University Press, 1965).

Public Papers of the Presidents of the United States: John F. Kennedy, 1961 (Washington, D.C.: United States Government Printing Office, 1962).

Public Papers of the Presidents of the United States: John F. Kennedy, 1963 (Washington, D.C.: United States Government Printing Office, 1964).

Roberts, Chalmers, *Washington Post*, March 19, 1961.

———, *Washington Post*, November 30, 1963.

SarDesai, D. R., *Indian Foreign Policy in Cambodia, Laos, and Vietnam, 1947–1964* (Berkeley: University of California Press, 1968).

Schelling, Thomas, *Arms and Influence* (New Haven: Yale University Press, 1966).

———, *The Strategy of Conflict* (New York: Oxford University Press, 1963).

Schlesinger, Arthur, Jr., *A Thousand Days* (New York: Fawcett World Library, 1965).

Sidey, Hugh, *John F. Kennedy, President* (New York: Atheneum, 1963).

"The Situation in Laos," *Department of State Bulletin* (April 17, 1961).

Smith, Roger, "Laos," in George Kahin, ed., *Governments and Politics of Southeast Asia* (2nd ed.) (Ithaca: Cornell University Press, 1964).

Sorensen, Theodore, *Kennedy* (New York: Bantam Books, 1965).

Stebbins, Richard, *The United States in World Affairs 1961* (New York: Harper & Row, 1962).

Sulzberger, C. L., *New York Times*, January 4, 1961.

Time. 1961.

Toye, Hugh, *Laos* (London: Oxford University Press, 1968).

U.S. Consulate General Hong Kong, *Survey of China Mainland Press*, No. 2485 (April 28, 1961).

———, *Survey of China Mainland Press*, No. 2490 (May 5, 1961).

Wall Street Journal. 1961.

Warner, Denis, *The Last Confucian* (New York: Macmillan, 1963).

Washington Post, 1961.

"What Is Washington Trying for in Laos?" *The Current Digest of the Soviet Press*, Vol. XIII, No. 17 (May 24, 1961).

Young, Kenneth, *Negotiating with the Chinese Communists* (New York: McGraw-Hill, 1968).

Zagoria, Donald, *Vietnam Triangle: Moscow, Peking, Hanoi* (New York: Pegasus, 1967).

3

Alexander L. George

THE CUBAN MISSILE CRISIS, 1962

I. THE DECISION TO TRY COERCIVE DIPLOMACY

"If we had to act on Wednesday in the first twenty-four hours" of the crisis, the president said later, "I don't think we would have chosen as prudently as we finally did." It was indeed fortunate that the high-level decision of September 10, 1962, to avoid overflights of western Cuba was finally set aside, permitting a U-2 photo reconnaissance flight on Sunday, October 14, which revealed secret Soviet preparations of medium range (MRBM) missile sites in that part of the island.[1] The discovery came before the Soviet missiles achieved operational readiness. Thus, Kennedy could deliberate at some length with his advisers as to how to respond to this unexpected development. It would be about ten days, intelligence specialists estimated, before the missiles would be ready for firing.[2]

One of the president's first decisions was that he would not be hurried into action but would take full advantage of the time available to consider the problem facing his administration from every standpoint. This decision, as the president's reflection on the crisis we have quoted suggests, was possibly momentous in its

86

consequences. For at first most of the members of the group of advisers Kennedy quickly assembled, which came to be known as ExCom (Executive Committee of the National Security Council), thought that the president would have to resort to an air strike in order to remove the missiles. "A so-called 'surgical' strike," Sorensen reports, appealed "to almost everyone first considering the matter, including President Kennedy on Tuesday and Wednesday." [3] The president had been convinced from the beginning, upon being shown the photographs and given the interpretation of their significance, that he would have to act, that the United States would have to bring the threat to an end one way or another.[4]

The belief that an air strike should be undertaken persisted several days though the number of advisers favoring it gradually declined. The strength and depth of this belief among its staunchest proponents is indicated by the fact that as late as 1969 Dean Acheson still believed that an air strike confined to the missile sites "was the necessary and only effective method of achieving our purpose." [5] Only remarkable luck, Acheson holds, enabled Kennedy to get the missiles removed without an air strike.

Though leaning toward an air strike, the president wanted to consider thoroughly all alternatives. He was careful not to let his own thoughts influence his advisers; and he encouraged them to try to think of other alternatives when for a moment on Tuesday the choice seemed to lie between an air strike and acquiescence.[6] On Wednesday McNamara developed the idea of a blockade, which had been briefly mentioned the preceding day.

We shall pass over the details of the debate within ExCom concerning the air strike and blockade options.[7] The president's interest in the blockade option was soon caught by the possibility that it might rescue him from the many-horned dilemma confronting him. He had quickly rejected acquiescence to the missile deployment in Cuba; to do nothing seemed to him the worst of all options. A purely diplomatic overture to Khrushchev — that is, words without action — would be not only ineffectual but dangerous. It could precipitate a crash effort by the Soviets to capitalize on their missile deployment. An air strike or invasion, on the other hand, would result in heavy casualties; moreover it carried grave risks of a strong Soviet response and the danger of war. Might a blockade somehow enable Kennedy to obtain removal of the missiles without having to take direct military action?

From the very beginning the idea of a blockade raised the question whether Khrushchev could be induced to remove the missiles. No one believed that Khrushchev would lightly forgo the considerable advantages he expected to obtain from his covert missile deployment or that he would tolerantly accept the loss of domestic and international prestige which would be associated with a blatant retreat. Pressure would be necessary. But were Khrushchev and other members of the Soviet government coercible on this matter? Were they capable of "retreating," as their doctrine enjoined them to do when faced with overwhelming danger? [8] Or were the Soviet leaders so committed to the daring venture on which they had embarked that, for them, there could be no turning back? This was indeed a critical question, but available accounts of the ExCom meetings hardly refer to it. An affirmative answer to the question was implicit in ExCom's analysis of the calculations of the Soviet decision to deploy the missiles. Most of Kennedy's advisers felt that the Soviet leaders had miscalculated the risks of their action and that once made aware of these risks they would be capable of retreating, at least in principle. But a theoretical answer to the question, while not without value, did not suffice. The more difficult question was the practical one: Could a way be found to induce the Soviet leaders to retreat? Adherents of the air strike, particularly those who remained committed to it, appear to have answered this question negatively. They did not see how the blockade option could generate enough pressure to achieve this result, certainly not before the missiles had been made operational, which everyone seemed to agree would drastically alter the situation in Khrushchev's favor.

In the end, however, the president's image of Khrushchev was decisive. "The President believed from the start," his brother reported "that the Soviet Chairman was a rational, intelligent man who, if given sufficient time and shown determination, would alter his position." [9] The president's answer, therefore, was that Khrushchev was capable of retreating and that an effort should be made to induce him to do so. At the same time, Kennedy was keenly aware of the danger of backing his opponent into a corner without leaving open a line of retreat.

Thus, Kennedy chose to try coercive diplomacy instead of opting immediately for the "quick, decisive" military strategy represented by the air strike. Kennedy chose this strategy even though he realized that its success would be jeopardized because a blockade — indeed any public demand for removal of the missiles — would inevitably engage Khrushchev's prestige. In fact, a blockade could well push both sides into "rigid postures of simultaneous commitment with regard to a specific and highly visible point of confrontation." [10] Kennedy was by no means oblivious of this danger. He felt he had no choice but to challenge Khrushchev's prestige if he wanted to get the missiles out before they became operational. Any diplomatic action by the United States that did not involve Khrushchev's authority was likely to be ineffectual. A blockade would at least engage his prestige less than an air strike. And, besides, as we shall see, Kennedy *was* prepared to help make it easier for Khrushchev to retreat, not merely by cooperating in perfunctory face-saving gestures but also by making a meaningful contribution of his own to a quid pro quo that would secure removal of the missiles.

II. KENNEDY'S VIEW OF THE STAKES

The president quickly perceived the multiple dangers implicit in Khrushchev's bold move. Robert Kennedy reported that his brother "knew he would have to act. The U.S. could not accept what the Russians had done. What that action would be was still to be determined. But he was convinced from the beginning that he would have to do something." [11] We need not exclude the possibility that the president momentarily wavered and wondered whether a strong response was necessary or feasible, or might even be postponed.* This possibility, however, is less important than his considered judgment that the stakes were very high indeed and that time was all-important.

Kennedy's motivation was complex. It was obvious to him and to others that, if allowed to succeed, Khrushchev's move could have a variety of damaging consequences for the United States position in the world, for Kennedy's foreign and domestic policies, and also for his ability to provide leadership thereafter. Not merely his personal prestige and his political future, but also the prestige and interests of the United States were at stake. It is idle to attempt to sort out and weigh separately, as some critics have tried to do, these two dimensions of the president's motivation.[12] A

* One story has it that, when the president was told by McGeorge Bundy that the missiles had been discovered, his initial response was to ask whether action could be deferred until after the congressional elections.

leader's sense of his personal stakes usually enters in some way into his judgment of his country's interests. And often, though not always, there is in fact some basis in reality to encourage the tendency to identify personal stakes in an issue with those of party or country.

Khrushchev could hardly have thought of a better way to ensure that both dimensions of Kennedy's motivation would be strongly aroused and, indeed, so fused as to become virtually inseparable. However hard the president might have tried in this situation, he could not have found a way to accept damage to his personal political stakes without also accepting damage to major United States interests. The kind of personal and political humiliation that the covert deployment of missiles would inflict upon the president could hardly have escaped Khrushchev's attention altogether when he planned and carried it out. Of those several aspects of Khrushchev's bold move that reflect bad judgment and miscalculation, his willingness to inflict personal and political humiliation upon Kennedy is by far the most irresponsible. If Eisenhower had inadvertently embarrassed Khrushchev personally and politically by his clumsy handling of the U-2 affair in May 1960, Khrushchev foolishly repaid Kennedy tenfold and under far more dangerous circumstances.

After the Bay of Pigs fiasco of April 1961 the administration had settled upon the indirect approach of attempting to isolate Castro diplomatically and of applying economic pressures. To many this policy seemed to underestimate the danger of allowing a Communist base to exist in the Caribbean from which revolution could be exported to other Latin American countries. As the Soviet military build-up in Cuba that began in July 1962 took on an ominous character during the summer, domestic discontent with Kennedy's Cuban policy was severely exacerbated and generated pressure for stronger measures. The Republicans announced that Cuba would be the dominant issue in the congressional elections in November. The administration, in turn, mobilized itself to reassure the voters that the danger was being exaggerated and that there was no reason for war-like measures. Administration spokesmen, including Vice President Johnson, rejected the call for blockade measures against Cuba on the ground that this would constitute an "act of war" against the Soviet Union. The administration disclosed considerable intelligence information at its disposal concerning the character of the Soviet military supplies and personnel flowing into

Cuba, hoping thereby to assure the public that it was well informed as to what the Soviets were and were not doing.

As much to calm the war psychosis encouraged by critics such as senators Keating and Goldwater as to deter the Soviets, Kennedy made his position explicitly clear on September 4 and again on September 13. He warned the Soviets that his administration would not tolerate the introduction of "offensive" weapons into Cuba.* The president thereby publicly pledged himself to act if missiles were introduced into Cuba. Kennedy did so perhaps largely, though certainly not exclusively, for domestic political purposes, for he thought it most unlikely that the Soviets would undertake such action. But once he had taken his stand on this issue, his public pledge to act thereafter if challenged was irrevocable.[13] Also, the president had become particularly vulnerable since he personally, as well as members of his administration, had persistently deemphasized the danger of a missile deployment in order to counter charges by Senator Keating and others that the Soviets were already secretly moving missiles into Cuba. When the missiles were finally discovered in mid-October, therefore, "the United States might not be in mortal danger but the Administration most certainly was." [14]

Even without the added impetus of Kennedy's personal political stakes, the need to find a way to remove the missiles before they became operational was compelling, but not because the missiles being placed in Cuba would shift the strategic military balance in Russia's favor. Had the Soviet deployment been of that magnitude, which it clearly was not, Kennedy's motivation would have been even stronger. Rather, initial intelligence on the Soviet missile deployment was such that it was possible for Secretary of Defense McNamara to argue that "a missile is a missile," and to suggest that the administration try to accept Soviet missiles in Cuba without creating a major international crisis.[15] Some critics of Kennedy's handling of the crisis have used the fact that the secretary of defense himself was not upset by the military signifi-

---

* Kennedy also warned the Soviets against taking other actions in Cuba as well that would "endanger or interfere" with United States security, "including our base at Guantanamo, our passage to the Panama Canal, our missile and space activities at Cape Canaveral, or the lives of American citizens in the country." American action was threatened also in case Cuba attempted "to export its aggressive purposes by force or the threat of force against any country in this hemisphere," or became "an offensive base of significant capacity for the Soviet Union."

cance of the Soviet missiles in Cuba to charge that the president created a dangerous crisis quite unnecessarily in order to preserve his personal political interests. Among the important factors this thesis overlooks is that McNamara's initial judgment of the military significance of the missiles was overly sanguine, that he initially ignored the political-diplomatic significance of the missiles, and that he shortly changed his mind regarding the importance of what was at stake.

Among those who quickly disagreed with McNamara's initial view of the military significance of the Cuban missiles was Paul Nitze, his assistant secretary of defense for international security affairs. Nitze felt that the missiles in Cuba would expose a large part of the American strategic bomber force, based in the southeastern states, to sudden attack by reducing the warning time from fifteen to two or three minutes.[16] The forty-two MRBMs and the twenty-four to thirty-two IRBMs that were already in Cuba or on the way, it was later estimated, did not give the Soviets a good first strike capability, but they did increase the destructive power that the Soviets could deliver on United States targets by about 50 per cent. Moreover, one could not ignore the possibiilty that Moscow might decide later to send still more medium-range missiles to Cuba. Even now, with additional time and the benefit of hindsight, efforts to assess the real military significance of the missiles quickly lead to intricate technical considerations. We forgo further discussion of this here, because the president and his advisers were swayed not by the military threat but largely by the important political-diplomatic advantages they saw accruing to Khrushchev if the missiles remained in Cuba.[17] As the president himself said later, after discounting the immediate military threat of the Cuban-based missiles, "It would have politically changed the balance of power. It would have appeared to, and appearances contribute to reality." [18]

No one could be certain what the Soviet leaders intended to do with their Cuban-based missiles. Many possibilities suggested themselves, and ExCom and the president gave considerable weight to the theory, supported by circumstantial evidence, that Khrushchev hoped his Cuban missiles would radically redefine the setting in which the Berlin problem could be reopened after the elections in November. Indeed, before the missiles were discovered, Khrushchev had indirectly warned that the Berlin problem would once again come to the forefront after the United States mid-term congressional elections. The threat was severe enough to lead Kennedy to obtain authorization from Congress in early September for a call-up of reserves.

The administration's specialists on Soviet behavior foresaw that Khrushchev would be able, if he wished, to draw many important advantages from the missiles in Cuba.* Khrushchev in effect was asking Kennedy to accept his assurance that this large missile force would be used only to deter an American attack on Cuba, that it would not be used psychologically, politically, and diplomatically to enhance other, even more important Soviet foreign policy objectives at the expense of the United States and its allies. That was an extraordinary thing to ask Kennedy to believe! [19]

Moreover, for the president to retreat from the explicit public commitment given as recently as September that he would not tolerate "offensive" missiles in Cuba would have eroded all United States commitments and invited Khrushchev and others to question Kennedy's future credibility in the most painful and dangerous way. To the familiar criticism that Kennedy over-reacted to what was really only a matter of prestige, Charles Burton Marshall later replied, "Why *only*? Prestige is the faculty enabling a great power to avoid final, miserable choices between surrender and war. Prestige is the ingredient of authority in international affairs. . . . The quality that demands being listened to is prestige — and a nation suffers loss of it at great peril." [20]

Finally, an important, long-range goal of the president's foreign policy was at stake. He came to office believing that the Cold War should be modified, that a mutually acceptable form of coexistence with the Soviet Union could be worked out through negotiation and serious exploration of each other's interests. "Braving criticism

---

* Hilsman, *To Move a Nation*, pp. 161, 164, reports that one group of Sovietologists in the State Department concluded that the decision to put missiles into Cuba was best viewed as "a generalized, strategic response to a whole set of problems, military, economic, and political" facing Soviet leadership in 1962. "A general improvement in the Soviet military position would affect the entire political context, strengthening their hand for dealing with the whole range of problems facing them. . . . If the move in Cuba were successful and the over-all Soviet position strengthened, their leverage on Berlin would indeed be improved. NATO would surely be shaken and the chances of the U.S. successfully creating a multilateral nuclear force reduced. In Latin America, other potential 'Castros' would be encouraged. American power would be less impressive and American protection less desirable."

from allies abroad and enemies at home," Pachter notes, Kennedy had made at least a start in this direction, seeking solutions for the Congo, Berlin, a test-ban treaty. The Cuban missile deployment was a blow at the very foundation of this policy aspiration. "He knew that, were he humiliated a second time in Cuba, he would lose all hopes for a stable world peace." [21]

Having characterized the multifaceted nature of Kennedy's perception of what was at stake, we should also mention some constraints and limits on his otherwise strong motivation to secure removal of the missiles. The question of motivation cannot be discussed independently of the objectives toward which it might be channeled. Kennedy's motivation was strong particularly insofar as it was focused and concentrated upon the limited objective he clearly set for his response and consistently followed — namely the removal of the missiles, no more and no less. His motivation was not oriented toward the objective of seizing the occasion to topple Castro and drive out Soviet influence from Cuba altogether. The probable costs and risks of this objective were perceived by him to be excessive and the strength of his motivation would not suffice if it were linked to this more ambitious goal.

Finally, even with respect to the removal of the missiles, we do not know for certain whether the value the president attached to this objective would have been strong enough to lead him to order an air strike in the event that his ultimatum of Saturday, October 27, failed to produce Khrushchev's compliance. Kennedy was moving toward that decision but had not yet committed himself to it when the crisis ended. Therefore, the possible limits of his motivation were not in fact fully tested. That the missiles were not yet operational offered Kennedy an opportunity to initiate action without war. In doing so, to be sure, he accepted the risk of war; but he did not behave recklessly to increase its probability. We can also say that there is nothing in the available materials to suggest that the president's judgment was distorted by an emotional response to being deceived by Khrushchev, by adherence to an extreme Cold War image of the Soviets, or by a desire to punish Khrushchev for his misbehavior—although certainly the president did feel it necessary to correct his opponent's mistaken notion that he lacked determination. Finally, while Kennedy was out to "win" the confrontation, "defeating Khrushchev," as Pachter states, "was not a final goal but a milestone beyond which lay war and peace." [22]

III. CHOICE OF THE BLOCKADE: ITS
USES AND LIMITATIONS FOR
COERCIVE DIPLOMACY

Despite the accomplishments of the ExCom during seven days of feverish planning, the administration entered the overt phase of the crisis on October 22 without having resolved a critical ambiguity in its strategy. The president chose the blockade option because it enabled him to postpone and control the risk of a major war better than an air strike would have. In this respect the blockade had advantages that the air strike option lacked altogether: it enabled the president to initiate the showdown with Khrushchev without immediate resort to force; it permitted him to retain personal control over United States actions and to be immediately responsive to changes in the situation; and it offered at least the possibility of coercing and persuading Khrushchev to remove the missiles voluntarily. The president still had to find a way of utilizing the blockade for this purpose, however.

Herein lay the critical gap in the ExCom's deliberations of the first seven days. The weakness and lack of relevance of the blockade for obtaining the withdrawal of missiles already in Cuba had been argued very cogently indeed by those ExCom members who advocated an air strike. The limitations of the blockade had been perceived and conceded also by those who opposed an immediate air strike and favored a blockade. But the advocates of the blockade had failed to come up with a specific plan for utilizing the blockade in order to obtain removal of the missiles, and they had only a vague and inadequate concept of how this might be done.

Aware of this gap in ExCom's planning, the president nonetheless decided to give priority for the time being to the imperatives of crisis management in order to avoid war if possible. He chose to employ a strategy of coercive diplomacy despite its ambiguities and uncertainties and to hold in reserve the military solution to the problem of the missiles. Notwithstanding the administration's successful application of coercive diplomacy earlier in Laos in 1961, it still lacked a clear concept of the nature of this strategy and an adequate understanding of its complex requirements.

As a result, the president entered the showdown with Khrushchev on October 22 with a serious disadvantage. He was caught squarely between the conflicting requirements of crisis control and those of coercive diplomacy. Fortunately he understood at least the first set of requirements quite well. Indeed, the president and his key advisers made imaginative use of the inherent flexibility of the blockade option to control its conflict potential. In contrast, the requirements of coercive diplomacy were less well understood and were given less weight in Kennedy's actions *until* Friday, October 25. Until then the president relied essentially upon a weak form of coercive strategy for persuading Khrushchev to remove the missiles * — what we have labeled the "try-and-see" approach. Then, driven by circumstances at the end of the week, Kennedy was forced to improvise a much stronger variant of coercive diplomacy, namely what we have called the "tacit-ultimatum" approach.

With these distinctions in mind, let us review ExCom's deliberations during the seven-day planning period preceding Kennedy's speech of October 22. The possibility of an ultimatum was considered only in connection with the air strike; it was never tied into or related to the blockade option. Even the idea of a private ultimatum threatening Khrushchev with an immediate air strike if he did not agree to withdraw the missiles was soon abandoned within ExCom, evidently because no feasible way of translating it into action could be envisaged. As Sorensen reports, "Many of those originally attracted to the air-strike course had favored it in the hope that a warning would suffice, and that the Soviets would then withdraw their missiles. But no one could devise any method of warning that would not enable Khrushchev either to tie us into knots or force us into obloquy." †

---

* As noted in Chapter One, while the blockade was a relatively weak strategy for persuading the opponent *to undo* or reverse what he had already done — remove the missiles in Cuba — it was a much stronger coercive strategy for persuading him *to stop* sending more missiles to Cuba. We focus our remarks here on the more ambitious and more difficult of these two objectives of Kennedy's coercive policy.

† Sorensen adds: "I tried my hand, for example, at an airtight letter to be carried out from the President to the Soviet Chairman by a high-level personal envoy. The letter would inform Khrushchev that only if he agreed in his conference with that courier (and such others as he called in) to order the missiles dismantled would U.S. military action be withheld while our surveillance oversaw their removal. But no matter how many references I put in to a summit, to peaceful intentions and to previous warnings and pledges, the letter still constituted the kind of ultimatum which no great power could accept, and a justification for either a preemptive strike against this country or our indictment in the court of history. From that point on, I veered away from the air-strike course." (Sorensen, *Kennedy*, p. 685)

Proponents of the blockade option were unable to envisage more than a try-and-see use of it. This was true even of McNamara's now celebrated argument of Thursday, October 18, in which he held that a blockade would "maintain the options." If the blockade failed, McNamara reasoned, the president would then have a choice of responses. He could decide to deny the Cubans other kinds of cargo — petroleum, for example — or he could move up the scale to an air strike. If one form of pressure failed in its purpose, then another, more severe pressure could be applied. Far from attempting to show how the threat of an air strike could be used to increase the coercive impact of the blockade, McNamara's concept of "maintaining the options" served merely to remind everyone that the blockade could be applied without losing the option to launch an air strike later.[23]

Insofar as McNamara's concept of "maintaining the options" had a strategic dimension, the strategy he had in mind was that of graduated escalation. But in the ensuing policy discussions of the next few days it became evident that there were two divergent, competing notions of how escalation strategy ought to be applied, should the blockade fail to persuade Khrushchev to remove the missiles. Some members of ExCom believed that, in that event, the president should proceed immediately to an air strike without going through many additional escalatory steps.[24] Others picked up and elaborated McNamara's image of a more gradual, step-by-step escalation with many intermediate steps before resorting to an air strike.[25] These competing images of gradual and abrupt escalation contained sharply different implications for policy, but the disagreement was not thrashed out in the ExCom meetings. In fact, this latent policy conflict remained unresolved throughout the entire crisis. The competing views as to escalation strategy were revived at the end of the week, but Khrushchev's acceptance on October 28 of Kennedy's formula for ending the crisis served to forestall a major clash over this issue. Both of these competing views of the blockade as the initial step in graduated escalation fell into the category of what we have called the "try-and-see" approach to coercive diplomacy. There is no indication that the proponents of either of these two concepts suggested that the coercive potential of gradual escalation could be enhanced by adding a time limit for compliance with the demand for removing the missiles, using the threat of an air strike to motivate Khrushchev's compliance.

Rather, the eventual conversion of the "try-and-see" approach into an ultimatum seems to have been entirely improvised at the last minute by President Kennedy himself.

IV. THE PRESIDENT'S PROBLEM: SIGNAL DETERMINATION WITHOUT RISKING WAR

The evidence indicates that for Kennedy, too, the attractiveness of the blockade option lay not in some pre-vision of how he could make it part of a tacit-ultimatum. Rather, he preferred the blockade for other reasons, some of which we have already indicated and one which deserves to be singled out before proceeding.

From the very beginning of the crisis the president, probably more so than most of his advisers, was deeply impressed — indeed, perhaps haunted — by the feeling that Khrushchev's missile gambit could be explained only in terms of a long-standing problem that had plagued Kennedy. Almost from the day he entered office the president had wrestled with the problem of how to convey his determination to the Soviet leader in order to prevent him from attempting dangerous encroachments on the world position of the United States. The disaster of the Bay of Pigs and Khrushchev's performance at the summit meeting at Vienna severely exacerbated Kennedy's problem and his concern. As the tension over Berlin mounted once again in the summer of 1961, the president unburdened himself to James Wechsler of the *New York Post:*

> What worried [Kennedy] was that Khrushchev might interpret his reluctance to wage nuclear war as a symptom of an American loss of nerve. Some day, he said, the time might come when he would have to run the supreme risk to convince Khrushchev that conciliation did not mean humiliation. "If Khrushchev wants to rub my nose in the dirt," he told Wechsler, "it's all over." But how to convince Khrushchev short of a showdown? "That son of a bitch won't pay attention to words," the President said bitterly on another occasion. "He has to see you move." [26]

As the prolonged negotiations over Berlin ground to an inconclusive halt during the summer of 1962, the administration readied itself for new Soviet pressure against West Berlin. Many indications pointed to the likelihood that Khrushchev was preparing another major challenge. Some of them were imbedded in his curiously juxtaposed assurances of September and October that

Soviet military assistance to Cuba was for purely "defensive" purposes and that he would not embarrass the president by raising the Berlin issue again until after the forthcoming congressional elections of November. In other ways, too, Khrushchev was suggesting a linkage between Cuba and Berlin. This was not lost upon the administration, but Kennedy and his advisers failed to penetrate the deception and to guess the linkage — and the trap — that Khrushchev was preparing. Even in September, Sorensen reports, Kennedy was concerned over the possibility that Khrushchev was giving increasing military assistance to Cuba in order to provoke Washington into another invasion of Cuba that would make a martyr out of Castro and wreck United States relations with Latin America, while the Soviets moved in on West Berlin. This suspicion was revived briefly after the missiles were discovered and is contained in one of the early theories, the "Diverting Trap" theory, that ExCom entertained when mulling over the motives behind the missile deployment.[27]

For many months, therefore, as Pachter puts it, "Kennedy had worried that Khrushchev might underestimate his determination and present him with an ultimatum [on the Berlin problem] he might have to reject. War might break out unless Khrushchev modified his overconfidence, or someone did it for him." [28]

This, then, was the president's mental set when he learned on October 16 that Khrushchev had been secretly putting missiles into Cuba even while systematically deceiving him with false assurances. Recovering from the shock, the president realized at once that the development he had long feared had now materialized, though not in the guise he had expected and not with immediate reference to Berlin. He realized, too, that — as he had expressed to Wechsler earlier — the time had come when he had no choice but to face "the supreme risk." Words alone would not suffice with Khrushchev; "he has to see you move."

Almost intuitively, the president saw that in the dangerous situation created by Khrushchev's miscalculation the only chance of getting the missiles out of Cuba without war lay in finding a way of impressing Khrushchev, as never before, with his determination. We may suppose that this perceived requirement contributed to Kennedy's instinctive decision not to disclose his knowledge of the missile deployment until he was ready to act and to seize the initiative. The same objective of correcting Khrushchev's image of his weak determination, it is clear, entered into other decisions and judgments the president was called upon to make throughout the crisis. It contributed, for example, to Kennedy's rejection of the advice that he start not with the blockade but with a purely diplomatic approach to Khrushchev. If Kennedy gave serious thought to the idea, noted above, of beginning the crisis by sending a private ultimatum to Khrushchev, he also probably wondered whether Khrushchev, still prone to question his determination, might conclude he was only bluffing.

The point we wish to emphasize here is that, in addition to the reasons already noted, the blockade option appealed to Kennedy because it offered him a badly needed opportunity to correct Khrushchev's misjudgment of his determination by means short of more dangerous, irreversible military actions. This was a tactical objective of an essentially psychological nature.* For Kennedy it was a necessary first step for achieving a peaceful and acceptable resolution of the crisis. Therefore, it assumed a priority of a special kind in Kennedy's calculations. It helped shape his strategy and tactics, both of which reflected a strong element of improvisation to be sure but one that was guided by a search for means of impressing Khrushchev with his strong motivation and by careful attention to indications of whether or not this message was getting through.

V. NEGOTIATIONS: THE IMPORTANCE OF TIMING

Having emphasized the importance to Kennedy of finding a way of impressing Khrushchev with his determination, let us now consider how this tactical requirement fitted into Kennedy's conception of the role that negotiation would eventually play in terminating the crisis. The president did not have a clearly defined image of the negotiating phase of the crisis that lay before him when he disclosed his knowledge of the missiles in Cuba and announced the blockade; rather, his view of negotiation was dominated by the conviction that he must impress Khrushchev with his determination before entering into the process of bargaining. The timing of negotiations was critical in this respect for, as the

* As Hugh Sidey puts it, Kennedy ordered the blockade of Cuba "not to stop ships from bringing in missiles — that did not matter in the time which the U.S. had to act — but as a device to send the message of our determination through clearly to Nikita Khrushchev." *Life* magazine, November 22, 1968.

president correctly perceived, if he tried to bargain with Khrushchev before correcting the Soviet leader's mistaken view of his determination, Khrushchev's appetite and expectations might well remain excessive and unrealistic. In that event either Kennedy would have to pay too high a price to secure removal of the missiles, or else the negotiations would become prolonged or break down and the president would be forced to take further actions that would risk war.

We must recall at this point our earlier remarks on the theory and art of coercive diplomacy. In Chapter One we emphasized that the feasibility of this strategy depends among other things on whether one combines threats with positive inducements. The addition of a "carrot" may make possible something the "stick" cannot achieve by itself, unless it is a very formidable one. Thus, a proper reading of Kennedy's success in coercing the Soviets to withdraw their missiles from Cuba must call attention not only to the president's threats but also to his willingness to give Khrushchev a substantial quid pro quo. Kennedy eventually offered not only a conditional pledge not to invade Cuba but — as his brother's posthumous account has now made clear — he also gave Khrushchev a private assurance that the Jupiter missiles in Turkey would be removed soon. (That Kennedy added the stipulation that the Turkish missile bases could not be considered to be part of the formal quid pro quo for settling the crisis substantially reduced but did not altogether eliminate their value as part of the "carrot.") *

It is clear that the "carrot" offered by Kennedy was a genuine payment, not merely an inconsequential concession to permit Khrushchev to save face. But it is also clear that this payment would not have been sufficient by itself — that is, the "carrot" alone without the "stick" — to induce Khrushchev to take the missiles out.

Of course, Kennedy might have tried to buy his way out of the

---

* Not only were the United States Jupiter missiles in Turkey few in number — far fewer than the number of missiles the Soviets deployed into Cuba — they were also an obsolescent first-generation missile that President Kennedy had already directed be dismantled and removed. Abel, *The Missile Crisis*, pp. 189–190. It can be safely assumed the Soviets knew that the Jupiters were few in number and of low quality. Therefore, the value of Kennedy's concession in removing them lay not in reducing the military threat to the Soviet Union but in the political significance of offering them as an open payment for removal of Soviet missiles from Cuba.

crisis without making a serious effort at coercion. A careful reading of the record, however, indicates that Kennedy was certain
that Khrushchev's price tag in that event would be too large. Accordingly, *Kennedy relied on coercion to reduce substantially his
part of the quid pro quo.* He did not rely on coercion exclusively to
secure removal of the missiles. This point is critical both for
understanding Kennedy's strategy and for tempering the temptation to misread the lessons of this case as supporting a simple-
minded and overly optimistic view of the utility and feasibility of
coercion as an instrument of foreign policy.

It may come as a surprise even to those who have followed
closely the literature on the Cuban missile crisis if we assert that
from an early stage the president believed he would probably have
to pay a price to get the missiles out. Not only the president himself but others within the ExCom as well believed this. The
president's rejection of Adlai Stevenson's more explicit and more
extreme views regarding what the United States ought to be prepared to contribute to a quid pro quo and the notoriety that
Stevenson's views achieved thereafter have obscured the fact that
others, too, entertained the belief that the United States might
have to, and ought to be willing to, make concessions in return for
the removal of the missiles. Even before Stevenson joined the late
afternoon meeting of the ExCom on Friday, October 18, "someone observed that the United States would have to pay a price to
get them out: perhaps we should throw in our now obsolescent
and vulnerable Jupiter missile bases in Turkey and Italy, whose
removal the Joint Congressional Committee on Atomic Energy as
well as the Secretary of Defense had recommended in 1961." [29]

The president gave an early hint of his view that a delay in the
timing of the offer of a quid pro quo was all-important. In the
ExCom planning session at which Stevenson outlined his thoughts
the president expressed the belief that such talk of negotiating
formulas was "premature." Rather, the president wanted to concen-
trate in his signaling and communications to Khrushchev "on a
single issue — the enormity of the introduction of the missiles and
the absolute necessity for their removal." [30]

The president's awareness of the eventual necessity of a two-
sided quid pro quo was conveyed more explicitly by his brother.
Schlesinger reports that after the president, Robert Kennedy,
Rusk, and others had finished going over the draft of the initial
speech on the crisis to be delivered by Ambassador Stevenson

before the United Nations, "The Attorney General drew me aside to say, 'we're counting on you to watch things in New York. . . . *We will have to make a deal at the end, but we must stand absolutely firm now. Concessions must come at the end of negotiations, not at the beginning.'* " [31]

The need to avoid being drawn into serious bargaining until he had impressed Khrushchev with his determination and developed important bargaining assets remained with the president as the crisis unfolded. We see this consideration at work when he and a few advisers were going over a draft of the important October 22 speech. Discussion turned to the question of what the president should say about negotiation in the speech. President Kennedy's answer, Sorensen reports, was in effect, "Nothing that would tie our hands, anything that would strengthen our stand." Furthermore, "*the President deleted from my* [Sorensen's] *original draft a call for a summit meeting,*" preferring to state simply, in the words of the speech as given, that "this nation is prepared to present its case against the Soviet threat to peace, and our own proposals for a peaceful world, at any time and in any forum . . . — *without limiting our freedom of action.*" [32]

Later on, when he became depressed and worried by signs that the Russians were about to challenge the quarantine, the president controlled his impulse to rush into negotiations prematurely. On Tuesday evening, October 23, his brother relayed a private conversation with the Soviet ambassador in which Dobrynin said he knew of no change in instructions in Soviet vessels nearing the blockade line and expected that they would attempt to go through to Cuba. The president, evidently agitated at hearing this, spoke at once about the possibility of arranging an immediate summit with Khrushchev, "but finally dismissed the idea, concluding that *such a meeting would be useless until Khrushchev first accepted, as a result of our deeds as well as our statements, the U.S. determination in this matter.* Before a summit took place, and it should, the President wanted to have some cards in his own hands." [33]

VI. IMPLEMENTATION OF THE BLOCKADE

During the three and a half days following his address of Monday, October 22, the president's actions were dominated by the priority he gave to the requirements of careful crisis management.

He was embarked on an effort to secure his objective, the removal of the missiles, by means of coercive diplomacy. But the bite and impact of this coercive strategy were diluted by the priority Kennedy gave to managing the crisis to avoid dangerous incidents. Kennedy took one small step at a time; when he saw that would not suffice he reluctantly took another step. There was, indeed, a strong element of improvisation in Kennedy's effort to devise a coercive strategy.

Missing, or only present in weak form, were two of the three components of the stronger, "ultimatum" variant of the strategy. In seizing the initiative on October 22, Kennedy stated clearly his demand for removal of the missiles. He also announced his intention to impose a naval quarantine on vessels bringing offensive weapons and related components to Cuba. But his speech of October 22 was considerably vaguer with respect to laying down a time limit for compliance with his demand and threatening a credible and potent punishment for non-compliance. These two components of the classical ultimatum were hinted but not sharply conveyed in Kennedy's opening speech. True, the president did state that "these actions may only be the beginning," and he emphasized that the quarantine and other actions he was announcing were "initial steps." He added, "Should these offensive military preparations continue, thus increasing the threat to the hemisphere, further action will be justified. I have directed the Armed Forces to prepare for all eventualities; and I trust that, in the interest of both the Cuban people and the Soviet technicians at the sites, the hazards to all concerned of continuing this threat will be recognized."

Here we have a clear reference to the possibility of further escalation and a veiled threat of an air strike against the missile sites. But, at the same time, the notion of a time limit or sense of urgency for compliance with the demand for removal of the missiles is lacking. Moreover, Kennedy by no means threatened that air action against the missile sites would be the next or even an early step in his threatened escalation. Rather, a quite different impression was given by his statement that the quarantine would be extended, "if needed, to other types of cargo and carriers," thus clearly implying a gradual, piecemeal escalation rather than an abrupt jump to the air strike. This image of a prolonged, slowly developing crisis could only be reinforced by the statement, toward the end of the speech, intended particularly for American listeners but, of course, heard also by Soviet leaders that *"many months* of sacrifice and self-discipline lie ahead — *months* in which both our patience and our will will be tested, *months* in which many threats and denunciations will keep us aware of our dangers."

Therefore, notwithstanding the clear hints and warnings of further actions, including a possible air strike, included in the speech, it fell far short of an ultimatum.* Moreover, there is nothing in the record to indicate that Kennedy strengthened the speech by coupling it with a private, informal ultimatum to Khrushchev, as he was to do later in the case of his October 27 letter.

That the speech of October 22 did not go further in specifying a time limit of some kind and a threat of punishment for noncompliance, we may assume, was deliberate on Kennedy's part. We have noted that there had been some discussion earlier in ExCom of the possibility of giving a private ultimatum to Khrushchev and that this idea was discarded on the grounds that it was impossible to implement properly as well as being risky. We also know that on October 22 the president vetoed a passage in a draft speech to be given by Stevenson at the United Nations that explicitly threatened an American strike if the Soviet build-up in Cuba continued.[34] † Kennedy's private letters to Khrushchev during the week, so far as we know, contained no wording suggestive of an ultimatum regarding the demand for removal of the missiles, though in these private communications as well as in most of his public statements on the issue Kennedy consistently portrayed this matter to be urgent or as having priority over other matters. Also, as the days passed, Kennedy and other administration spokesmen repeatedly pointed out that work on the missile sites was still proceeding.

Kennedy was undoubtedly right in believing that the tough, determined opponent he faced would not be particularly impressed by words alone but would be watching to see what Kennedy was

* We do not take up here other important aspects of the October 22 speech that do not bear on the points being made. Thus, for example, the speech included a threat of massive retaliation against the Soviet Union if any missiles were fired from Cuba against any country in the Western Hemisphere. This was a deterrent threat, not directly employed to coerce Khrushchev into removing the missiles. Kennedy did not repeat it during the crisis. Of course, Kennedy's statement was also a bid for hemispheric solidarity.

† Schlesinger, who was present, adds that Kennedy implied or stated that he preferred to leave the possibility of an American strike to Moscow's imagination.

doing. Indeed, the president did a great deal, both before and after his opening speech of October 22. He put into effect a full strategic alert and conducted an unprecedented mobilization of tactical forces poised for action in the Caribbean.

But much was at stake for the Soviet Union, too, and it quickly became evident that its leaders, though taken by surprise, were not going to conduct a hasty retreat. They might have to take out the missiles, but they would attempt to salvage as much as possible from their Cuban venture. The time afforded them by Kennedy's prudent approach to crisis management offered them useful opportunities to exert counter-pressure against his stance, to test the depth and scope of his determination, and to mobilize world opinion roused by the danger of war to undermine and soften, if possible, the American position. It became clear rather soon, therefore, that the mere announcement of a blockade would not suffice and that its implementation would have to play an important role in Kennedy's strategy. His opponent would not cave in merely because of the impressive build-up of United States strategic and tactical forces. We must examine more closely, therefore, the way in which Kennedy chose to implement the blockade and the effect this had on the Soviet government's behavior.

In the ExCom deliberations the blockade was favored as the initial step, to be followed by others as necessary. As it turned out, however, when Kennedy turned his attention to implementing the blockade option he began his actions many rungs of the ladder below the final act of blockade. Why he did so is important. The president foresaw that the critical and most dangerous point in the blockade scenario would be reached when American naval vessels would be called upon to stop and inspect a Soviet vessel. Unless one or the other side backed away from this confrontation, or unless Soviet vessels bound for Cuba submitted to the United States Navy's procedures for boarding and inspecting, the confrontation would result in a dangerous military clash.

While such a confrontation would indeed display United States determination, Kennedy was mindful of its risks and shied away from it. All accounts indicate that he thought it quite likely that Khrushchev would feel himself obliged to retaliate, most likely by some action against West Berlin. Accordingly, the president felt it necessary to give Khrushchev time to consider what he would do and time to issue new orders to the captains of the vessels bound for Cuba. And he hoped desperately that something short of actually boarding and inspecting a Soviet vessel would suffice to signal his determination sufficiently to persuade Khrushchev not to attempt to force the blockade. What that lesser action might be, and even whether a lesser action would suffice, remained to be seen.

Kennedy inserted several discrete steps into his implementation of the blockade to put off a direct, possibly fateful confrontation on the high seas. As the Wohlstetters have observed, Kennedy's behavior in this respect shows that "where the alternative is to be ruled by events with such enormous consequences, the head of a great state is likely to examine his acts of choice in crisis and during it to subdivide these possible acts in ways that make it feasible to continue exercising choice." [35]

The logic of Kennedy's tactic of subdividing the blockade option, we may add, grew out of his recognition that the possibility for careful presidential control of the conflict would decline rapidly once a military incident occurred. He was concerned throughout the crisis that it would reach the dangerous point of no return toward war; he spoke movingly of his fear that, as had happened at the outset of World War I, the momentum of events would at some point sweep aside efforts to maintain control of the conflict. Accordingly, the president jealously safeguarded his options and withheld use of them as long as possible to avoid reaching that dangerous threshold too soon and perhaps unnecessarily. At the same time he was imaginative in subdividing one option into several smaller ones so as to slow up the momentum of the unfolding crisis and retain personal control of it. Ironically, the desperate feeling that he was about to lose control over the momentum of events at the end of the week forced him to pass from the careful "try-and-see" approach to an ultimatum. Let us review quickly the way in which Kennedy introduced the blockade in a deliberately slow, piecemeal fashion.

In his speech of Monday, October 22, Kennedy announced his intention to impose a quarantine. He waited until after obtaining approval from the Organization of American States on Tuesday, to issue the official proclamation of the quarantine. In turn, the proclamation stated that the interdiction of vessels bound for Cuba would begin on the following day, at 2 P.M. Greenwich time, Wednesday, October 24.

Late Tuesday evening the president moved the original blockade line that stretched out 800 miles around Cuba back to 500 miles. The circumstances and motivation for this decision are a revealing example of the way in which political desiderata in crisis management can dominate military considerations. Earlier in the evening the president and his advisers had learned that an extraordinary number of coded messages had been sent to all the Russian ships on their way to Cuba. "What they said," Robert Kennedy reported, "we did not know then, nor do we know now." But it was clear that the Soviet vessels as of that moment were still on a straight course for Cuba. Information about the coded messages came to Kennedy's attention some hours after he had received a private letter from Khrushchev in which the Soviet leader asserted in unmistakable language that the Soviet Union would not observe the blockade. Khrushchev added that the Soviet Union would not give instructions to the captains of the vessels bound for Cuba to obey the orders of American naval forces. To this he added the threat that if any effort were made to interfere with Soviet ships, "we would then be forced for our part to take measures which we deem necessary and adequate in order to protect our rights. For this we have all that is necessary." [36] Khrushchev's threat was similar to other efforts being made at this time by Soviet diplomatic and military personnel to convey a hard, "burned bridges" Soviet posture vis-à-vis the blockade.[37]

The president immediately composed a letter to Khrushchev asking him to observe the quarantine and making it clear that the United States did not wish to fire on Soviet vessels. Other decisions then taken in the Tuesday evening meeting reveal the president's heightening concern to find ways of reducing and controlling the risks of an untoward incident. If a confrontation took place with a vessel refusing to cooperate with the interdiction procedures, the navy was to shoot at the rudders and propellers of the vessel in order to avoid loss of life or the sinking of the ship. The ExCom also considered ways and means whereby vessels clearly not carrying military equipment might be let through without being boarded and searched.

At the close of this ExCom meeting, the president sent his brother to see Soviet Ambassador Dobrynin, among other reasons to find out the import of the coded messages of a few hours ago from Moscow to the Russian vessels en route to Cuba. At the end of their conversation Robert Kennedy asked Dobrynin if the Soviet vessels were going to go through to Cuba. Dobrynin replied that that had been their instructions and he knew of no changes.[38] According to another account, Robert Kennedy reported back to the president late that evening that Dobrynin had "seemed very shaken, out of the picture and unaware of any instructions," and that "this meant the imposition of the quarantine the next day might well bring a clash." [39]

Then British Ambassador Ormsby-Gore, a close friend of the president who was present when Robert Kennedy relayed his account of the conversation with Dobrynin, suggested that the line of interception for the blockade might be shortened. Otherwise an interception might take place within a few hours. "Why not give them more time," he asked, "to analyze their position?" Thereupon the president, fearful that the Soviets were still moving to confront the quarantine, called McNamara and shortened the interdiction line to 500 miles.[40] This action was taken before the quarantine was scheduled to go into effect the following day, il-lustrating the recurring tension in crisis management between political and military requirements for use and control of forces, to which we called attention in Chapter One. The navy had wanted the interdiction line 800 miles out from Cuba in order to reduce the vulnerability of its warships to MIG's stationed on Cuba. This military consideration gave way to the over-riding political consideration though not, it is reported, without adding to the tension between military and civilian chiefs in the Department of Defense.[41]

The next morning, Wednesday, the quarantine went into effect. Tension immediately mounted in the ExCom as reports came in that Russian vessels were approaching the blockade barrier. The moment had arrived when the president could no longer find a way of postponing further confrontation and the necessity of impressing Khrushchev with his determination. "We either had to intercept them or announce we were withdrawing," the president's brother reported later.[42]

As is well known, Khrushchev pulled back at the last moment. At 10:25 A.M. a preliminary report indicated that some of the Russian ships had stopped dead in the water. Shortly thereafter, this report was confirmed and amplified. The twenty Russian ves-sels closest to the interdiction barrier had stopped dead in the water or turned around.* Later that day it emerged that fourteen of the Soviet ships had stopped or turned back. Most of those continuing were tankers. One of them, the *Bucharest*, reached the barrier during the day. After identifying itself it was allowed, because it was a tanker, to pass without being boarded and inspected. This evidently followed from an instruction issued hurriedly by the president when he learned that some Soviet vessels were turning back; he directed that no ships should be stopped or intercepted for the time being in order to give them a further opportunity to turn back. The president's decision was sharply challenged by other ExCom members who felt that the *Bucharest* should be stopped and boarded, so that Khrushchev would not be misled as to the administration's intent and will. The president postponed a final decision and ordered the *Bucharest* shadowed by American warships after it had passed the quarantine line.[43]

In the following days an East German passenger ship was allowed to go through, again after strong arguments against doing so within the administration; and finally on Friday morning, October 26, the first vessel was stopped and boarded. This vessel, the *Marucla*, was carefully selected by the president for this purpose. Since it was not a Soviet vessel but a Panamanian-owned, Lebanese-registered vessel under Soviet charter, it could be stopped without offering a direct affront to the Soviets. At the same time, by stopping and searching a vessel carrying Soviet cargo the president would demonstrate to Khrushchev that he was going to enforce the quarantine fully.

But by Friday, when the *Marucla* was boarded, it had become somewhat less urgent and certainly far less risky to stage this confrontation. For Khrushchev had already been impressed with Kennedy's determination. The Soviet leader had stopped many of his vessels that were bound for Cuba — presumably those carrying weapons. He had already accepted conditionally U Thant's first proposal of Wednesday, October 24, coupling a "voluntary suspension of all arms shipments to Cuba" with "the voluntary suspension of the quarantine measures involving the searching of ships bound for Cuba."

U Thant's first proposal in effect clearly favored Khrushchev

---

* The significance of this Soviet action was not immediately evident. Some of Kennedy's advisers thought that the Soviet ships were changing course or waiting in order to join up with Soviet submarines before challenging the blockade.

since it would relax the blockade in return for suspension of further arms shipments without any reference to those already in Cuba. Thus, it would have hampered Kennedy in his effort to use the blockade to increase pressure and a sense of urgency with respect to his demand for removal of missiles already in Cuba. For this reason it was quickly turned down by the president.

U Thant's first appeal of October 24 to Khrushchev contained no reference at all to the importance of stopping work on the missile sites. Instead, U Thant directed such an appeal to Castro simultaneously with his joint proposal to the United States and Soviet leaders. Khrushchev's reply accepting U Thant's proposal made no reference to the appeal to Castro or, indeed, to the continuation of work on the missile sites in Cuba.*

When the *Marucla* was boarded on Friday morning Khrushchev had before him a new proposal from U Thant, received on the preceding day. In it the United Nations secretary general diluted his first proposal in order to make it more acceptable to Kennedy. U Thant now called upon Khrushchev "to instruct the Soviet ships already on their way to Cuba to stay away from the interception area for a limited time only." In return, Kennedy was "to do everything possible to avoid direct confrontation with Soviet ships in the next few days in order to minimize the risk of any untoward incident." In effect, U Thant's new proposal asked Khrushchev to formalize and accept openly what he had already accepted in fact on Wednesday in the first dramatic turning point of the crisis when he ordered Soviet vessels to turn back. Still, Khrushchev's acceptance of the proposal would be of considerable value for it would constitute Moscow's first formal acceptance of the quarantine and offer some assurance against a resumption of a direct Soviet challenge of the blockade.

U Thant's second proposal was valuable also because it offered Khrushchev a quick face-saving formula for reducing embarrass-

* In the absence of a reply from Castro, U Thant renewed his appeal to him on Friday, October 26, and requested an affirmative reply "very urgently." Castro replied on the following day indicating he "would be prepared to accept the compromises you request as efforts in favor of peace, provided that at the same time, while negotiations are in progress, the United States Government desists from threats and aggressive actions against Cuba, including the naval blockade of our country." (The relevant documents are reproduced in Pachter, *Collision Course*, and also in David L. Larson, ed., *The "Cuban Crisis" of 1962: Selected Documents and Chronology* [Boston: Houghton Mifflin Co., 1963].) But by then, Khrushchev had already set into motion his feelers regarding a quid pro quo for removal of the missiles.

ment caused by the retreat forced upon him on the high seas by Kennedy's determined application of the blockade the preceding day. U Thant's constructive, well-timed second proposal may have been influenced by United States diplomacy.* Certainly U Thant's second proposal received prompt attention and immediate acceptance by the president on the very same day it was made. And Khrushchev accepted it the following day, Friday, October 26.†

We have suggested that the boarding and inspection of the *Marucla* on Friday was not the decisive point of the confrontation. Let us consider in more detail now earlier actions that may have impressed Khrushchev with the strength of Kennedy's determination and caused him to pull back vessels carrying weapons to Cuba. We can only speculate on the basis of available facts. Despite disclosures regarding the events of Wednesday made by United States sources on various occasions and, in particular by Robert Kennedy in *Thirteen Days*, important details are still lacking. It appears likely that the decisive action that convinced Khrushchev to pull back was the American navy's actions against Soviet submarines that were leading and attempting to shield the merchant vessels approaching the interdiction line.[44]

On Tuesday Kennedy learned that Russian submarines were beginning to operate in the Caribbean. "The President ordered the Navy to give the highest priority to tracking the submarines and to put into effect the greatest possible safety measures to protect our own aircraft carriers and other vessels."[45] On Wednesday morning when two Soviet ships, the *Gagarin* and the *Komilies*, were within a few miles of the quarantine barrier, it was reported that a Soviet submarine had moved into position between them. Robert Kennedy's account of the response to this new threat is revealing:

> It had originally been planned to have a cruiser make the first interception, but, because of the increased danger, it was decided in the past few hours to send in an aircraft carrier, supported by helicopters, carrying antisubmarine equipment,

---

* This hypothesis is supported by Elie Abel's report that on Wednesday night Undersecretary of State Ball asked Stevenson to suggest to U Thant that he issue an appeal to the Russians to stop their ships for a while. Stevenson finally agreed, after a second call from Ball, to wake U Thant and to put the time-buying proposition before him. Abel, *The Missile Crisis*, p. 138.

† Knowledge of Khrushchev's acceptance of the second U Thant proposal probably arrived in Washington after the decision made very early Friday morning to board the *Marucla*.

hovering overhead. The carrier *Essex* was to signal the submarine by sonar to surface and identify itself. If it refused, said Secretary McNamara, depth charges with a small explosive would be used until the submarine surfaced.[46]

Robert Kennedy does not report explicitly what then happened. He implies that the submarine was forced to surface, but whether depth charges were dropped is not clear. He further implies that action against the submarine or submarines preceded the turning point already referred to, namely the turning back of the Soviet vessels. The United States Navy continued its harassment of the Soviet submarines: "All six Russian submarines then in the area or moving toward Cuba from the Atlantic were followed and harassed, and at one time or another, forced to surface in the presence of U.S. military ships." [47] * Details are lacking as to the nature of the harassment and the precise time at which these events, particularly the important initial encounter, took place.[48]

Robert Kennedy does not explicitly say so, but it would appear from his account that the president's quest for a means of impressing Khrushchev with his determination was provided — rather unexpectedly, it would seem — by United States naval harassment of the Soviet submarines. This may well have impressed Khrushchev and his military chieftains with Kennedy's willingness to use his superiority in conventional forces to enforce the blockade. Of course the navy's action against the Soviet submarines took place in the context of a highly menacing build-up of United States strategic and tactical forces.

If this interpretation regarding the significance of the navy's action against the submarines is correct, it is ironic that the presi-

---

* Similarly in an early account of the Cuban missile crisis two journalists, James Daniel and John G. Hubbell, reported that "the Russian subs were 'found' immediately. Wherever they moved, they were followed. Aware, through their own sonar devices, that they were being tracked on the surface, cat-and-mouse fashion, the Russians could only go on as long as possible while submerged, then prepare to come face to face with American warships as they surfaced to charge their batteries." *Strike in the West* (New York: Holt, Rinehart and Winston, 1963), p. 1965. An article by Commander Andrew J. Valentine (U.S.N.), "Rx:Quarantine," *U.S. Naval Institute Proceedings* (May 1963), was accompanied by a photograph of a United States Navy CH 19-E helicopter hovering over a Large Attack Type Russian F-Class submarine during the Cuban quarantine operations. This information accompanied the photograph; there was no discussion of the subject in the article itself. The *New York Times*, November 10, 1962, also published a photograph of a United States helicopter observing a Soviet submarine, which was cruising on the surface in Caribbean waters during the quarantine operations.

dent wavered at the last minute and was inclined to avoid the confrontation with the Soviet submarine on Wednesday morning. "Isn't there some way we can avoid having our first exchange with a Russian submarine — almost anything but that?" McNamara held the President firm. "No, there's too much danger to our ships. There is no alternative," said McNamara. "Our commanders have been instructed to avoid hostilities if at all possible, but this is what we must be prepared for, and this is what we must expect." [49] Some minutes later the preliminary report arrived stating that some Russian ships had apparently stopped dead in the water.

In reflecting on this phase of the crisis it is worth observing that the blockade, while initiated and implemented on a "try-and-see" basis, always contained the latent threat of a de facto ultimatum. [50] Thus, Kennedy demanded that Khrushchev stop doing something he was already doing, namely sending vessels with "offensive weapons" to Cuba. In case of non-compliance with this demand, Kennedy threatened to stop Soviet vessels and prevent those carrying such cargo from proceeding. The other component of an ultimatum — a time limit for compliance — was less obvious, but also present in the situation since the United States Navy interposed itself between the Soviet vessels and Cuba. There need be no explicit time limit for compliance since the blockade was self-enforcing in this respect. Not only was Khrushchev forced to judge whether Kennedy was bluffing but, because of the structure of the situation, he was forced to initiate risky actions — i.e. allowing Soviet vessels to reach and attempt to pass the interception line — in order to find out. As we have seen, Khrushchev made some efforts to test and weaken Kennedy's resolution and to find out whether Kennedy's threat was credible; but the Soviet leader did not call Kennedy's bluff in the most direct and also the most risky manner by attempting to send the vessels carrying "offensive weapons" through the interception barrier. Perhaps, as we suggested earlier, Kennedy's threat of preventing such vessels from proceeding had gained the final necessary credibility in Khrushchev's eyes as a result of the harassment of Soviet submarines. On the other hand, given the fragmentary information available, we cannot exclude the possibility that the Soviet leaders would have turned back these vessels even in the absence of the harassment of their submarines.

Clearly, Khrushchev accepted the blockade and was presumably impressed with Kennedy's determination. But most of the missiles were already in Cuba and the effort to bring them to operational readiness was proceeding at a rapid pace. Would a continuation of the blockade help coerce Khrushchev into removing them? Or would Kennedy have to step up pressure in a more substantial manner?

VII. FROM "TRY-AND-SEE" TO ULTIMATUM

The successful boarding of the *Marucla* notwithstanding, a feeling of gloom began to settle over the ExCom on Friday morning, and for good reason. Soviet acquiescence to the blockade did indeed cut off the flow of missiles and related weapons to Cuba, but United States intelligence reported that at least thirty MRBM's were already in Cuba. (In fact, as was learned later, forty-two had already arrived.) True, the blockade had enabled Kennedy to really impress Khrushchev with his determination. This was an important achievement that would contribute eventually to the termination of the crisis, perhaps even more than Kennedy could perceive on Friday morning. But the determination which Kennedy had conveyed and the successful imposition of the blockade still did not add up to the leverage needed to secure the president's irreducible objective: the removal of the missiles. And every successive intelligence report had indicated that work on the missile sites was continuing at a rapid pace and that they would soon be operational.

As seen by the president and his advisers, therefore, the situation on Friday morning was a most difficult one and would rapidly get worse. Khrushchev was still in a position to gain the upper hand without having to directly challenge the blockade. For three and a half days, Kennedy had adhered faithfully to his conviction that he must slow up events leading to a confrontation in order to give Khrushchev time to reflect, time to reconsider and alter his policy, time to issue new directives to his vessels approaching the blockade line. Thereby, a possibly dangerous confrontation on the high seas had been avoided. But the same time given Khrushchev for this purpose had also enabled the Russians to rush the missiles already in Cuba toward completion and to devise and put into effect a counter-strategy for salvaging as many gains as possible.

Thus the president had paid a price — how large and serious it would turn out to be no one yet knew — for his faithful adherence thus far to prudent crisis management principles. He had knowingly decided to do so a week earlier when in the ExCom planning sessions he had listened carefully to the arguments against the blockade option, accepted their validity, and decided nonetheless that the blockade was preferable to the air strike. And since then he and other members of the ExCom had seen the predicted disadvantages of the blockade option begin to materialize one by one. Indeed, sober forecasts by ExCom of the blockade's chief limitations and risks had been remarkably prescient. "At first there had been very little support of a blockade," Sorensen recalls, for "it appeared almost irrelevant to the problem of missiles. . . . The greatest single drawback to the blockade was time. Instead of presenting Khrushchev and the world with a *fait accompli*, it offered a prolonged and agonizing approach, uncertain in its effect, indefinite in its duration, enabling the missiles to become operational, subjecting us to counter-threats from Khrushchev . . . and in all these ways making more difficult a subsequent air strike if the missiles remained." [51] Nonetheless, the president had finally chosen the blockade option because the disadvantages and risks of the alternatives to it seemed even worse.

When he announced his choice of the blockade to the ExCom, the president, striving to pull together the badly divided group, had said half jokingly that those whose advice on what to do had been rejected were the truly fortunate ones since they would be able later to say they had been right! [52] That time was at hand on Friday, October 26, and even more so the following day. Now the fact that even a successful blockade would not remove the missiles from Cuba, and the additional fact that the Russians were rapidly bringing the missiles to a state of readiness reactivated the powerful voices of the air strike advocates. Their arguments took on new force and relevance that could not be turned aside so easily as before. Their pressure on Kennedy mounted with every passing hour, with every new disturbing development that Friday and especially Saturday brought.

During these two days, as a matter of fact, two distinct phases can be detected in Kennedy's response to the situation. On Friday morning, when he began to tighten the screws, he distinctly confined his actions to a "gradual increase in pressure." [53] There is no indication at this stage that the president was thinking of moving beyond gradual increase in pressure to an ultimatum. He ordered more low-level flights and, significantly, as evidence of the gradual escalation he had in mind at this stage he asked the State and

Defense departments to prepare to add petroleum and lubricants to the embargo list.

"But privately," his brother reports, "the President was not sanguine about the results of even these efforts. Each hour the situation grew steadily more serious." [54] Recognizing this and looking ahead to actions he might be forced to take, the president also ordered the State Department to proceed with preparations for a "crash program" on civil government in Cuba after a United States invasion.

On Friday, even while stepping up the pressure, the president was still trying to retain some of his earlier allegiance to ultra-prudent crisis management principles. Lincoln White, the State Department press officer, went somewhat beyond his instructions in threatening additional action by calling attention to that sentence in the president's speech of October 22 which stated that "further action will be justified" if work on the missile sites did not stop. This triggered headlines that an invasion was imminent. Kennedy immediately rebuked White and made his displeasure known also to Rusk and others.* His major interest at this time was to communicate, which he did in various ways, the American sense of urgency that work on the missile sites must stop very soon. But added to the signal that emerged, whether or not the president fully intended it, was the widespread interpretation that the United States could hold off its next step for no more than a few days. While members of the administration may have fostered rumors and leaks to this effect, the president was not officially committed thereby even though he may have instigated some of these reports himself. Kennedy was moving toward a full-fledged ultimatum, but he had still to formulate it explicitly and give it to the Soviet government directly.

A step in this direction occurred when Rusk took advantage of an unexpected opportunity on Friday afternoon. John Scali, a State Department correspondent, received a telephone call from

---

* An interesting indication that even at this stage in the crisis the president envisaged the possibility that it might drag on for a considerable period is contained in his rebuke to the State Department for White's press conference. According to Sorensen, *Kennedy*, p. 712, the president argued that "this was going to be a prolonged struggle . . . requiring caution, patience and as little public pressure on him as possible." But in the next twenty-four hours the president joked about White's unauthorized statement saying that it may have helped the Soviets realize how urgent the situation really was. Hilsman, *To Move a Nation*, p. 214.

Aleksander Fomin, a counselor at the Soviet Embassy, requesting an immediate meeting. When they met shortly thereafter Fomin urged Scali to find out whether the administration would be interested in a solution to the crisis whereby the Soviet government would remove the missiles, with United Nations inspection, in return for a public pledge by the United States not to invade Cuba. Rusk, after discussion with other members of the ExCom including the president, authorized Scali to reply that the United States was interested, but that it was his [Scali's] "impression" that "time is very urgent." [55]

Khrushchev now resolved an important question the president had not yet faced. Kennedy had refused, as we observed earlier, to begin serious bargaining with Khrushchev over the terms of a quid pro quo for ending the crisis until he had succeeded in impressing the Soviet leader with his determination and accumulated some bargaining assets. So far as can be established from available materials, Kennedy had not developed a formula of his own for a quid pro quo which he was holding back to introduce at the right moment. The subject had not been discussed much in the ExCom — indeed the president had actively discouraged discussion of whether the United States should pay a price to secure voluntary removal of the missiles. Lack of preparation on the subject is evidenced in accounts of ExCom's somewhat desperate last-minute efforts on Saturday to consider how the Turkish bases might be offered up as part of the quid pro quo.[56] Very conveniently for Kennedy, Khrushchev took the initiative in signaling on Friday, October 26, that the time for serious bargaining was at hand.* Some time before Fomin's call to Scali at 1:30 P.M. — how much before is critical for reconstructing and explaining more fully the factors and events that influenced the Soviet decision, but this is not known — Khrushchev evidently decided that it was time to begin a serious exploration of how to bring the crisis to an end and to find out how much he could hope to salvage out of it.

The interpretation advanced here is that Khrushchev opened the bargaining without having made a firm decision to end the

---

* Khrushchev employed multiple channels for this purpose. At about the same time that Fomin was talking to Scali, Schlesinger, A Thousand Days, p. 827, reports, "in New York . . . we heard that Zorin had advanced the same proposal to U Thant, and that the Cubans at the UN were beginning to hint to unaligned delegates that the bases might be dismantled and removed if the United States would guarantee the territorial integrity of Cuba."

crisis immediately and without a fixed view as to the terms of an acceptable settlement. It is possible, as some commentators have suggested, that Khrushchev's decision early on October 26, or even on October 25, went beyond this, that he and his associates "decided that the game was up: the U.S.S.R. would yield." [57] Such an interpretation, however, is too simple a post hoc explanation; it reads back from Khrushchev's later actions that a clear-cut decision to yield must have been made earlier and it leaves out intervening events. It also overlooks the possible impact on Soviet policy of the increase in Kennedy's pressure on Friday and Saturday, and it ignores the fact that work on the missile sites continued while Khrushchev opened the bargaining. This latter point — that Khrushchev continued work on the missile sites — is critical. Evidently, for the time being, Moscow preferred the bargaining advantages expected from bringing the missiles to a state of readiness to the calming effect a cessation of work on the missile sites would have imposed on Kennedy and the more hawkish of his advisers.

Had Khrushchev's top priority been to de-fuse the danger that the crisis might suddenly and uncontrollably erupt into war, *he had only to stop work on the missile sites.* For it was this, obviously, that was driving the president, otherwise reluctant to escalate, to increase pressure. Here was an option of considerable potential utility to Khrushchev. At some point he could have stopped further work on the missile sites *without beginning to dismantle them;* and then, after waiting for the steam behind Kennedy's momentum to dissipate, as it surely would have if work on the missile sites stopped, he could have renewed the bargaining in a more leisurely fashion in order to extract as high a price as possible for an agreement to dismantle and remove the missiles. Such a bargaining strategy would have capitalized more effectively on the widespread support at the United Nations and throughout the world for the proposal the Soviets finally unveiled on Saturday, October 27, for a swap of Turkish and Cuban bases. Instead, the Soviet leaders, perhaps divided on this issue, chose to couple this bid for a bigger pay-off with a decision to continue work on the missile sites, gambling that this would pressure Kennedy to cave in and agree to remove his Jupiters from Turkey as well as pledge himself not to invade Cuba.

Some indirect evidence indicates that the Soviet government finally decided to call off work on the missile sites, just when they were becoming operational,[58] but without agreeing as yet to dismantle and remove them. Khrushchev's letter of Sunday morning, October 28, which accepted Kennedy's formula for removing the missiles, contained a cryptic reference to "earlier instructions on the discontinuation of further work on weapons constructions sites" in addition to which, Khrushchev added, he had now "given a new order to dismantle the arms which you described as offensive, and to crate and return them to the Soviet Union." It is possible, of course, that Khrushchev's reference to an earlier order was contrived so as to present as a matter of his own decision what was in fact forced upon him by Kennedy.

Available materials do not indicate that Khrushchev attempted to bring such an earlier order to Kennedy's attention. Indeed, none of the commentaries and analyses of the crisis that I am familiar with have taken note of this passage in Khrushchev's letter. If the Soviet government finally resorted to this option because it was suddenly impressed with the danger of an American attack — before or after receiving Dobrynin's account of Kennedy's ultimatum — then it had waited too long to put into effect the attractive bargaining strategy described in the preceding paragraphs. At this late stage Khrushchev could no longer be sure that an offer to stop work on the missile sites would de-fuse the momentum of Kennedy's ultimatum.* We note, finally, without being able to clarify it, the possible link between Castro's belated reply to U Thant earlier on Saturday in which he conditionally agreed to a cessation of work on the missiles, and Khrushchev's reference to such an order as having been given in his letter to Kennedy. Castro's acquiescence may have been considered as desirable, if not necessary, before ordering work to stop on the missile sites; but this in itself does not clarify the other components of the Soviet decision.

Whatever Khrushchev's reasons for opening the bargaining on Friday, it is likely that his initial calculations shifted in response to new developments. It is also possible that disagreements divided Soviet leaders so badly as the crisis intensified that they no longer followed a consistent, well-integrated policy. Whatever the calculations of Soviet policy-makers, however, events themselves make clear that two coercive processes were going on simultaneously on Friday and Saturday, one in each direction. The president was

---

* The details of Kennedy's ultimatum are presented below.

stepping up pressure for getting the missiles out and was still trying, as he had all week, to keep down the price he knew he would probably have to pay as his contribution to an eventual quid pro quo. At the same time, however, Soviet leaders were engaged in a crash effort to blackmail Kennedy into paying as much as possible, even while cooperating in the essential aspects of crisis management in order to avoid war.

Before we turn to the often confused bargaining that occurred, particularly on Saturday, we should make several additional observations. Earlier in the week, as various commentators have noted, tacit cooperation in careful crisis management had developed between Kennedy and Khrushchev. Even while the Soviet leader blustered and exerted pressure of his own in order to undermine Kennedy's resolve and his ability to implement a coercive strategy, Khrushchev nonetheless also "went to great lengths to guarantee the avoidance of a clash at sea. Submarines were not used to interfere with the blockade and no attempt was made to break it with surface vessels." Instead, he "abided by the American rules for the blockade and submitted to all the demands of the American Navy." [59]

Once the confrontation on the high seas was safely accomplished, however, United States and Soviet cooperation in managing the crisis began to break down on Friday as Kennedy deliberately stepped up pressure and the Soviet government insisted nonetheless on rushing the missile sites to completion. As a result, the tempo of events speeded up and a startling lack of synchronization began to characterize the interaction between the two sides. The context and meaning of certain possibly critical moves and communications that one side was making became confusing to the other. Deciphering the intentions and calculations behind the specific moves of the opponent became difficult. We know that Kennedy experienced this problem acutely and we have to assume that his adversary felt the same unsettling phenomenon in Moscow. There was real danger in this, but the disturbing sensation that things were getting out of control and the mounting fear that one side or the other might miscalculate was probably not without value in helping to bring the crisis to a sudden halt on early Sunday morning.

United States policy-makers and those writing about the crisis since then have found it difficult to explain the discrepancy between Khrushchev's more personal and more emotional private

letter of Friday evening, in which he suggested removal of the
missiles in return for a pledge of non-invasion of Cuba, and the
more formal and composed letter which he issued publicly on Saturday morning demanding that the United States remove its missiles from Turkey as well. Various interpretations were entertained
at the time and have been offered since. One interpretation that
attracted considerable support initially is Henry Pachter's ingenious and plausibly argued thesis that Khrushchev's second letter
was written first but was delayed because of Soviet clearance procedures or because it was timed for release on Saturday morning in
order to secure maximum impact at the United Nations.[60] Pachter
interprets Khrushchev's Friday night letter as being a hurried improvisation by a man who was responding desperately to growing
signs earlier in the day that Kennedy was getting ready for a major
escalation of the crisis. Consistent with Pachter's interpretation is
that the Friday night letter asked less of Kennedy by way of a
quid pro quo than did the Saturday morning letter. Presumably
Khrushchev made a quick decision to lower the price because he
feared that the situation was about to get out of hand. That the
Saturday letter was then issued, even though it was out of date,
can be explained variously: either Khrushchev and his aides ne-
glected to cancel the delayed release of the first letter or perhaps
the "hawks" in the Kremlin insisted it, too, should go out.

Pachter's interpretation is weakened, however, when we consider
additional facts, not available to him when he wrote in 1963. Not
knowing of Fomin's approach to Scali early Friday afternoon and
similar Soviet initiatives in the United Nations corridors, Pachter
did not know that Khrushchev's Friday evening letter contained
essentially the same feelers that Fomin and Soviet diplomats had
unveiled earlier in the day before the burden of Kennedy's new
pressure was felt. Thus the decision to probe Kennedy's bargaining
position had been made much earlier, no later than Friday morning. The Friday night letter, then, was not as hurried and belated
an improvisation as Pachter believes and this, in turn, weakens the
thesis that Khrushchev suddenly wrote it on Friday night because
he was responding to signs during the day that Kennedy was getting ready to escalate.

A slightly different interpretation holds, more simply, that the
hawks in the Kremlin, learning of and disapproving Khrushchev's
personal initiative of Friday night, overruled him and wrote a new
letter that demanded more. This thought occurred to members of

the ExCom at the time and was an additional source of confusion and anxiety.[61]

Still another interpretation, somewhat different from each of the preceding, seems worth considering. Having learned from their probe on Friday via the Fomin-Scali exchange that the president was immediately willing to pledge the United States not to invade Cuba in order to get the missiles out, Soviet leaders may have decided to bargain harder in order to find out whether Kennedy would be willing to contribute more than that to a quid pro quo. The tactic of raising the price after an opponent has agreed to your first proposition, in effect trying to get him to pay twice for the concession made to him, is a familiar aspect of Soviet and other negotiating styles. In any case, we can assume that upon learning of Kennedy's immediately favorable response to their first overture, Khrushchev and his colleagues wondered whether the president was prepared to pay an even bigger price for removal of the missiles. The more modest quid pro quo offered the president on Friday could be expected — and perhaps was intended — to calm down the pressure building up in the administration for further escalation. Perhaps it was safe now to try to raise the price. Was it so unlikely that the president would agree to throw in removal of the obsolescent Jupiter bases in Turkey? There was, after all, Walter Lippmann's article of Thursday, October 25, suggesting that the president do so. Soviet leaders might well have thought this was a trial balloon inspired by the more dovish members of the administration and, additionally, they might have noticed that the administration did not disassociate itself from Lippmann's position.

Even before Lippmann's article appeared, the Soviet government had been preparing the ground for a demand for a "symmetrical" trade of United States and Soviet overseas bases. Thus, although the Soviet government had carefully refrained from threatening action in Berlin in response to the blockade, it had been exerting counter-pressure with regard to United States bases in Turkey.* Removal of the Jupiter missiles from Turkey would

---

* As early as Tuesday, October 23, Soviet Defense Minister Malinosky, in a conversation with a Western diplomat, had compared Cuba and Turkey. In the middle of the week, according to unconfirmed sources, the Soviet ambassador in Ankara had threatened annihilation of Turkish cities in case the American bases there were not soon dismantled. On Friday the Red Army paper, *Red Star*, referred to the idea of a trade of the Cuban and Turkish bases. (Pachter, *Collision Course*, pp. 49–52.) The idea of such a base swap

not constitute the large gains Khrushchev had expected when he deployed missiles secretly into Cuba, but his problem now was to salvage as much as he could. Besides, to force Kennedy into agreeing to remove the bases in Turkey would by no means constitute an insignificant prize — not because of the military significance of the Jupiters to either the United States or the Soviet Union but because such a concession under duress would have damaging political-diplomatic consequences for the American position in NATO.

According to this interpretation, some of the disturbing Soviet actions of Saturday constituted a deliberate increase of pressure designed to motivate Kennedy to accept the latest base swap proposal. A U-2 was shot down over Cuba; two other reconnaissance planes were shot at as they swooped low over the missile sites Saturday morning; outside the quarantine line a single Soviet ship detached itself from the others and headed for the blockade line.

In Washington these actions were interpreted, not surprisingly, as grim indications that the Soviets had decided to test United States determination. Some ExCom members reasoned that since the Soviets must have realized shooting down U-2s would force the United States to take direct action against the SAMs, "their action seemed to mean that they had decided on a showdown." [62] There was speculation as to whether Khrushchev was still in charge in the Kremlin, and contradictory speculation that Khrushchev was trying to extract a higher price. The president would have to decide what to do next under the burden of considerable uncertainty and confusion as to what was going on in the Kremlin.

Whether or not the shooting down of the U-2 was a calculated part of Soviet bargaining strategy,* it served as the critical trigger that pushed the president before the day was over into giving Khrushchev a tacit ultimatum.[63] Kennedy withstood pressure from

had received sympathetic mention in the British press early in the week and attracted widespread support in the United Nations where to many representatives it appeared to be a natural and reasonable way to end the dreadful danger of war.

* Other possibilities are that the U-2 was shot down by the Soviet SAM crew on the initiative of local Soviet commanders in Cuba without authorization from higher authorities, or that the timing of the incident was fortuitous, with Soviet forces having orders to use the SAMs as soon as they became operational. Hilsman, *To Move a Nation*, p. 183, states that the SAMS and their associated radar nets did not become operational as a system until about October 27, when the U-2 was shot down, or at most a day or two earlier.

his advisers to put into effect contingency plans calling for a retaliatory air strike against one SAM site in Cuba, but it was clear
that the reconnaissance flights would have to continue and that if
another one were shot down he could not hold off a reprisal attack
against SAM sites. What would happen, thereafter, he feared
could lead to uncontrollable escalation.[64] An immediate effort to
end the crisis before it went out of control was necessary. Motivated as never before — not merely by a desire to get the missiles
removed but by a desperate need to try to end the crisis before it
resulted in war — Kennedy was finally ready to give Khrushchev
an ultimatum.*

He accepted his brother's suggestion to reply to Khrushchev's
contradictory two letters by ignoring the Saturday morning demand for an exchange of bases and "accepting" Khrushchev's
earlier suggestion of a quid pro quo linking removal of the missiles
with a United States pledge not to invade Cuba. Kennedy's formal
letter to Khrushchev did not hint at an ultimatum, though it conveyed a sense of urgency. The ultimatum was transmitted orally
by his brother when he gave the letter to Soviet Ambassador
Dobrynin in the early evening of Saturday, October 27. Robert
Kennedy summarized what he told Dobrynin: "We had to have a
commitment by tomorrow that those bases [missiles in Cuba]
would be removed. I was not giving them an ultimatum but a
statement of fact. He should understand that if they did not remove those bases, we would remove them. . . . Time was running
out. We had only a few more hours — we needed an answer immediately from the Soviet Union. I said we must have it the next
day." [65]

Thus, to his long-standing demand for removal of the missiles
the president had finally added the two missing elements of a
classical ultimatum — a time limit for compliance and a credible
threat of punishment for non-compliance. On the next day, Sunday, October 28, Khrushchev accepted Kennedy's formula — taken
from Khrushchev's feelers of the preceding Friday — for settling
the crisis. A few months later, on December 12, 1962, Khrushchev

* As Richard Smoke has noted (in a personal communication), Kennedy
was evidently led to escalate from try-and-see to ultimatum at this point quite
paradoxically by both coercive-diplomatic and crisis-managerial considerations.
This state of affairs is rather odd and unexpected since one expects that crisis-
management considerations normally encourage the more cautious try-and-see
strategy.

defended his conduct of the Cuban venture in a major speech to the Supreme Soviet. He did not mention or allude to an ultimatum per se. However, he did go very far toward indicating the urgent pressure under which he had been placed:

> In the morning of October 27 we received information from our Cuban comrades *and from other sources* which directly stated that this attack would be carried out within the next two or three days. We regarded the telegrams received as *a signal of utmost alarm,* and this alarm was justified. Immediate actions were *required* in order to prevent an attack against Cuba and preserve the peace.[66]

VIII. WHAT IF?

What would Kennedy have done if Khrushchev had not accepted the ultimatum of Saturday, October 27? Would he have then ordered the air strike or would he have tried to find still other ways of persuading Khrushchev to remove the missiles? While an answer to this question is necessarily speculative, the available evidence strongly suggests that the president would not have resorted immediately to the air strike option.

Before we review the material bearing on this question, let us recall that during the planning period an important split had emerged among members of the ExCom regarding the way in which graduated escalation should be applied. Some felt that there should be relatively few, if any, intermediate steps between the blockade and an air strike. Others thought in terms of a series of intervening steps or options which would permit the president to increase pressure more gradually in the hope that at some point short of an air strike Khrushchev would agree to remove the missiles. A more finely graduated escalation appealed to them also because it would enable the president to retain control over the momentum of events for as long as possible.

Disagreement on this critical issue among Kennedy's advisers during the ExCom planning sessions had not been resolved; rather, it was set aside when Kennedy chose to start with the blockade option. The issue was coming to the fore again at the end of the week, however, for it was now clear that the partial success of the blockade notwithstanding, more pressure would have to be applied to get Khrushchev to remove his missiles. The issue was further sharpened by the possibility that continued SAM attacks against United States reconnaissance planes flying over Cuba might force the president to put into effect the contingency plan for retaliatory attacks against the SAM sites which, in turn, could have set off an escalatory spiral.

On Saturday afternoon and evening, even while the tacit ultimatum to Khrushchev was being planned and delivered, Sorensen reports, "the Executive Committee was somewhat heatedly discussing plans for the next step. . . . The POL [petroleum products] blockade, air-strike and invasion advocates differed over what to do when." [67] Consistent with his earlier advocacy of the gradual, slow approach to escalation, McNamara was now in favor of tightening the blockade rather than going immediately to the air strike. The secretary of defense later recalled that while the air strike would have been ready to go in thirty hours, it "would not have been my next recommendation. I had told Ros Gilpatric [Deputy Secretary of Defense] that I would recommend deferring the air-strike option. I would have added POL to the contraband list and tightened the blockade instead." [68] The next morning, Sunday, McNamara rose early to draw up a list of "steps to take short of invasion." [69]

The Joint Chiefs of Staff and others in ExCom who had favored the air strike earlier were now pressing the case for it with renewed vigor.* Since the sense of urgency behind Kennedy's pressure on Khrushchev had always been geared to the expectation that the missiles would soon be operational, what the latest intelligence estimates were saying on this critical question is quite relevant. The information available on this point is fragmentary and by no means provides the detailed picture we would like. On Friday morning, October 26, the latest aerial photographs indicated that the Russians were racing to put the missile sites into operation. "Time was running out," Elie Abel states in his account of the ExCom meeting that morning. "In a matter of hours, the Soviet missiles could be ready to fire. Some said the lesser danger was to knock them out before they could threaten the United States." [70] Essentially the same intelligence picture was reported to the ExCom the following morning, Saturday, October 27.[71]

* On Saturday night, Sorensen recalls, the president adjourned the ExCom meeting "as the hawks began to dominate the discussion and to urge an immediate air strike." (Theodore Sorensen, *The Kennedy Legacy* [New York: Macmillan, 1969], p. 190.)

However, Hilsman flatly states that "all the MRBMs were operational by October 28," the day on which Khrushchev agreed to the president's formula.[72]

Indeed, if all or many of the missiles were thought to be operational on October 28, the question arises whether Kennedy would have been inhibited thereafter from ordering an air strike out of fear that some missiles would survive and be fired against American cities. Various other arguments against an air strike could also have been raised at this juncture by those who favored a tightening of the blockade. McNamara, for example, believed that the fact that the Soviet air defense missiles (SAMs) were operational made the air strike riskier than a tightening of the blockade. He said, "I would rather have sunk a Russian ship than bombed the missile sites." [73] Moreover, by this time intelligence had established that the missile sites were guarded by Soviet ground combat units equipped with tactical nuclear weapons. Under these circumstances an American air strike and invasion, as Hilsman remarks, would have been awesome to contemplate.[74]

Kennedy's advisers later offered other predictions as to what he would have done next had Khrushchev turned down the ultimatum or temporized. Robert Kennedy states that on Saturday night neither the president nor he was optimistic as to Khrushchev's acceptance of the ultimatum they had just passed on to him; rather, their expectation was that events were moving to "a military showdown by Tuesday and possibly tomorrow." Yet, on Sunday morning the attorney general took his daughters to a horse show — hardly the action of a man who expected an important decision to be made momentarily — where at 10:00 A.M. he received a call from Secretary of State Rusk saying that Khrushchev had agreed to remove the missiles. As for Sorensen, in his judgment the president "would not . . . have moved immediately to either an air strike or an invasion; but the pressures for such a move on the following Tuesday were rapidly and irresistibly growing." [75]

It is clear enough that at the Saturday-night meeting of the ExCom "no decisions were made, except to call up twenty-four troop carrier squadrons of the Air Force Reserve," which would be needed if it became necessary to invade Cuba.[76] While this was no bluff, as Elie Abel notes, and while the president was inching toward such a decision, he had not yet made it, and he was still trying to keep his options open. The president did not himself know what he would do next if Khrushchev turned him down. Probably much would have depended on the way in which Khrushchev turned down or temporized over Kennedy's demand and on what the president then concluded regarding the utility of further bargaining. It is interesting to speculate, therefore, how the president would have reacted had Khrushchev announced that he had stopped all work on the missile sites but that he would need a more equitable quid pro quo which included the Turkish bases before he would agree to dismantle and remove his missiles.

Dean Acheson, a strong advocate of the air strike, has stated that the president was "phenomenally lucky" to have obtained the removal of the missiles without an air strike. Elaborating, Acheson refers to "the luck of Khrushchev's befuddlement and loss of nerve. . . . He went to pieces when the military confrontation seemed inevitable. But he need not have done so." Acheson adds that his reading of Robert Kennedy's account of the crisis, *Thirteen Days*, "does not convince me that an attack would have been inevitable if Khrushchev had 'played it cool.' " [77]

Indeed, there is some uncertainty, as we have tried to indicate, as to what the president would have done next if Khrushchev had not obliged him. But the threat of an air strike and invasion was not, after all, a case of bluff, pure and simple. The preparations had been made; and Kennedy had already managed to convey his determination to Khrushchev by implementing the blockade. Moreover, it is only by ignoring the fact that Kennedy did improvise and apply a strong coercive strategy on Saturday that Acheson is able to arrive at his sweeping conclusion as to Kennedy's "phenomenal luck" and Khrushchev's "befuddlement and loss of nerve." Curiously, Acheson makes no mention of the ultimatum transmitted to Khrushchev; he fails to appreciate why the Soviet leader would find it necessary to credit the ultimatum with sufficient credibility; he passes over too lightly the risks Khrushchev would have run had he rejected it; and he fails to consider that Khrushchev received a meaningful quid pro quo and did not act exclusively out of "befuddlement and loss of nerve." Good fortune was not missing from the equation. But to regard Kennedy as having been "phenomenally lucky" fails altogether to appreciate that by Saturday night Kennedy had earned the remaining luck he needed to persuade Khrushchev to pull out the missiles.

IX. LESSONS AND CONCLUSIONS

Critics have chided Kennedy for going to the brink unnecessarily, a judgment they feel justified since the missiles in Cuba did not reverse the strategic balance in Russia's favor. Other critics, agreeing with the administration's judgment that the missiles were a threat which had to be removed, have professed to believe that Kennedy could have persuaded Khrushchev to remove the missiles through quiet diplomacy without creating such a dangerous crisis. Understandably appalled by the danger of war that Kennedy's response to the missiles created, most critics have generally failed to credit him for having withstood pressures to resort to military action, for having refused advice to step up demands on Khrushchev once the latter began to retreat, for having been guided throughout by a desire not merely to secure the removal of the missiles but to do so in a way that would create a stepping stone toward détente, serious arms control agreements, and a new form of coexistence to replace the Cold War.

While it is still too early to judge whether the outcome of the Cuban missile crisis marked a turning point in the Cold War, its immediate consequences for Soviet-American relations were beneficial. The crisis was hardly over before cautious cooperation in seeking a more general relaxation of tensions emerged. As on earlier occasions in history when one or both sides stepped back from the brink of war,[78] a détente quickly followed and policies that had dangerously exacerbated the earlier conflict of interests were re-examined. Within ten months of their dangerous brush with war, the two leaders had cooperated in bringing about a partial test ban treaty.

From his success in the Cuban crisis Kennedy obtained, therefore, not only the removal of the missiles but also an important modification of the offensive thrust of Khrushchev's policies toward the West. This is not the place to trace the important shift in the priorities and operating objectives of Soviet foreign policy following the Cuban crisis,[79] but contrary to all indications prior to the discovery of missiles in Cuba, including Khrushchev's own intimations, the Soviet government did not resume pressure against West Berlin. Nor have Khrushchev's successors returned to this familiar Cold War battleground. At the very least Kennedy's handling of the Cuban crisis gained an important, prolonged respite in the dangerous clash over unresolved European issues. That better use has not been made of this reprieve to deal constructively with the requirements for creating a more stable world system can be acknowledged and deplored without losing sight of Kennedy's attempt to convert the Cuban missile crisis into an opportunity to initiate meaningful steps in this direction.

Paradoxically, the most important lesson of Kennedy's success in this crisis is that it is extremely difficult to apply coercive diplomacy effectively even when one possesses overall military superiority and other advantages as well. I have chosen to stress this in the preceding account of the crisis because I think it is important to draw from historical experience a better understanding of the practical difficulties of applying the theory of coercive diplomacy.

As we noted in the Introduction, the missile crisis was hardly over when some members of the administration, including the president himself, cautioned against the temptation to generalize from its successful outcome. Inadequate and incomplete analysis of the Cuban crisis, however, inevitably encouraged oversimplified formulations of the theory and practice of coercion. On the side of theory, neither those who participated in the administration's handling of the crisis nor those who wrote about it subsequently distinguished clearly between the try-and-see and the ultimatum variants of the strategy, so evident in the evolution of Kennedy's handling of the crisis. They directed attention, rather, to questions such as the respective merits of rapid, large-step escalation against a more gradual piecemeal increase in pressure. This was, as we have described, a controversial issue among United States policymakers during the Cuban crisis, and it has remained controversial since then. It erupted once more during the controversy over policy in the Vietnam War.

While the argument over gradual versus rapid escalation is also important, it has not been related to the more fundamental distinction between the try-and-see and the ultimatum variants of coercive diplomacy. Both the rapid, large-step and the gradual, piecemeal types of escalation can be conducted in the try-and-see manner, that is, without specifying a time limit for compliance and a credible threat of punishment. Similarly, an initially cautious piecemeal type of escalation can be converted into an ultimatum, as in the Cuban missile crisis, without actually engaging in a rapid, large-step escalation. Hence, the strategy of coercive diplomacy cannot be adequately described or discussed solely in the terms in which the argument over rapid versus piecemeal escalation has been conducted.

Some observers have incorrectly drawn support from the Cuban missile crisis for a concept of this strategy that rests exclusively on coercive threats. Their theory of coercive diplomacy makes no provision for the carrot as well as the stick. Or, to put it another way, their theory envisages that one offers an opponent only face-saving gestures on trivial or peripheral matters. Thus, they overlook the possibility that coercive diplomacy in any given situation may be facilitated by, if indeed it does not require, genuine concessions to the opponent as part of a quid pro quo that secures one's essential demands. Coercive diplomacy, therefore, must be distinguished from pure coercion; it includes bargaining, negotiations, and compromise as well as coercive threats.

Some observers are overly impressed by Kennedy's success. Once the president's attempt at coercive diplomacy succeeded, relieving the acute anxieties the crisis had engendered — and still engenders among those who read graphic accounts of it — his accomplishment looked far easier than it had been in fact. Kennedy's success was certainly spectacular. It was all too easy at the time and since then to regard him as a masterful virtuoso who pulled just the right strings to bring about Khrushchev's defeat — a heroic image that the humility with which Kennedy spoke of his achievement only succeeded in swelling further.

For such grateful admirers, Kennedy's handling of the crisis quickly became, as Pachter says, "a feat whose technical elegance compelled the professionals' admiration." Denis Healy, the British Labour party expert on defense and a man noted for a critical attitude toward United States foreign policy, exclaimed afterwards that Kennedy's handling of the crisis "could be cited as a model in any text-book of diplomacy." One can only hope that the difficulties Kennedy experienced in applying coercive diplomacy as well as his ultimate success will be recorded in the textbooks. Even Khrushchev is supposed to have confided to a Western diplomat: "Had I been in the White House instead of the Kremlin, I would have acted like Kennedy" — a compliment to the president, as Pachter states, that was no doubt meant to reflect back favorably on the speaker.[80]

American experts with special policy axes to grind quickly passed over the president's difficulties in making his strategy of coercive diplomacy work. For them, the compelling need was not to reflect soberly on the problems that had beset Kennedy; rather, it was to provide explanations for his success that would support their favored positions on matters of doctrine and force posture. Advocates of United States strategic nuclear superiority argued that it had played the decisive role in forcing Khrushchev to back down. Firm believers in the virtues of ample conventional military capabilities, on the other hand, saw Khrushchev as having been checkmated by the superior conventional capabilities the United States had quickly mustered in the Caribbean. Nonpartisans in this dispute exercised the wisdom of eclecticism by observing that Khrushchev had been squeezed between American strategic and local superiority.

This competition in locating the basis for Kennedy's success in one or another component of the United States military posture obscured a much more significant point about the crisis: how difficult it had been for the president to utilize his combined strategic and local superiority in order to find a way of imposing his will on Khrushchev without going to war!

What then did the Cuban crisis reveal about the problems of utilizing the strategy of coercive diplomacy? First, even when strongly motivated a responsible leader will draw back from the risks of giving an ultimatum to an opponent who is also strongly motivated and commands formidable military capabilities of his own. A leader must consider whether an ultimatum threat will be credible; whether the recipient will regard it as a bluff and, if so, whether the side that issued it will be prepared to demonstrate otherwise; or whether the ultimatum will provoke the recipient into seizing the initiative himself to engage in a major escalation of the conflict.

Kennedy felt that he must first find a safe way to impress Khrushchev with his determination so that Khrushchev would believe him if and when it became necessary to press harder to secure removal of the missiles. He chose the blockade option as the vehicle by which he would demonstrate his resolve and rid himself of the image of weakness in Khrushchev's eyes. To achieve his important tactical objective, Kennedy had to implement the blockade with careful attention to the requirements of crisis management lest the blockade measures provoke Khrushchev and lead to war.

One important policy dilemma revealed by the Cuban crisis was that prudent crisis management generally tends to conflict with the requirements for strong coercive diplomacy. As a result, the decision-maker may well end up — as Kennedy did during the first part of the crisis — having to dilute the content and impact of his attempt at coercive diplomacy. And yet, paradoxically, special crisis management considerations toward the end of the week also pushed the president into issuing an ultimatum!

The strategy of coercive diplomacy may require that at some point in the crisis a sense of urgency be created for the opponent's compliance. However, the practice of deliberately slowing up and spacing out military actions, which crisis management requires, may be difficult to reconcile with the need to generate the sense of urgency for compliance. Another principle of crisis management, giving the opponent enough time to receive and reflect on the signals directed toward him and to reconsider his policy and set into motion the desired changes, also dilutes the necessary sense of urgency and also inevitably carries with it the risk that the opponent will use that time in other ways. He may mount counterpressure to undermine the strategy of coercive diplomacy directed toward him, he may increase his own military preparations, or he may even seize the military initiative. Crisis management considerations dominated Kennedy's handling of the crisis in the first three and a half days. Only several unusual developments in the situation — the fact that work on the missile sites was bringing them to the point of operational readiness, which would have drastically altered the bargaining context in Khrushchev's favor, and the fact that a U-2 reconnaissance plane was shot down over Cuba, which increased pressure on Kennedy to retaliate and thereby possibly lose control over events — forced the president finally to summon the nerve and determination to convert the try-and-see approach he had been following into an ultimatum. Thus, although the theory of coercive diplomacy may emphasize the general advantages of the ultimatum over the try-and-see approach, it is evidently not very easy in practice to adopt the ultimatum variant of the strategy. Moreover, since each approach may have advantages under difficult conditions, flexibility and timing may be all-important.

Another problem in utilizing the strategy of coercive diplomacy concerns the difficulty of achieving optimum timing of negotiations. Kennedy's task was to delay serious bargaining until he had succeeded in impressing Khrushchev with his determination. If he had entered negotiations prematurely, Kennedy would have been at a serious bargaining disadvantage. In the Cuban case Kennedy was successful in delaying the bargaining until he had forced

Khrushchev to back down over the blockade and had accumulated other important bargaining assets. Kennedy achieved this, moreover, without having to pay a high price in terms of negative domestic or international reactions to his delaying negotiations. In other situations — for example, Vietnam — it is not so easy for the president to delay serious bargaining in order to acquire negotiating assets without paying a heavy price.

Closely related to the need for a sense of urgency and the difficulty of timing is the problem of impressing an opponent with the strength of your motivation before subjecting him to the strong form of coercive diplomacy. The Cuban crisis stands out as a case in which a relatively small and carefully applied amount of force — the blockade — when combined with the threat of additional force — the ultimatum — sufficed to secure the objective without major escalation or prolongation of the conflict. What helped the strategy of coercive diplomacy succeed in this case was that the implementation of the blockade and the United States Navy's harassment of the Soviet submarines strongly impressed the opponent with Kennedy's determination. This, together with the menacing United States military build-up, very much strengthened the credibility of the later threats Kennedy made when he passed the ultimatum on to Khrushchev. But the initial actions taken in a crisis, on which one hopes to build a strategy of coercive threats, may not always signal strong determination to the opponent. Rather, they may inadvertently and incorrectly signal timidity and irresolution.

A fourth problem of utilizing coercive diplomacy concerns the need to formulate the content of the carrot and stick so that it is commensurate with the magnitude of the demand made on the opponent. The task of coercive diplomacy can be relatively easy or quite formidable, depending on what one demands of the opponent and how strongly he is motivated not to do what is asked of him. To employ the strategy of coercive diplomacy successfully, therefore, necessitates finding a combination of carrot and stick that will suffice to overcome the opponent's disinclination to yield. What is demanded of the opponent, that is, must be less unattractive to him than the threatened consequences if he does not acquiesce. And if the threatened consequences are not potent enough for this purpose, then concessions must be offered to the opponent as well so that the combination of negative and positive inducements directed toward him will outweigh the unattractiveness of what is demanded. In the Cuban case Kennedy was able to formulate a combined carrot and stick that neutralized Khrushchev's initially strong motivation not to yield to the demand that the missiles be removed. Indeed, as we have seen, Khrushchev actually helped Kennedy to do this by initiating the quid pro quo himself. In other circumstances and in other cases, however, the opponent who is the target of coercive diplomacy may not be so cooperative in helping to formulate a quid pro quo. In that event, the United States may have great difficulty in formulating a carrot and stick inducement that suffices to overcome the opponent's strong reluctance to do what is demanded of him before the United States threat to escalate is called and American leaders are faced with the decision to act or back away from their demand.

This suggests a fifth problem of utilizing coercive diplomacy. Not merely the timing of negotiations but, more specifically, the timing of the carrot and stick may be critical. An otherwise serviceable and workable quid pro quo may be offered too late, after one's military operations have hardened the opponent's determination and made it more difficult for him to accept what is demanded of him. Kennedy's timing, it turned out, was just right, neither too early nor too late.

The question of timing, of course, calls attention to the importance of skill in applying the strategy of coercive diplomacy. We consider this problem in more detail in Chapter Five. Here it will suffice to say that, judging by the results, Kennedy dealt with the problems of the strategy of coercive diplomacy skillfully. But there was no guarantee that he would and no way of predicting. The results could easily have been otherwise. Besides, certain underlying situational conditions favored skillful implementation of the strategy of coercive diplomacy in this case. We have not discussed these conditions explicitly in this chapter but will do so in the final chapter after examining the Vietnam case, characterized by a more complex set of conditions that made the adoption and skillful implementation of the strong variant of coercive diplomacy more difficult.

NOTES

[1] The decision to halt U-2 flights over western Cuba was taken on September 10 to avoid the possibility of a U-2 being shot down. Information on this aspect of the United States intelligence "failure" emerged only belatedly. See Elie Abel, *The Missile Crisis* (Philadelphia: J. B. Lippincott Co. 1966), p. 14; Roger Hilsman, *To Move a Nation* (New York: Doubleday, 1967), pp. 174–190; Graham T. Allison, "Policy, Process and Politics: Conceptual Models and the Cuban Missile Crisis," (Unpubl. Ph.D. diss., Harvard University, 1968), pp. 192–201, 283–291.

[2] Arthur Schlesinger, Jr., *A Thousand Days* (Boston: Houghton Mifflin Co., 1965), p. 803.

[3] Theodore C. Sorensen, *Kennedy* (New York: Harper & Row, 1965), p. 684.

[4] Schlesinger, *A Thousand Days*, p. 801; Sorensen, *Kennedy*, pp. 682–683; Robert F. Kennedy, *Thirteen Days* (New York: Norton, 1969), p. 33; Hugh Sidey, *John F. Kennedy, President* (New York: Atheneum, 1963), p. 327.

[5] Acheson distinguished the concept of a smaller-scale air strike confined to the missiles, which he favored, from the larger air strike proposed by the Joint Chiefs of Staff, which included other targets as well. Dean Acheson, review of Robert F. Kennedy's *Thirteen Days*, in *Esquire*, February, 1969.

[6] Schlesinger, *A Thousand Days*, p. 803.

[7] In addition to materials on the ExCom policy deliberations in Abel, *Missile Crisis*; Sorensen, *Kennedy*; Schlesinger, *A Thousand Days*; Hilsman, *To Move a Nation*; Acheson, review of *Thirteen Days*; and Kennedy, *Thirteen Days*, see the perceptive analysis of the politics of decision-making provided by Allison, *Policy, Process and Politics*. A condensed version appears under the title "Conceptual Models and the Cuban Missile Crisis," *American Political Science Review*, LXIII (September 1969), pp. 689–718.

[8] See, for example, Nathan Leites, *A Study of Bolshevism* (New York: Free Press, 1953).

[9] Kennedy, *Thirteen Days*, pp. 126–127.

[10] Oran Young, *The Politics of Force* (Princeton: Princeton University Press, 1968), pp. 258–259.

[11] Kennedy, *Thirteen Days*, p. 33.

[12] A recent article which emphasizes Kennedy's personal stakes is Thomas M. Mongar, "Personality and Decision-making: John F. Kennedy in Four Crisis Decisions," *Canadian Journal of Political Science*, II (1969), pp. 200–225.

[13] Sorensen, *Kennedy*, p. 674.

[14] Hilsman, *To Move a Nation*, pp. 196–198; see also Allison, *Policy, Process and Politics*, pp. 283–287.

[15] Abel, *The Missile Crisis*, pp. 51, 60; Hilsman, *To Move a Nation*, pp. 195, 197; Sorensen, *Kennedy*, p. 683.

[16] Abel, *The Missile Crisis*, pp. 52, 59–60; Hilsman, *To Move a Nation*, p. 195.

[17] In addition to the accounts by Sorensen, *Kennedy*; Hilsman, *To Move a Nation*; Schlesinger, *A Thousand Days*; and Abel, *The Missile Crisis*, see also the discussion of the significance of the missiles by Dean Acheson in review of *Thirteen Days*; Arnold Horelick, "The Cuban Missile Crisis: An Analysis of Soviet Calculations and Behavior," *World Politics*, XVI (April 1964), pp. 364–377; Albert and Roberta Wohlstetter, "Controlling the Risks in Cuba," Adelphi Paper No. 17, Institute of Strategic Studies, London, April 1965.

See also the briefing of February 6, 1963, by John Hughes, Special Assistant to General Carroll, reprinted in *Department of Defense Appropriations for 1964*, U.S. Congress, House of Representatives, 88th Session, Part I, 1963, Washington, D.C.

18 Interview with President Kennedy, *Washington Post*, December 18, 1962.

19 Horelick, "The Cuban Missile Crisis," p. 366, argues persuasively that so large and expensive an offensive capability would not have been placed in Cuba had Khrushchev's objective been limited to deterring a United States attack on Cuba or had it also included removal of United States Jupiter missiles from Turkey.

20 Charles Burton Marshall, *Cuba: Thoughts Prompted by the Crisis* (Washington, D.C.: Washington Center of Foreign Policy Research, n.d.), p. 3.

21 Henry M. Pachter, *Collision Course* (New York: Praeger, 1963), p. 13.

22 *Ibid.*

23 Abel, *The Missile Crisis*, p. 81. McNamara's argument had been anticipated and partly formulated in earlier ExCom meetings, *ibid.*, p. 62, though evidently not phrased so colorfully and appealingly in terms of "maintaining the options."

24 At the Friday night (October 19) session of the ExCom, for example, Paul Nitze recalls having stated that "it [the blockade] might or might not work. But if, after a reasonable period we saw that the Russians were going ahead with their missile bases or uncrating the Il-28 bombers just delivered, *then we would go to an air strike.*" *Ibid.*, p. 89. Italics added. This was true also of Nitze's written recommendation of Sunday, October 21, as quoted *ibid.*, p. 94.

25 In a final presentation to the president at the ExCom meeting of Saturday, October 20, "the choices put before Kennedy that afternoon were two: begin with the naval blockade and, if need be, *move up the ladder of military responses, rung by rung;* or begin with an air strike, then move almost certainly to a full-scale invasion of Cuba." *Ibid.*, p. 93. Italics added. The available historical sources do not make clear the nature and number of intermediate escalatory steps envisaged by the advocates of the slow, graduated escalation strategy.

26 Schlesinger, *A Thousand Days*, p. 391.

27 Sorensen, *Kennedy*, pp. 671, 677, 681. The linkage of the unresolved Berlin problem to the Cuban missile deployment is traced by Jack M. Schick in "The Berlin Conflict, 1958–62" (unpubl. ms.).

28 To this perceptive observation Pachter, *Collision Course*, p. 84, adds, with some embellishment, that "Kennedy was waiting to be tested. He needed an opportunity to show his mettle. That this opportunity came in Cuba may have given him additional satisfaction. Here was a chance to cancel out last year's humiliation."

29 Schlesinger, *A Thousand Days*, p. 807.

30 *Ibid.*, p. 810.

31 *Ibid.*, p. 811. Italics added.

32 Sorensen, *Kennedy*, p. 699. Italics added.

33 Kennedy, *Thirteen Days*, pp. 66–67. Italics added.

34 Schlesinger, *A Thousand Days*, p. 811.

35 Wohlstetter and Wohlstetter, "Controlling the Risks in Cuba," p. 19.

36 Kennedy, *Thirteen Days*, pp. 79–80.

37 See, for example, Abel, *The Missile Crisis*, pp. 133–134, 151.

38 Kennedy, *Thirteen Days*, p. 66.

[39] Schlesinger, A Thousand Days, p. 817.

[40] Kennedy, Thirteen Days, p. 67.

[41] Schlesinger, A Thousand Days, p. 818; Sorensen, Kennedy, p. 710. Abel, The Missile Crisis, pp. 154–156, and Hilsman, To Move a Nation, p. 215, report that a similar clash over implementation of the blockade took place on the following day. Allison, writing before Robert Kennedy's Thirteen Days became available, offers a different interpretation of these events which suggests that the navy did not observe Kennedy's Tuesday night order to pull back the blockade line. See "Conceptual Models and the Cuban Missile Crisis," p. 706.

[42] Kennedy, Thirteen Days, p. 68. This book, relied on heavily here, provides the most detailed public account of the critical events of the Wednesday morning confrontation at the blockade barrier.

[43] Ibid., p. 74.

[44] Brief references to the navy's shadowing of Soviet submarines in the Caribbean and forcing them to surface appeared in earlier accounts: Schlesinger, A Thousand Days, p. 822; Abel, The Missile Crisis, p. 155; and Hilsman, To Move a Nation, p. 214.

[45] Kennedy, Thirteen Days, pp. 61–62.

[46] Ibid., p. 69.

[47] Ibid., p. 77; see also Abel, The Missile Crisis, p. 155.

[48] Admiral Anderson, Chief of Naval Operations, was less specific than Abel and Robert Kennedy in his public references to the navy's anti-submarine activities. See his speech to a Navy League banquet, November 9, 1962, New York Times, November 10, 1962; and his testimony, cited in Allison, Policy, Process, and Politics, before the House Armed Services Committee in 1963, Hearings on Military Posture, 88th Congress, 1st Session, 1963, p. 897.

[49] Kennedy, Thirteen Days, p. 70.

[50] I am indebted to David Hall for this interpretation of the blockade.

[51] Sorensen, Kennedy, pp. 687–688.

[52] Ibid., p. 694.

[53] Kennedy, Thirteen Days, p. 83; see also Hilsman, To Move a Nation, pp. 213–214; Abel, The Missile Crisis, p. 173; and Sorensen, Kennedy, p. 711.

[54] Kennedy, Thirteen Days, p. 83.

[55] This quotation is taken from Hilsman's record of what Rusk wrote on a piece of paper for Scali to say. However, Rusk was evidently more specific in his verbal instructions to Scali; according to Hilsman, Rusk told Scali to say that "no more than two days" remained. Hilsman, To Move a Nation, p. 218. Italics added. We have no independent account of what formulation of the sense of urgency Scali actually transmitted to Fomin when they met again at 7:35 P.M. Detailed accounts of the Scali-Fomin meetings, which continued into November, appear also in Abel, The Missile Crisis, pp. 175–177, and particularly in Pierre Salinger, With Kennedy (New York: Doubleday, 1966), pp. 341–348.

[56] See particularly Abel, The Missile Crisis, pp. 194–195.

[57] Adam Ulam, Expansion and Coexistence (New York: Praeger, 1968), p. 674.

[58] See p. 64.

[59] Young, The Politics of Force, pp. 330–331.

[60] Pachter, Collision Course, pp. 67–68.

[61] Michael Tatu, Power in the Kremlin (New York: Viking, 1969), p. 263; Hilsman, To Move a Nation, pp. 220–221; Abel, The Missile Crisis, pp. 188–189.

[62] Hilsman, To Move a Nation, p. 220.

[63] Robert Kennedy in *Thirteen Days*, p. 97, referred to the shooting down of the U-2 as the event which was "to change the whole course of events and alter history."

[64] Hilsman, *To Move a Nation*, p. 220; Kennedy, *Thirteen Days*, p. 98; Sorensen, *Kennedy*, p. 713.

[65] Kennedy, *Thirteen Days*, p. 109. Robert Kennedy initially disclosed his role in the ultimatum six months after the crisis in a speech prepared for delivery in Columbia, South Carolina, on April 25, 1963. See *New York Times*, April 26, 1963. This account of it was less detailed than that which he gave later and there are, as a result, some discrepancies. Another statement about the ultimatum was given by Robert Kennedy for quotation in a memorial volume for his brother. As quoted on this occasion, he erroneously indicated that the deadline for compliance was contained in the president's letter. See Goddard Lieberson, ed., *John Fitzgerald Kennedy, As We Remember Him* (New York: Atheneum, 1965). Reference to a deadline for compliance or an ultimatum is contained in a number of other accounts: Pachter, *Collision Course*, pp. 54–55; Schlesinger, *A Thousand Days*, p. 829; Sorensen, *Kennedy*, p. 715; Abel, *The Missile Crisis*, p. 199; Hilsman, *To Move a Nation*, p. 224. The possibility that not all members of ExCom and lesser officials in the administration knew that an ultimatum was given, even for some time after the crisis, cannot be excluded. Unnamed "high officials" who took part in the critical decisions of October 27, asked to comment on Robert Kennedy's disclosure in his speech in Columbia, South Carolina, stated "that they knew of no secret messages or ultimatum. They supported the attorney general's statement that Major Anderson's death was a major element in bringing this country to the edge of drastic action, such as an air strike on Cuban bases. But they said the warning to Mr. Khrushchev—the 'notification' — was by way of deeds, not words." *New York Times*, April 26, 1963.

[66] Quoted from *Pravda*, December 13, 1962, by Horelick, "The Cuban Missile Crisis," p. 368.

[67] Sorensen, *Kennedy*, p. 715.

[68] Abel, *The Missile Crisis*, p. 193.

[69] Sorensen, *Kennedy*, p. 716. Unnamed White House sources told the *New York Times* shortly after the end of the crisis that any next step would almost certainly have been an expansion of the blockade rather than an attack. "Invasion was hardly ever seriously considered," another official stated. "Chronology of Cuban Missile Crisis," *New York Times*, November 3, 1962.

[70] Abel, *The Missile Crisis*, p. 173.

[71] *Ibid.*, pp. 186, 192.

[72] Hilsman, *To Move a Nation*, p. 227. The same disclosure was made by John Hughes, Defense Department photo interpretation specialist, in his authoritative briefing to the House Appropriations Committee, *Department of Defense Appropriations for 1964*, 88th Congress, 1st Session, 1963, p. 12.

[73] Abel, *The Missile Crisis*, p. 193.

[74] *Ibid.*, p. 227; Hilsman, *To Move a Nation*, p. 227.

[75] Kennedy, *Thirteen Days*, pp. 109–110; Sorensen, *Kennedy*, pp. 715–716.

[76] Abel, *The Missile Crisis*, pp. 178–179; see also Sorensen, *Kennedy*, p. 717; *New York Times*, November 3, 1962.

[77] Acheson, review of *Thirteen Days*.

[78] See Herbert Dinerstein, "The Transformation of Alliance Systems," *American Political Science Review*, LIX (September 1965).

[79] See, for example, Ulam, *Expansion and Coexistence*, pp. 677 ff.

[80] Pachter, *Collision Course*, pp. 87, 89.

BIBLIOGRAPHY

Abel, Elie, *The Missile Crisis* (Philadelphia: J. B. Lippincott Co., 1966).

Acheson, Dean, Review of R. F. Kennedy's *Thirteen Days, Esquire*, February 1969.

"After Cuba," *The Economist*, November 3, 1962.

Allison, Graham T., "Policy, Process and Politics: Conceptual Models and the Cuban Missile Crisis" (Unpubl. Ph.D. diss., Harvard University, 1968).

————, "Conceptual Models and the Cuban Missile Crisis," *American Political Science Review*, LXIII (September 1969), pp. 689–718.

Baldwin, Hanson W., "The Growing Risks of Bureaucratic Intelligence," *The Reporter*, August 15, 1963.

Ball, George, "Lawyers and Diplomats," Address before the New York Lawyer's Association, New York, December 13, 1962, reprinted in Department of State, *Bulletin*, December 31, 1962, pp. 987–991.

Brown, Seyom, *The Faces of Power* (New York: Columbia University Press, 1968).

Bundy, McGeorge, "The Presidency and the Peace," *Foreign Affairs*, XLII (April 1964).

Chayes, Abram, Thomas Ehrlich, and Andreas F. Lowenfeld, "The Cuban Missile Crisis," *International Legal Process* (Boston: Little, Brown and Co., 1969), II, 1057–1149.

Crane, Robert D., "The Sino-Soviet Dispute on War and the Cuban Crisis," *Orbis*, VIII (Fall, 1964), pp. 537–549.

"Cuban Crisis: A Step-by-Step Review," *New York Times*, November 3, 1962.

Daniel, James, and John G. Hubbell, *Strike in the West* (New York: Holt, Rinehart and Winston, 1963).

Dinerstein, Herbert, "The Transformation of Alliance Systems," *American Political Science Review*, LIX (September 1965).

Gerberding, William P., "International Law and the Cuban Missile Crisis," in *International Law and Political Crisis*, ed. Lawrence Scheinman and David Wilkinson (Boston: Little, Brown and Co., 1968).

Greene, Fred, "The Intelligence Arm: The Cuban Missile Crisis," in *Foreign Policy in the Sixties*, ed. Roger Hilsman and Robert C. Good (Baltimore: Johns Hopkins Press, 1965), pp. 127–140.

Halle, Louis J., *The Cold War as History* (London: Harper & Row, 1967).

Hearings, Department of Defense Appropriations for 1964, U.S. Congress, House of Representatives, 88th Congress, 1st Session, Part I, Washington, D.C., 1963.

Hermann, Charles F., *Crises in Foreign Policy* (Indianapolis: Bobbs-Merrill, 1969).

Hilsman, Roger, *To Move a Nation* (New York: Doubleday, 1967).

Holsti, Ole R., Richard A. Brody, and Robert C. North, "Measuring Affect and Action in International Reaction Models: Empirical Materials from the 1962 Cuban Crisis," *Journal of Peace Research* (1964), pp. 170–189.

Horelick, A., "The Cuban Missile Crisis, An Analysis of Soviet Calculations and Behavior," *World Politics*, XVI (April 1964).

————, and M. Rush, *Strategic Power and Soviet Foreign Policy* (Chicago: University of Chicago Press, 1965).

Horowitz, David, *The Free World Colossus* (New York: Hill and Wang, 1965).

Hyland, William, and Richard W. Shryock, *The Fall of Khrushchev* (New York: Funk & Wagnalls, 1968).

"Interview with President Kennedy," *Washington Post*, December 18, 1962.

Kateb, George, "Kennedy as Statesman," *Commentary* (June 1966).

Kennedy, Robert F., *Thirteen Days* (New York: Norton, 1969).

Knorr, Klaus, "Failures in National Intelligence Estimates: The Case of the Cuban Missiles," *World Politics*, XVI (April 1964), pp. 455–467.

Knox, W. E., "Close-up of Khrushchev During a Crisis," *New York Times Magazine*, November 18, 1962.

Kolkowicz, Roman, "Conflicts in Soviet Party-Military Relations: 1962–1963," The RAND Corporation, RM-3760-PR, August, 1963.

———, *The Soviet Military and the Communist Party* (Princeton: Princeton University Press, 1967).

Krock, Arthur, *Memoirs* (New York: Funk & Wagnalls, 1968).

Larson, David L., ed., *The "Cuban Crisis" of 1962: Selected Documents and Chronology* (Boston: Houghton Mifflin Co., 1963).

Leites, Nathan, *A Study of Bolshevism* (New York: Free Press, 1953).

Lieberson, Goddard, ed., *John Fitzgerald Kennedy, As We Remember Him* (New York: Atheneum, 1965).

Linden, Carl A., *Khrushchev and the Soviet Leadership, 1957–1964* (Baltimore: Johns Hopkins Press, 1966).

Lockwood, Lee, *Castro's Cuba, Cuba's Fidel* (New York: Macmillan, 1967).

Marshall, Charles Burton, *Cuba: Thoughts Prompted by the Crisis*, (Washington, D.C.: Washington Center of Foreign Policy Research, n.d.).

Mongar, Thomas M., "Personality and Decision-making: John F. Kennedy in Four Crisis Decisions," *Canadian Journal of Political Science*, II (1969), pp. 200–225.

"Speech by Robert F. Kennedy at Columbia, South Carolina," *New York Times*, April 26, 1963.

"Speech by Robert F. Kennedy on Cuban Missile Crisis, October 13, 1964, at Huntington, Long Island, New York," *New York Times*, October 14, 1964.

Pachter, Henry M., *Collision Course* (New York: Praeger, 1963).

———, "JFK as an Equestrian Statue: On Myth and Mythmakers," *Salmagundi* (Spring, 1966).

Salinger, Pierre, *With Kennedy* (New York: Doubleday, 1966).

Schelling, Thomas C., *Arms and Influence* (New Haven: Yale University Press, 1966).

Schick, Jack M., "The Berlin Conflict, 1958–62" (unpubl. ms.).

Schlesinger, Arthur, *A Thousand Days* (Boston: Houghton Mifflin Co., 1965).

Sidey, Hugh, *John F. Kennedy, President* (New York: Atheneum, 1963).

Sorensen, Theodore C., *Kennedy* (New York: Harper & Row, 1965).

———, *The Kennedy Legacy* (New York: Macmillan, 1969).

Steel, Ronald, "Endgame" (review of Robert F. Kennedy's *Thirteen Days*), *New York Review of Books*, March 13, 1969.

Stone, I. F., "The Brink" (review of Elie Abel's *The Missile Crisis*), *New York Review of Books*, April 14, 1966.

Sulzberger, C. L., articles in *New York Times*, October 20, 22, 24, 1962; February 25, 1963.

Tatu, Michael, *Power in the Kremlin* (New York: Viking, 1969).

Ulam, Adam, *Expansion and Coexistence* (New York: Praeger, 1968).

Valentine, Andrew J., "Rx:Quarantine," *U.S. Naval Institute Proceedings* (May 1963).

de Vosjoli, Philippe Thyrand, "So Much Has Been Swept Under the Rug," *Life*, April 26, 1968.

Weintal, Edward, and Charles W. Bartlett, *Facing the Brink* (New York: Charles Scribner's Sons, 1967), chap. 4, "Challenge on the Doorstep."

Wohlstetter, Albert, and Roberta Wohlstetter, "Controlling the Risks in Cuba," Adelphi Papers, No. 17, Institute of Strategic Studies, London.

Wohlstetter, Roberta, "Cuba and Pearl Harbor," *Foreign Affairs* (July 1965).

Wolfe, Thomas, *Soviet Strategy at the Crossroads* (Cambridge, Mass.: Harvard University Press, 1964).

Young, Oran R., *The Politics of Force* (Princeton: Princeton University Press, 1968).

4

William E. Simons, Colonel, USAF
THE VIETNAM INTERVENTION, 1964-65

I. BACKGROUND

On February 7 and again on February 11, 1965, aircraft from United States carriers in the Gulf of Tonkin attacked military targets in North Vietnam in reprisal for Viet Cong assaults on United States and South Vietnamese installations. On February 8 and 11, United States Air Force (USAF) aircraft based in South Vietnam escorted South Vietnamese Air Force (VNAF) strike sorties on similar missions. During the weeks that followed, commentators interpreted these events and related official statements to mean that the objective of the United States was coercive; that is, it was attempting to pressure the government in Hanoi into abandoning its support of the insurgency in South Vietnam. As the tempo of the bombing increased during March and April — no air strikes occurred between February 11 and March 2 — this inter-

This chapter has been adapted with the permission of the RAND Corporation from William E. Simons, Lt. Col., USAF, *Coercion in Vietnam?* Memorandum RM-6016-PR (Santa Monica, Calif.: The RAND Corporation, May 1969).

pretation became commonplace as one of the explanations for United States actions.

The public record contains little conclusive evidence that this coercive objective was, in fact, a major element of the administration's policy. Even if it had been, there were sound operational and political reasons why the president would not have openly identified such an objective. Still, reports that factions within the government were advocating military operations for this purpose had appeared in the press on the occasion of every major policy review since early in 1964.

The first suggestion that the government may have chosen such a policy came in reaction to the announced rationale for the second set of strikes on February 11. Official statements accompanying both of the reprisal actions used similar language: they described the United States and South Vietnamese reprisals as a "response" to "provocations" directed from Hanoi and they specifically described the triggering Viet Cong actions as including attacks on South Vietnamese and United States installations. Still, newspaper accounts stressed "implications" in the second statement that the rationale had changed somewhat. As one commentator wrote, "It is at least implied that the policy might be to respond with air action in North Vietnam to Viet Cong attacks on South Vietnamese military and civil targets." [1] The accounts claimed administration sources for some of their ideas, and speculation along this line was undoubtedly encouraged by interviews on February 9 with United States officials who advised that future retaliatory strikes would not necessarily be tied to attacks on United States forces. Moreover, the Joint Chiefs of Staff were reported as having advised the president that one-shot reprisal attacks such as those following the attacks on United States destroyers — in August 1964 — and on Pleiku had little value.[2]

Following the reprisals, these and other leaks gave rise to a series of press analyses linking the most recent and the anticipated air strikes to implied threats of extensive future damage to North Vietnam if it refused to alter its policies. The remarks of Ambassador Maxwell Taylor that "our objective is limited — namely, to oblige Hanoi, to persuade Hanoi, to desist in its efforts to maintain the insurgency" were significant. Explaining that the bombing effects were primarily psychological, he added, "The limited actions which we have taken have been deliberately planned, moderately sponsored, to suggest the possibility of other and bigger forms of reactions." [3]

This interpretive line received authoritative reinforcement on February 17 when President Johnson appended to a speech on the domestic economy a statement on Vietnam that said, "We will persist in the defense of freedom and our *continuing actions* will be those that are made necessary by *the continuing aggression* of others." [4] High-level government spokesmen frequently referred to this remark in explaining United States policies, particularly with respect to the pattern of more frequent bombing raids beginning in mid-March. Its theme was made even more explicit in the State Department white paper, released on February 27, which stated that "the choice now between peace and continued and increasingly destructive conflict is one for the authorities in Hanoi to make." [5] When the bombing was resumed three days later, this statement served to confirm the view of many commentators that the administration had decided to force Hanoi, by military means, into a decision to halt its sponsorship of the insurgency in the South.

To what extent was some attempt at coercion actually made during the early months of 1965? Determining this is complicated by the lack of a single, commonly accepted model of political-military coercion with which the record of United States decisions and actions can be compared. It is also complicated because administration policy-makers of the time have denied being guided by any such theory. For example, Secretary of Defense Robert McNamara stated, "We never believed, and we don't believe today, that bombing of the North will drive the North Vietnamese to the bargaining table or force them to cease their . . . subversion of the political institutions of the South." [6] However, adequate evidence demonstrates that administration officials were not unfamiliar with this kind of concept.

Throughout 1964, the possibility of using direct military means — principally air strikes — to exert added pressure on Hanoi was a frequent topic for public speculation. Statements by high-level administration officials gave evidence that the government was at least considering this possibility as an option. [7] Some public accounts even went so far as to identify various officials by name as either favoring or opposing military actions against the North.

During the latter part of the year, leading officials perceived that various forms of limited air attack offered increasingly interesting possibilities for exerting pressure on the government in

Hanoi. Not only would air attacks enable the United States to pursue several different objectives, but they also appeared to provide psychological advantages. If employed in a steadily intensifying manner, limited air attacks would signal to the opponent a vivid threat of still more intensive attacks to come. Some officials were reported to believe that such a threat might even deter Hanoi's continued infiltration in support of the insurgency.[8]

Of course, the really critical factor affecting the possibility that infiltration itself could be deterred — and that a coercive objective could be successfully pursued — was the intensity of the North Vietnamese government (DRV) resolve to continue its existing policies toward South Vietnam. In 1964 no one could have known the exact price that Hanoi would be willing to pay to achieve its ends in the South. Still, some administration officials apparently believed that the DRV would not risk losing its newly acquired industrial capital in the North.[9] Although members of the administration generally conceded that compelling Hanoi to change its policies could not be undertaken with high confidence of success, nevertheless they had some interest in such an objective.

Whether or not a coercive objective was pursued in some form within the government in 1965, the intellectual and strategic climate of the mid-1960s was certainly conducive to thinking about the coercive possibilities of the limited use of force.* Conceptual awareness in this regard derives from four broad patterns of experience, wholly or partially shared by the administration officials involved in decision-making.

First, the force posture and strategy dialogues that had occupied the Department of Defense since 1961 had made many administration officials conversant with the general concept of persuading or inducing an opponent to terminate a conflict on terms favorable to the United States. They believed that in a nuclear era characterized by an assumed mutual incentive to limit the extent of warfare, the United States could achieve early termination through coupling the specter of its massive destructive capacity with carefully restrained application of a modest portion of this capacity designed to demonstrate a resolve to come to the defense of allies faced with aggression. Although this concept originated with the discussions of nuclear strategy — the "cities in hostage" theme of the McNamara counterforce strategy — it

* See Chapter One, pp. 5–8.

permeated many aspects of the New Frontier's "flexible response" philosophy. For example, it played a central role in the conventional defense strategy developed for NATO.

Also, many administration officials and key foreign policy advisors had great faith in — and Americans in general were bedazzled by — the technological, material, and intellectual resources amassed by the United States and the margin of advantage which these presumably provided over other powers. This faith manifested itself in various ways, not least of which was the apparently high expectations associated with the clearly superior air and naval power of the United States. Since 1951, the idea had permeated United States defense thinking that America's technologically superior air and naval forces coupled with well-trained indigenous ground forces would provide an adequate deterrent to major regional aggression. This idea was an important root for the New Frontier's emphasis on counter-insurgency training and its exportation through the Military Assistance Advisory Group structure. As late as 1965, Bill D. Moyers reports, there was an "unspoken assumption" that as soon as the United States indicated its willingness to use its power "the other people would fold." He quotes one civilian official as dismissing the suggestion that defeating the Viet Cong might take as long as it took the British to win in Malaya with "We are *not* the British." [10]

Third, as Moyers and others have also suggested, officials of the administration had been greatly encouraged and inspired with confidence as a result of their experiences in the Cuban missile crisis. Of paramount influence was the apparent success of their efforts in that crisis. President Kennedy and his advisors, most of whom still occupied key positions in 1964 and 1965, had coerced an infinitely more powerful enemy than North Vietnam into backing down from a publicly aggressive posture. Moreover, they had done it with the kind of means available for use in Vietnam, and they had developed a once-tested approach to the problem of coercive diplomacy. In essence, this approach consisted of: (1) stating clear and simple demands regarding the opponent's compliance behavior; (2) applying limited force and avoiding incidents or clashes of arms that would provoke the opponent into an impulsive military response; (3) conveying a threat of punitive measures to follow in the event of the opponent's failure to comply; (4) applying additional pressure on the opponent through international diplomatic activity; (5) maintaining a graduated scale of options so as to preserve freedom of action for the United States; and (6) being prepared to provide a public quid pro quo in return for the opponent's compliance.[11]

Finally complementing and serving to focus these more general conceptual influences was the idea that external instigators and suppliers of insurgencies should be rendered vulnerable to direct pressure as a legitimate means of coping with the insurgent problem. Walt Whitman Rostow first made this idea public as early as June 1961 in a speech to a Special Forces graduating class at Fort Bragg. As head of the State Department's Policy Planning Council, he is reported to have encouraged President Johnson to adopt such an idea.[12] Early in March 1964, *Newsweek* attributed to him a certain "Plan No. 6," which purported to call for a series of graduated actions against North Vietnam, including a blockade of Haiphong, PT-boat raids on coastal installations, and air strikes, all of which were to end as soon as Hanoi called off its support for the Viet Cong.[13] Similar proposals, emphasizing the threat of further damage rather than the actual effects of immediate actions, were attributed to Maxwell Taylor during the autumn of 1964.[14]

From such conceptual threads we can identify four actions that officials in the administration quite probably would have thought necessary at minimum if they had intended to coerce Hanoi.[15] These include:

1. Stating a demand that Hanoi stop aiding and directing the insurgency in South Vietnam.[16]
2. Making limited use of air strikes against North Vietnam, stressing their psychological and deterrent values rather than their military and destructive effects.[17]
3. Staging the military operations so as to give the impression of steadily rising pressure which could conceivably culminate in attacks on North Vietnam's urban industrial complex. If United States demands were not complied with, urban targets would be held in hostage and exploited for their threat potential, in line with the prevalent belief that the DRV valued its economic and industrial achievements highly and feared their loss.
4. Waging a campaign to document and exploit Hanoi's guilt as instigator of the aggression against South Vietnam as a means of enlisting international support for the correctness

of the United States demands. Such support would then serve to focus additional pressure against Hanoi in the normal diplomatic and negotiating arenas.

Today, looking back upon the three-and-one-half-year period of nearly continuous bombing, at times reaching levels of intensity well beyond those indicated here, these actions may not seem credible as elements of a coercive process. They were, however, relevant to the policy constraints of the time and, consequently, when compared with the administration's behavior in the first few months of 1965, they provide a fair test of its minimum coercive intent. That is, if the administration had intended to coerce Hanoi, it is fair to expect that it would have undertaken at least those actions indicated. But before comparing these minimally coercive actions with actual behavior, let us first consider more carefully the political-military context of the administration's decisions.

II. THE CONTEXT FOR DIRECT UNITED STATES INTERVENTION

Press reports throughout 1964 to the effect that air strikes were being advocated within the United States government as a means of persuading Hanoi to halt its support of the Viet Cong insurgency gave every indication of being reliable. Subsequent disclosures have corroborated that they were.[18] The Joint Chiefs of Staff urged such measures on several occasions during 1964, and several other officials endorsed the principle if not the particular approach which the military advisers favored. On at least two occasions during the last half of 1964, high-level strategy sessions considered the desirability of adopting such a policy.[19] Both times those present reaffirmed the reprisal precedent established after North Vietnamese attacks on United States destroyers in the Tonkin Gulf, but disapproved deliberate and systematic attacks on North Vietnam and set the idea aside for future reconsideration. In addition to the general reluctance to extend military involvements imposed by the presidential election campaign, advisers clearly perceived the uncertainty of obtaining even temporary reduction of Hanoi's support for the Viet Cong through limited applications of force. On the other hand, they thought the use of harsher measures would incur serious risks of reactions that could widen the conflict or otherwise damage United States interests.[20]

At the time of these assessments, certain perceptions of the context for action in Southeast Asia were prevalent in the administration. There was considerable concern over the influence and potential roles of Communist China in the Vietnam conflict. For example, assessments of "enemy" reactions often dealt with Hanoi and Peking as if they worked in concert. Concern over a Chinese military reaction in the event of direct United States intervention was acute. Although the administration regarded North Vietnam as the principal actor on "the other side," it saw China's role as significant and potentially dominant. It considered Peking, not Hanoi, as the major benefactor should United States policies and actions be discredited — particularly with respect to the viability of Peking's professed doctrine of encouraging "wars of national liberation." [21]

The administration also perceived a lack of public indignation over Hanoi's involvement in the South Vietnamese insurgency and a lack of public feeling that something should be done about it. Always sensitive to the vocal policy critics who challenged government claims of DRV duplicity in the Viet Cong insurrection, officials believed that a much larger segment of the United States public was simply unconcerned about, or at least unconvinced of, the part Hanoi was playing.[22] Moreover, in this respect they were faced with a troublesome policy dilemma.

Though it asserted DRV instigation and direction of the insurgency campaign during 1964, the United States government was reluctant to document publicly its ample evidence. For example, information indicating an increasing rate of infiltration assembled several months earlier was not released until late in January 1965.[23] Throughout most of the previous year the administration had seen the national interest as best served by avoiding a polarization of opinion regarding next steps, either withdrawal or bombing, to be taken in Vietnam. As Philip Geyelin explained, officials had stressed publicly and privately that the insurrection in the South was largely indigenous to South Vietnam and that most Viet Cong weapons came "from capture, purchase and local manufacture." Thus, if properly led and equipped, South Vietnamese forces should be able to cope with the military threat, and abandoning resistance or extending the war outside South Vietnam was unnecessary. To begin now to emphasize the problems posed by the infiltration from the North — particularly before either United States policy regarding further measures had been set or progress toward GVN stability had been assured — threatened to increase the strength of those who urged solutions at either extremity.[24]

Several writers, Geyelin included, have chosen to link this rationale with President Johnson's election strategy. In fact, the administration's concerns transcended the election. They were also entirely compatible with the then prevailing perceptions of the GVN: that real security for South Vietnam depended on creating a stable government and that organization of an effective campaign to combat the insurgents would provide a necessary motivating force.

Although the administration regarded the political situation in Saigon as dangerously unstable in the autumn of 1964, it hoped that the civilian government under Premier Huong would establish increasingly effective control. It generally conceded that for additional military pressures to have substantial effect, a non-Communist government in Saigon would first have to demonstrate genuine staying power. Consequently, United States efforts to assist in that development were assigned highest priority.[25]

These attitudes regarding Vietnamese trends, and the alternatives available to help improve the situation, were apparently formed under an assumption that the Soviet Union would continue its hands off policy of the previous three years. Until late December and January large-scale Soviet assistance to North Vietnam was not regarded as a significant potentiality in the developing Southeast Asian problem.

By early February 1965, the context for any actions in Southeast Asia had changed somewhat, and in ways that certainly had direct impacts on United States calculations with respect to further intervention. First, contrary to administration expectations, the political situation in Saigon had become even more chaotic. Dissolution of the civilian regime's High National Council by South Vietnam's military leaders, in mid-December, was followed by a brief reconciliation. However, toward the end of January, General Khanh had again seized power in the wake of widespread Buddhist protest demonstrations against both the Huong government and the United States ambassador. Despite official statements conveying calm resignation, Washington had little confidence that the new military regime could be relied upon — even to continue in power, much less to cooperate with United States policies. In fact, throughout much of January deeply concerned officials feared that continued political upheaval in South Vietnam would lead to eventual collapse of resistance to the Viet Cong insurgency.[26]

Another development of considerable significance was the re-emergence of the Soviet Union as an active participant in the politics of Southeast Asia. Despite high-level United States conversations with Soviet diplomats, one of the apparent purposes of which was to impress them with the seriousness of the United States resolve to stand by the GVN in the face of North Vietnamese aggression, Moscow agreed publicly to provide North Vietnam with military assistance. On several occasions during late December and January, Soviet spokesmen repeated a pledge to come to the aid of North Vietnam if the United States extended the war to its territory. Moreover, these affirmations were made at a time of public agreements with the Hanoi regime for trade and greatly expanded Soviet economic aid and of much closer working relations with South Vietnam's National Liberation Front.[27] Although it marked a major reversal of public policies, there was little doubt of the genuineness of the renewed Soviet involvement, prompted largely by the struggle with the Chinese for global leadership among Communist revolutionary factions. Given such strong political motivation, and with a Peking-directed spotlight focused on its every move, Moscow could not have been expected to deviate substantially from its public pledge to support North Vietnam in resisting United States pressures. Thereafter, the administration was obliged to take into account more closely the impact of its action upon Soviet policy.

One other factor that figured in United States calculations early in 1965 was a growing concern on the part of many administration officials over the president's disinclination to respond to direct Communist provocations against United States facilities and personnel in South Vietnam. Following the Viet Cong attacks on the air base at Bien Hoa (November 1, 1964) and again on the Brink officers' billet in Saigon (December 24, 1964), the United States had failed to retaliate. Moreover, the president had decided against reprisal actions despite tacit acceptance of the principle, as in the Tonkin Gulf, and public statements to the effect that repetition of such behavior would not be tolerated.[28] Administration officials felt great concern over this apparent inconsistency between word and action lest the Communist governments and the Asian allies of the United States both come to doubt our resolve to continue to resist aggression.

Thus, the political context of early 1965 hardly encouraged a United States attempt to coerce the government of North Vietnam. On the one hand, strong motivation existed to take action that would restore the credibility of United States declaratory policy to oppose Communist aggression in Southeast Asia. This credibility would be essential if the administration expected to use threats of further punishment to get Hanoi to alter its policies toward South Vietnam. On the other hand, to carry out such threats at that time appeared quite likely to bring the Soviet Union more directly into public alignment with North Vietnam, thus bolstering Hanoi's resistance to United States demands with Soviet as well as with Chinese support. Moreover, aware that as yet there was little support for substantially increasing the American commitment in Vietnam, the administration was hardly in a position to insist that Hanoi comply promptly with its demands under explicit threat of punitive action. Then, too, there was little reason to expect mere threats to convince Hanoi of the futility of its policies as long as political upheaval in Saigon prevented effective GVN action to counter the insurgency engulfing most of South Vietnam.

In addition to the political aspects of the possible intervention, the administration also had to consider the military means available to it. Beyond further increases in the United States advisory function, what were its options? Conceivably, the administration could have sent ground forces to Indochina, either to aid in combat operations against the Viet Cong or to relieve Army of the Republic of Vietnam (ARVN) units for such roles by taking over the static defense of bases and of administrative capitals in South Vietnam. It could have used air and naval forces in an attempt to close off North Vietnam's major port facilities and destroy its economic and industrial potential. It could have credibly threatened such actions by demonstrating its willingness to strike or blockade such targets. It could have used air forces to strike carefully limited targets in North Vietnam. Or could it, in fact, have done all of these things?

President Johnson most certainly had no interest in January–February 1965 in sending United States ground combat forces into Southeast Asia. On the contrary, he would have wished to avoid this for good reasons. During his election campaign, the president had taken a strong public stand against such a course, proclaiming repeatedly that he did not intend to send "American boys to do the fighting for Asian boys." [29] He was very conscious of the strong congressional opposition to such an alternative, expressed in the hearings prior to passage of the Tonkin Gulf Resolution, and more recently during the January 1965 Senate debates on Asian policy. Moreover, he was aware of the strong "never again" sentiment regarding large-scale land war commitments that resided within the Joint Chiefs of Staff.[30] In fact, the president would have had sufficient reasons to regard avoidance of the use of United States ground forces in Vietnam as a major criterion for eventually settling upon a policy alternative.

Thus, the only military options congenial to the administration were different variants of air operations against North Vietnam. But even among these, the choice was not as free as it may appear. Before undertaking high-intensity air and naval operations against North Vietnam, the administration quite probably would have needed to feel that it enjoyed a large measure of domestic and international support. However, in actuality, it was clearly troubled that it lacked even a clear-cut public conviction of Hanoi's guilt. Moreover, it was conscious that it had just received an overwhelming mandate based in part on its expressions of resolve not to commit more American forces to an extended military involvement in Asia. Thus, at the beginning of 1965, it was faced with a national emotional climate that encouraged caution — unlike public opinion at the time of our discovery of Soviet missile sites in Cuba.* The administration no doubt perceived that high-intensity air and naval operations would risk the loss of much public confidence.

International opinion likewise was less than encouraging for bold action. The issue that the administration regarded as serious enough to warrant the possible risk of war — the need to contain the expansion of Chinese influence and revolutionary doctrine — was believed in Europe and in some Asian countries not to be at stake in Vietnam.[31] Therefore, the administration expected harsh punitive measures against North Vietnam — for example, denying

* Even during the Cuban missile crisis, certain of the national leaders who could expect to receive public censure if their countermoves failed to halt Soviet MRBM emplacement refused to risk military blows against Cuba that might have damaged the American conscience.

it the use of its ports — to cause a sharply adverse reaction internationally. A similar reaction was also foreseen in the event that United States moves against the DRV precipitated a significant widening of the war — a possible outcome to be given careful evaluation in view of the strong, public Soviet and Chinese commitments to come to North Vietnam's aid. Thus, a heavy air and naval campaign against North Vietnam's economy and industry could conceivably find the United States committed to a large-scale conflict in Asia without the support of several of its allies.

As a result, in early 1965 the administration could only consider two military options as realistic or politically viable. Both involved demonstrative and somewhat limited air attacks, one against high-value military and industrial targets, presumably largely for punitive and threatening purposes, and the other against more modest military targets associated directly with the infiltration into South Vietnam. Being of a limited nature, both offered the inherent advantage of being carried out by forces already deployed. Each could be ordered and executed promptly — as a retaliation for another Viet Cong provocation. Although either of these would be less committing and less costly than a full-fledged air and naval campaign, however, demonstrative attacks on high-value targets carried political risks similar to those inherent in a full-scale campaign. If the initial attacks failed to bring about a satisfactory response from Hanoi, pressure would likely be generated for keeping on with them, until the distinction between the demonstrations and the full-fledged campaign became blurred.

Of course, the results expected from limited demonstrative attacks would be difficult to appraise. Such attacks gave little promise of doing more than slowing down the military infiltration into South Vietnam. Military advisers consistently cautioned that significant damage to the flow of men and supplies could not be achieved without "sustained and heavy bombardment" of communication routes and military targets in North Vietnam.[32] Also, despite increased air operations against the infiltration routes in Laos, it was evident by late January that the flow of Communist forces into that country had actually increased.[33] But a demonstrative option could serve to either reassert the United States resolve to continue its opposition to aggression in Southeast Asia, bolster South Vietnamese will to continue their resistance to the Viet Cong insurgency, or show that North Vietnam would no longer be considered a sanctuary. Moreover, if applied in reprisal for Communist provocations, demonstrative air strikes might conceivably deter further acts like the Viet Cong attacks on United States and South Vietnamese military installations.

Here again, limited attacks on the more modest targets appeared to offer an additional advantage. Starting with modest targets provided the opportunity for steadily increasing the intensity of the attacks — implicitly posing the threat of more to come — without encountering too early the political risks associated with higher-value targets. To avoid those political risks, however, the administration could not afford to state an explicit intention to intensify its attacks until it forced Hanoi's compliance. At least, it could not permit this to be regarded as its sole reason for actions that would constitute a major departure from its current behavior.

At best, within the context of the political and military environment of early 1965, the administration must have perceived a concerted attempt to coerce Hanoi as an action of potentially high risks and costs. That is, the various constraints imbedded in the political-military-diplomatic situation at this time virtually excluded the use of the strongest variants of coercive diplomacy. To the extent coercive diplomacy was contemplated, only a "try-and-see" variant could have appeared attractive.

III. THE NATURE AND INTENT OF DIRECT UNITED STATES INTERVENTION IN VIETNAM

In view of the very visible risks and costs of any attempt to coerce the DRV in 1965, how can we explain the administration's decisions to intervene directly in Vietnam with airpower, and later with ground forces? Certain alternative hypotheses exist: the administration regarded the coercive objective of pressuring Hanoi to cease assistance to the Viet Cong as central to its actions and employed measures which it believed would produce adequate coercive effects; or the administration was determined to coerce Hanoi but felt constrained by the context to limit itself to measures which provided low confidence of producing the desired results; or the administration hoped to coerce Hanoi but decided to pursue other objectives as well; or the administration abandoned hope of coercing Hanoi and sought to accomplish different objectives.

Actions and statements by the administration were consistent at different times with one or another of these hypotheses, depending upon the particular phase of the intervention. Moreover, statements — particularly unattributed statements — varied somewhat with respect to the hypotheses, depending on the officials who issued them. These factors suggest that administration objectives may have changed or assumed varying degrees of importance at different times during the period examined, and that individual officials may have had different understandings of what the objectives were at any particular time. For analytical purposes, we will create three successive chronological periods. Period one covers roughly the first three weeks of February 1965; period two covers approximately February 20 through March 20, 1965; and period three runs from the end of March until the public commitment of United States ground combat forces in July 1965.

1. Period One: Initiating Direct Military Intervention

The first acts of direct United States military intervention in the war in Vietnam came on February 7 and 11, 1965, in reprisal for Viet Cong attacks on United States and South Vietnamese installations. From the limited nature of these initial United States bombing attacks and from what is known of administration assessments of Hanoi's likely responses to such attacks, evidently the administration did not intend significant military results. Therefore, the conclusion is that the actions were intended primarily to convey a signal. What were these signals and to whom were they being sent?

One obvious answer is that they were sent to the Communists — in particular, the leaders of Red China and North Vietnam. The DRV was certainly an intended recipient, and under the circumstances of the intervention, the administration could have had a variety of messages in mind. These messages could have included: (1) U.S. forces could no longer be attacked without reprisal; (2) continued aggression against South Vietnam could be carried out only at a price; and (3) only a change of DRV policy could avoid future destruction. Such mild action against North Vietnam — especially in light of earlier air operations in Laos — could have served as a warning to China, to indicate that the home territory of those aiding the guerrillas in South Vietnam would not be treated as a sanctuary. No doubt it was also intended to emphasize that the United States was still actively involved in

Vietnam on behalf of its ally, that it had not lost any of the resolve to protect its interests in Southeast Asia that it had demonstrated at the time of the Tonkin Gulf incident.

The latter message — applicable to Hanoi, Moscow, and Peking alike — reflected a deepening administration concern. Throughout the previous year, the United States had hewed carefully to a policy of assisting the South Vietnamese improve their own military efforts by ostensibly limiting United States forces to advisory roles and avoiding deeper, direct military involvement. In effect, the United States government had made clear its unwillingness to undertake operations appropriate for countering the kind of aggression occurring in Vietnam. In December, after its well-publicized strategy review session, it implied publicly that further United States military contributions would be contingent upon a substantial strengthening of South Vietnam's government operations.[34] Officials were apprehensive that United States policy during the closing months of 1964, including the decisions not to retaliate following Viet Cong attacks on the Bien Hoa base and the Saigon billet, had been interpreted as a sign of flagging United States will. Certain congressmen of both parties and leading spokesmen for the Republican party publicly expressed similar concerns.[35] Clearly, if officials had any hope of forcing Hanoi to change its policies, dispelling doubts about the resolve of the United States would have been important, as in the early phase of the Cuban missile crisis, for establishing the credibility of coercive signals.

However, if the administration wanted to signal strong resolve to the North Vietnamese, it also wanted to convince others — in particular the GVN and the South Vietnamese military — of its intention to hold fast. During the first week of February, as the president's assistant for national security affairs, McGeorge Bundy, and other officials were departing on an undisclosed special mission to Saigon, there were well-informed reports of growing uneasiness in Washington over the specter of a South Vietnamese collapse.[36] Pointedly, Bundy's first message to the GVN on February 4 was a renewed pledge of continued United States support: "The record of the last 25 years all around the world shows that those who stand firm for their own freedom can be confident of the strong and untiring support of the United States of America." Later, he cited as one of three reasons for the United States policy of bombing in the North the need to let the people and leaders of South Vietnam know that we and they were striking back against the source of their troubles.[37] Still another White House staff member at the time has confirmed that the president was being advised that Saigon's morale could be revived only if the United States assured the South Vietnamese of its determination to uphold its commitments to them by bombing military targets in North Vietnam.[38]

We can reasonably assume that the administration was sensitive as well to the attitudes of neighboring governments in Laos, Thailand, and Malaysia. Caution in handling air operations in Laos gave clear evidence of concern by the United States for the delicate position of Premier Souvanna Phouma. The administration was also well aware of Thailand's interest in assuring a firm United States stand against the Communist threat in Vietnam.[39] Now, both governments were publicly identified by the Communists as targets for further guerrilla activity. United States officials were also concerned about the threatened development of a "Jakarta-Peking Axis" and saw Malaysia as a logical focus for aggressive pressure from that source.[40] Consequently, all these governments appear as logical audiences for demonstrations of a United States resolve to strike back in the face of Communist aggression.

The White House also could have wanted to convey a signal to the American public. Spokesmen for the political right were becoming apprehensive that the administration might neglect the goal of a non-Communist South Vietnam. The president's resistance to their urging, and to that of the Joint Chiefs of Staff, of retaliation for earlier Viet Cong provocations was the basis for this apprehension, and these spokesmen threatened to become increasingly vocal in their opposition. On the other hand, the president's reelection campaign — consciously inflating the image of the president as a man of peace and restraint — encouraged somewhat those political leaders who wished to see the United States pull back from its involvement in Southeast Asia. This group, too, became increasingly vocal; Senator Church, later encouraged by Senate Majority Leader Mansfield, proposed a policy shift in support of the neutralization of all Southeast Asia, and Senator Morse criticized the unilateral involvement of the United States in South Vietnam's fight.[41] This group gained added strength in mid-January from angry congressional reactions to news-service disclosures of the use of U.S. aircraft in operations over Laos.[42]

Given the rising sentiment for disengagement among the doves and increasing restiveness among the hawks, the president may have believed that some sort of bold action was needed to reassert the firmness of his perception of the national commitment. Tom Wicker reported, for example, that immediately after becoming president, Johnson told Ambassador Lodge and others, "I am not going to lose Vietnam. I am not going to be the President who saw Southeast Asia go the way China went." [43] Similarly, many months after the bombing began and sometime after United States troops were fighting in South Vietnam, he remarked to reporters, "I am not going to be the first American President to lose a war." However, according to a number of journalists covering the White House, the Johnson style of dealing with diametrically opposed political forces was to advance measures designed to give a little to each, but to alienate neither.[44] Limited attacks against North Vietnam, under circumstances that did not constitute an abrupt departure from existing policy, satisfied these criteria.

For several reasons then — or perhaps, more properly, for several audiences — the administration had reason in February 1965 to demonstrate its willingness to strike a blow directly against North Vietnam. More than one White House observer has suggested that one reason for the Bundy mission to Saigon on February 4 was to determine the capability of South Vietnam, under a new government since January 27, to withstand possible responses to, and to support, such new United States actions.[45] Philip Geyelin, citing a "high State Department official" as the source, states that "the Johnson Administration had, by the first week of February, made up its mind to expand the war." [46]

However, for both domestic and international political reasons it would have to be done carefully. Premier Kosygin was visiting Hanoi during the first week of February, presumably, among other things, to test North Vietnamese interest in a Laos conference and to establish the extent of new Soviet aid programs. Deliberate actions against North Vietnam during his visit would have threatened to damage whatever chances there were that the Soviet Union would attempt to dampen tendencies within the DRV leadership to escalate the conflict. In addition, by taking action against the North, the administration would have appeared to embrace too warmly the new military regime of General Khanh at a time when it had already strongly endorsed the idea of a more broadly based civilian regime in Saigon. Moreover, there was no guarantee that Khanh's military junta would last any longer than its predecessor. At home, whatever actions were contemplated would have to avoid encouraging more aggressive advocacy among the hawks and avoid ruffling too abruptly the feathers of the doves.

The Viet Cong attack on the United States compound at Pleiku on February 6 provided a suitable situation for military action that would satisfy the operative political criteria. A master of political timing, President Johnson was adept at taking controversial action at times when the influence of his political opponents was weakened by events. The Viet Cong provocation offered such a moment. It provided the administration with a clear political and military justification for the reprisals that followed. It allowed flexibility for developing the subsequent public United States policy position, depending on such variables as enemy response and public reactions. In some ways it was a repetition of the Tonkin Gulf incident under circumstances that did not expose the United States to possible charges of deliberate staging.

The official statements that accompanied the reprisal strikes were careful to link the events to the Tonkin Gulf precedent. Particularly stressed through this association were the limited nature and the appropriateness of the retaliatory acts. Thus, the White House announcement stated:

> Today's joint response was carefully limited to military areas which are supplying men and arms for attacks in South Vietnam. As in the case of the North Vietnamese attacks in the Gulf of Tonkin last August, the response is appropriate and fitting.[47]

Ambassador Stevenson made the same point in his report to the president of the United Nations Security Council. He emphasized that such actions were justified as measures of self-defense against the type of aggression faced by South Vietnam and in view of the United States "public commitment" to assist in its defense.[48]

Statements by officials also stressed what the administration believed to be the political significance of the attacks, and their comments gave a clear indication of an immediate purpose for the United States response. Ambassador Stevenson called the Viet Cong attacks "politically timed . . . to test the will of the Republic of Vietnam and the United States to resist." At a press conference the same day, Secretary McNamara and Undersecretary of State George Ball made nearly identical comments on this point:

> This was a test of the will, a clear challenge to the political purpose of both the United States and South Vietnamese Governments. It was a test and challenge therefore which we could not fail to respond to . . . without misleading the North Vietnamese as to our intent and the strength of our purpose to carry out that intent.[49]

Thus, in some respects the reprisal strikes of February 7 — and those by the South Vietnamese Air Force on February 8 — served a rather specific, immediate purpose. They provided a means of demonstrating the United States will to resist aggression against its ally. Indeed, given the perceived deterioration in South Vietnam and the increasing doubts about United States policy, the administration could not afford *not* to retaliate at this time — at least, as McNamara stated, not "without misleading the North Vietnamese." Of course, he could well have added, "and without misleading the South Vietnamese, the Laotians, the Thais, and our other Asian allies." Moreover, the reprisal for the Viet Cong attacks could be carried out without committing the administration to any particular course of action in the future. The United States government was careful to stress this in its public statements, and in a special communication to the Soviet Union it took pains to give assurances that its actions were nothing more than a retaliation in kind.[50] Because of the domestic and international opposition to an expanded war, the United States could not afford to react to this provocation with irreversible steps. Neither could it afford to risk frightening the Communists into precipitate counter-responses. For example, when a reporter attempted to fix the limits of United States policy, Secretary McNamara was quite emphatic in denying that administration responses should be interpreted as a threat or ultimatum.[51] Thus we see the requirements of crisis management, described in Chapter One, operating in this crisis.

Yet, his answer to an earlier question emphasized quite another aspect of the recent United States behavior. Unlike the reprisals for the attacks in the Tonkin Gulf, the secretary was careful not to "characterize this as a tit-for-tat raid." Significantly, the actions taken after Pleiku asserted a principle going beyond the precedent established in the retaliation of the previous August. The United States was responding again with a strike in North Vietnam, but this time in retaliation not to a North Vietnamese attack in international waters but in answer to an attack by Viet Cong forces inside South Vietnam.

Official statements were quite explicit in linking the Viet Cong attacks to direction from Hanoi. Referring to the attacks as "a direct provocation ordered and directed by the Hanoi regime," a White House announcement stated that they were part of "a more aggressive course of action" ordered from Hanoi "against both South Vietnamese and American installations." [52] Secretary McNamara explained that this conclusion was based on official intelligence sources, which included documentation of the increased infiltration of Communist manpower into South Vietnam. This infiltration, which the White House statement asserted had made the attacks possible, was given major attention by Ambassador Stevenson. Characterizing it as "a sustained attack for more than six years across a frontier set by international agreement," he related it to "a pattern of military operations directed, staffed, and supplied in crucial respects from outside the country." This, he charged, making specific reference to the Geneva agreements, was

> a pattern, in short, of deliberate systematic and flagrant violations of international agreements by the regime in Hanoi which signed them and which by all tenets of decency, law, and civilized practice, is bound by their provisions.[53]

By these statements, the administration publicly linked its new form of participation in the Vietnam conflict to the objective of returning to the stipulations of the Geneva settlements. By implication, therefore, the bombing of North Vietnam was injected into the contest of opposing pressures by which the political future of Vietnam would be determined. True, Secretary McNamara had rejected the idea of an ultimatum or threat and only barely hinted that the United States would use bombardment to force a settlement. Yet he planted the thought. In euphemistic terms, the White House announcement — pointedly repeated by each of the administration's spokesmen — affirmed that

> we seek no wider war. Whether or not this course can be maintained lies with the North Vietnamese aggressors. The key to the situation remains the cessation of infiltration from North Vietnam and the clear indication by the Hanoi

regime that it is prepared to cease aggression against its neighbors.[54]

In responses to reporters' questions McNamara and Ball sharpened the language somewhat. Declining to speculate on the future, the defense secretary stated, "Our actions will depend upon the degree to which the North Vietnamese carry out previous international agreements." Referring to the reprisals, Mr. Ball expressed hope that "as a consequence of this action," the North Vietnamese would realize "that it is not in their interest to try to continue this aggression." [55]

Thus, administration actions and statements after the attacks near Pleiku at once projected an assurance of restrained behavior and conveyed a menacing posture toward North Vietnam. In the days that followed, the administration's behavior did little to clarify the ambiguities in its public stance. On the morning following his return from Saigon and his initial report to the president, McGeorge Bundy spoke of the effect of the retaliatory raids in pulling South Vietnamese and American officials together. He emphasized, however, that such actions could not eliminate guerrilla attacks and were no substitute for improved military operations inside South Vietnam.[56] Following the air raid against North Vietnamese targets by the Vietnamese Air Force on February 8, administration officials released word of a White House decision to hold off on any further strikes while it assessed Communist reactions. The requirements of crisis management were once again very much in evidence. One knowledgeable reporter stressed the value of such a pause in reinforcing the message of restraint sent earlier to the Soviet Union. At the same time, however, the president and his advisors refused to rule out further retaliatory actions or to define the circumstances that might precipitate them.[57] The following day, officials elaborated on this theme as if to counteract any overemphasis that may have been placed on the administration's restraint. The retaliations following the attack on Pleiku, they said, should not be considered a precedent. Future counterstrikes would not necessarily be limited to reprisals for attacks on United States forces. These officials warned that retaliation might be ordered for attacks on South Vietnamese units or "whenever it is justified in our view." [58]

Newspaper accounts implied that government officials were not all of one mind concerning how to exploit the Viet Cong provocation or how strong a signal to communicate to Hanoi. Max Frankel disclosed that the targets struck in two days of reprisal attacks represented only a part of four areas that had been previously designated for simultaneous attack in the event of a provocation. Further, he reported that "some military advisors" now wanted to strike the other two.[59] Hanson Baldwin reported that "the military," apparently the Joint Chiefs of Staff, regarded "one-shot attacks," such as the recent reprisals, as perhaps useful only in warning against further Viet Cong assaults on United States installations. To affect the course of the war, they felt that only "a pattern of sustained and heavy bombardment of communication routes and military targets" would help.[60] Other accounts reflected the concern of some officials that the United States stance following Pleiku had in some ways limited its future options — that it had given the initiative and control to the enemy. Now more than before, they apparently felt, any future challenge from the Communists would have to be met with a response at least as strong as before, a process which conceivably could lead to the "wider war" the president wished to avoid. Moreover, they argued, it flung back a "test of will" challenge which the Communists could scarcely refuse to accept, thus making any possibility of soliciting help from Soviet moderating influences much more difficult.[61]

Such were the circumstances when the Viet Cong struck the American enlisted billet at Qui Nhon on the night of February 10. Following this apparent mockery of United States deterrent warnings, the United States response was little different from that of four days earlier. Nearly one hundred United States carrier-based aircraft and twenty-eight Vietnamese fighter bombers struck military barracks and training facilities in North Vietnam. This raid involved almost twice as many United States aircraft as the first, but the targets were quite similar and still roughly fifty miles north of the 17th Parallel. As in the case of the first incident, the White House announcement specified that the Viet Cong provocations for which the reprisals were taken included attacks on both South Vietnamese towns and installations and United States facilities and personnel. It also mentioned terrorist activities and Viet Cong attacks on South Vietnam's railroads, and implied that these provocations had occurred over a period of three days ("since February 8"). However, the announcement was not accompanied by further explanation or by any further statements relating United States actions to broader policy implications.[62]

This dearth of official comment regarding the policy on which the United States was now embarked was to continue for nearly two weeks. It gave rise to considerable speculation and statements of concern in the press. Amid reports of "considerable pressure from military leaders for permission to continue raids against North Vietnam," there were statements attributed to "Administration officials" insisting that the president had resisted these demands. These officials were reported as stressing that there was still a "distinction between outright war against North Vietnam and retaliatory air strikes." [63] Other interpretations stressed the political significance of the apparent United States decision to deny sanctuary status to North Vietnam. One commentator asked if it did not signal a major challenge to the Communists' global strategy of "wars of national liberation," while others stressed its more immediate suggestion that the DRV's prized industrial assets would be equally vulnerable to attack if Hanoi continued to encourage the insurgency in the South.[64] The latter view gained considerable stature from Ambassador Taylor's apparently authorized radio interviews, in which he stressed North Vietnam's loss of a sanctuary and asserted a deliberate United States attempt to "suggest the possibility" of more destructive actions.[65] Still other accounts linked United States actions to a possible desire to negotiate a settlement after first improving the United States bargaining position. One related that "the Johnson Administration was reliably reported" to be on the verge of announcing "that while the United States favored peace and negotiations, the preconditions for any talks must be a cease-fire by all sides." [66] Still, neither the president nor his immediate advisors had issued any public statements to clarify the direction of United States policy since the attack on Pleiku, and this fact received increasing attention from the news analysts as the weeks of February passed.[67]

The lack of clarity was regarded by many as deliberate, as it became evident that a policy debate was under way among the president's advisors. At issue in the reported discussions were (1) the extent to which bombing raids should continue against North Vietnam, (2) the possible reactions in Hanoi, Moscow, and Peking, and (3) the appropriate position regarding a negotiated settlement.[68] Different views on these issues were reportedly held even by different groups within the same department. In the latter part of February, the president was under pressure from within his administration to speak out and put speculation to rest. His speech of February 17 before the National Industrial Conference Board, wherein he said that "our continuing actions will be those . . . that are made necessary by the continuing aggression of others," was regarded as merely perpetuating the apprehension and the confusion regarding his real intentions. Those who favored continuing the official silence based their position on a generally held administration fear that premature references to a negotiated settlement would undermine the anti-Communist resolve in South Vietnam. Their arguments exploited the possibility that United States ambiguity might give the Communist powers pause without a need for further commitments and that, being unsure of the United States position, Hanoi and Peking might be encouraged to be more cautious and, perhaps, even to propose a more conciliatory solution. Those favoring a more forthright expression of the administration's policy argued that

> North Vietnam's control over the guerrillas in the South should be demonstrated to the world; . . . delay dissipates the political value of this month's air strikes and makes them appear to be merely retaliatory. . . . Various Communist governments as well as the Western allies and American people are confused, or even misled by silence and speculation here, and . . . the rebels and their supporters in fact and in appearance retain the initiative.[69]

2. Period Two: Increasing the Pressure

The solidification of the administration's policy position occurred almost simultaneously with the attempted coup d'etat in Saigon on February 19. This event dramatized what some advisers and commentators had warned against: that South Vietnam's sense of national purpose would be subject to periodic erosion unless the United States undertook a more sustained demonstration of its intent to make North Vietnam bear a greater cost for its role in the war. The earlier and purely retaliatory strikes had apparently had some salutary, if temporary, effect on Saigon's morale. Moreover, other developments had crystallized in a manner favorable to more resolute United States behavior.

In the last week of February both the climate of United States public opinion and military events in South Vietnam were com-

patible with a less ambiguous posture on the part of the administration. On February 22, a Harris opinion poll indicated that 83
per cent of those surveyed supported the president in ordering the
retaliatory bombings and that attitudes regarding further bombing
depended heavily on the degree of risk of Chinese intervention
imposed by the nature of the raids. Although 75 per cent favored
eventual negotiations, a clear majority of these saw the necessity of
waiting until the position of the United States and South Vietnam
became stronger and South Vietnam became more secure.[70] On
the previous day, the United States Information Agency had released the results of its survey of foreign editorial reactions to the
United States air strikes, which indicated a generally sympathetic
attitude. Only in France, Pakistan, and in the predictably hostile
nations of Africa and the Arab world was editorial opinion
strongly opposed.[71]

Meanwhile, the series of attacks which had provoked the United
States reprisals were being viewed as having a strategic significance.
The Viet Cong assaults on Pleiku and their several attacks in
Binh Dinh Province had apparently been part of a pattern of
actions enabling Communist forces to control a strip of territory
which, in effect, would cut South Vietnam in half.[72] While not
representing an immediate threat, the move portended ominous
consequences if the Communists could use their new holdings as a
base for expanded operations against government control in central Vietnam. This potentiality was given emphasis by the discovery near Tuy Hoa on February 19 of an arms cache containing
4,000 weapons and about one million rounds of ammunition
manufactured in China, the Soviet Union, and several Communist
nations in Eastern Europe. Apparently off-loaded from a camou-
flaged North Vietnamese ship that had recently been detected and
sunk, the discovery provided dramatic public evidence that large
quantities of military supplies continued to flow to the Viet Cong
under Hanoi's direction in direct support of a coordinated plan of
operations against South Vietnam.[73]

The administration's new public posture was given form through
State Department statements on February 25 and 27. On the
former occasion, Secretary Rusk reiterated the United States
charge that North Vietnam had disregarded the Geneva agreements of 1954 and 1962 and continued to wage "a systematic campaign of terror and guerrilla action aimed at the overthrow of the
Government of South Vietnam and the imposition by force of a

Communist regime." He promised "a full and up-to-date summary of the evidence" to support these charges in a "very few days." He went on to convey a coercive threat by drawing particular attention to President Johnson's statement of a week earlier that it was the purpose of the United States "to join in the defense and protection of freedom" of the South Vietnamese people against the attack directed "from outside their country." And that "our continuing actions" would be "fitting and adequate," as made necessary by "the continuing aggression of others." For the first time, he linked this warning with a listing of formal congressional and executive pledges of the United States intention to resist aggression in Southeast Asia. In it he made detailed reference to the August 1964 resolution, "as the President determines, to take all necessary steps, including the use of armed force, to assist any member or protocol state [i.e., South Vietnam] of the Southeast Asia Collective Defense Treaty." [74]

Two days later, the promised summary of infiltration evidence was released to the public. A State Department White Paper presented a variety of historical and current documentation — including that of the recent massive arms capture — describing the extent of North Vietnam's role in aiding and directing the guerrilla war against the government of South Vietnam. The document assessed the evidence as indicating that this role, and the pressure it exerted on South Vietnam, was increasing in the face of greater efforts by South Vietnam, with help from its allies, to resist. Stressing that both the governments of South Vietnam and of the United States had in the past hoped to cope with the aggression "within South Vietnam itself," the White Paper evaluated Hanoi's response as "apparently interpret[ing] U.S. restraint as indicating lack of will." It went on to state that "clearly the restraint of the past was not providing adequately" for South Vietnam's defense, and that, "therefore, air strikes have been made" in a "limited response fitted to the aggression that produced them." It then asserted a thinly veiled coercive threat:

> Until the regime in Hanoi decides to halt its intervention in the South, or until effective steps are taken to maintain peace and security in the area, the governments of South Vietnam and the United States will continue necessary measures of defense against the Communist armed aggression coming from North Vietnam.

The choice now between peace and continued and increasingly destructive conflict is one for the authorities in Hanoi to make.[75]

As correctly interpreted in the press, the administration had presented a public justification for exerting greater pressures on the Communists and had threatened the DRV with increasing destruction if it did not halt its aggressive policies. The pressures took many forms. In South Vietnam, the arrival of the earliest contingent of 2,000 South Korean engineer troops dramatized South Vietnamese, and United States', efforts to enlist increased international assistance in the struggle to contain the insurgency. On February 26, Secretary McNamara announced that previously approved, but long delayed, plans to expand South Vietnam's army by 100,000 would be carried out, but he would not confirm intentions announced in Saigon to send more United States ground troops to advise this additional force. Two days earlier, the Saigon Embassy had confirmed that United States jets had been employed "at the request of the Government of South Vietnam" in air strikes against Viet Cong troop concentrations in Binh Dinh province and had been used in similar operations "on a number of occasions during the past week." Later, a State Department spokesman linked the actions with the congressional resolution of August 1964, in language quite similar to that used by Secretary Rusk on February 25.[76]

Air action against North Vietnam did not occur until March 2. However, on March 1, Jack Langguth reported from Saigon that "qualified American sources" claimed that a mission had been scheduled for the previous Friday — February 26, the day before the release of the White Paper — but that it had been cancelled due to bad weather.[77] The raids that were carried out were the largest yet, involving nearly 130 United States and Vietnamese air force aircraft in strikes against the Quang Khe naval base and an ammunition storage depot at Xom Bang. The official White House announcement of these attacks stated that they represented "no change" in policy. Press Secretary George Reedy linked them specifically to President Johnson's statement of February 17 — continuing actions in response to continuing aggression — which had been given a more pointed context by Mr. Rusk on February 25.

Despite official portrayal of these raids as representing no departure from past policies, their real significance did not go unnoticed.

Observers particularly noticed that officials carefully refrained from linking the strikes, as in the past, to specific enemy provocations. Reporting that "official spokesmen . . . allowed the inference that [the raids] would continue as long as North Vietnam continued to support and supply" the Viet Cong, Max Frankel also described these spokesmen as acknowledging in private that the raids "represented a major tactical change and a form of stepping up the war in Vietnam." According to these views, the administration hoped to elicit a decision from Hanoi to avoid further raids by curtailing its infiltration of men and supplies into South Vietnam, a decision that could be communicated either "by formal agreement or tacit understanding." However, the administration declined to make its objectives explicit so as not to provoke the Communists into responding with an escalation of their own.[78] Indeed, it took special pains as it had in the past to assure the Soviet Union of its desire to avoid wider war in Southeast Asia, but it reportedly emphasized that it was "determined to take whatever measures it considered necessary" to stop the continuing aggression.[79]

Many accounts stressed the primarily political and diplomatic impact intended for the raids, but some also called attention to a degree of ambiguity regarding the outcomes expected by the administration. United States officials in both Saigon and Washington reportedly understood that the administration's purpose was to improve the opportunities for negotiating a reasonable settlement of the Vietnam question. According to Peter Grose, an "official estimate" in Saigon assumed that "it might take two or three months" of similar air attacks to bring this about. However, just what action Hanoi could take to get the United States to call off the attacks and move to the negotiating table had not been made clear. By implication only, the attacks would continue as long as Hanoi persisted in supporting Viet Cong actions, but there was no sense of urgency communicated regarding Hanoi's compliance. The only enemy steps called for by United States spokesmen had been for Hanoi to indicate that it was "prepared to stop doing what it is doing to its neighbors." Furthermore, the government's tough insistence on what would be, in effect, a cease-fire before negotiations was contrary to the nature of guerrilla warfare. Robert Kleiman suggested as a more productive tack that "the level of military activity on both sides could be reduced progressively while a settlement is worked out." [80]

One reason implied for what were characterized as unclear diplomatic signals was that the president reluctantly had derived the administration's position himself, piecing it together from alternatives debated among his advisors. Different accounts reported that the Joint Chiefs of Staff had been urging the president to approve a sustained campaign of air strikes long before his decision, but that they doubted the effectiveness of sporadic attacks.[81] Another account reported a proposal for unacknowledged, small-scale air strikes, to be accompanied by a diplomatic initiative, that had apparently lost out in the debate. However, since the "planned" attacks for which Saigon officials were reportedly alerted in mid-February bore some similarities to those in the proposal, the account speculated on the current status of what it called the "diplomatic track." [82] Since the new administration position was apparently the result of an ad hoc weighting of such different patterns of advice, it is possible that the United States diplomatic tactics had not yet been fully determined.

Another explanation for the lack of clear signals regarding negotiations may have been the widely recognized lack of a favorable bargaining position for the United States. Both the administration and Congress had been troubled by this lack since early in the year, and several newspaper accounts referred to it in their appraisals of the government's public posture in late February.[83] Apparently, the public was also aware of it. Louis Harris reported that in his survey of February 22, 75 per cent of the interviewees favored a negotiated settlement as the ultimate objective, although most of them recognized the need to delay until the negotiations could be conducted from a position of strength. Accordingly, by insisting on what would amount to a cease-fire before talks could begin, the administration sought to discourage negotiations until it could achieve a position of strength.

Its immediate motivations were quite apparent. In the wake of the initial reprisal against North Vietnam, the pressures for negotiations intensified. On February 10, French President de Gaulle renewed his plea for an end to all foreign intervention in South Vietnam and for settlement of the Vietnam question through negotiations. In a matter of days, similar appeals were voiced by the Government of India and by the United Nations secretary general. Within the United States, as the intra-administration policy debate continued, public debate on the subject of negotiations also intensified. United States Senate moderates Church and McGovern joined the already outspoken critics of administration policy, senators Gruening and Morse, in advocating prompt efforts on behalf of negotiations, while Senate Majority Leader Mansfield, on at least one occasion, urged the administration to consider the possibility of neutralizing Southeast Asia through a negotiated settlement.[84] Liberal senators McCarthy, Nelson, and Young also expressed misgivings about the prevailing policy and, along with McGovern and Church, became the focal point of a special White House effort to explain it. As columnists Evans and Novak have argued:

> The Senate only reflected the larger political spectrum. Although previous concern over Washington's support of Saigon had been pretty much limited to the far left, now it spread into the volatile, vital liberal wing of the Democratic Party.
>
> All this could not be ignored by Johnson as he had ignored Morse and Gruening.[85]

Still another explanation for the administration's apparent lack of interest in negotiations may have been indicated by the interesting undercurrents following the return of Soviet Premier Kosygin from Hanoi. Aside from negotiating a defensive arms and economic aid agreement, the purpose of his visit had been unclear from the start. The American press cited two broader political possibilities: that the Soviet Union was moving to preempt Chinese influence in Hanoi, perhaps even by mediating a settlement that would serve to remove the United States peaceably, but in a face-saving manner, from Vietnam; and that the Soviet Union had concluded that the Chinese were correct in their dictum that "wars of national liberation" did not threaten serious escalation and wished to renew their links with the revolutionary factions in Hanoi, believing that the United States had become resigned to failure in Vietnam.[86]

Kosygin's return touched off conflicting reports from Moscow concerning Soviet interest in encouraging a negotiated settlement. According to one interpretation, both Tass and *Pravda* were cautiously dropping hints of Soviet favor for new negotiations regarding Vietnam. Another account cautioned against over-optimism regarding Soviet policies, arguing that the Kremlin regarded negotiations as premature and that Kosygin was believed to have urged Hanoi's leaders to hold their course but to avoid provoking a wider war.[87] The views of Soviet intentions contain a split that corresponded roughly to that characterizing differing opinions on the proper course for United States policy.

A series of authoritative reports from Great Britain, however, indicated that the Soviet Union was indeed seeking an active role in a peaceful settlement. Moscow was reported as passing word to the British government on two separate occasions during the week of February 15, that it wished to see Southeast Asia rid of the specter of Chinese-inspired guerrilla warfare and that it wanted to resume informally its role as co-chairman of the Geneva conference. According to this same account, British Prime Minister Harold Wilson was so encouraged by this expression of interest that he sought clarification from the Johnson administration as to the kind of settlement it would regard as acceptable.[88] Later, Wilson stated publicly that his government was "actively engaged in diplomatic consultations of a confidential nature: to seek a basis for peacefully settling the Vietnam conflict." The "consultations" were somewhat less active than the statement implied, reportedly consisting mainly of a series of diplomatic notes passed in Moscow, which attempted to determine the extent to which the Soviets were prepared to go in reviving the Geneva machinery.[89] Finally, on February 23, the Soviet government publicly declared its support for a negotiated settlement through reconvening the Geneva conference on Indochina (the position advocated by President de Gaulle of France). Still, it was not clear how strongly the Russians, in their co-chairman role, were prepared to urge Hanoi's cooperation or whether they were prepared to undertake discussions to seek agreement on mutually acceptable preconditions.

Public sources do not make clear the extent to which the United States administration encouraged exploratory peace efforts on the part of the Geneva co-chairmen, or embraced such explorations as part of its policy. Clearly, United States spokesmen were careful not to relate the American position to the diplomatic initiatives. On the day that Soviet support for a reconvened Geneva conference was announced, United States officials stated that the British and other foreign governments had made inquiries in Washington to determine United States attitudes on prospects for a settlement in Vietnam. The State Department acknowledged that "a full account of the situation [in Vietnam] and our views" were given to these governments but said little more. As observed by more than one reporter, the administration wanted to eschew any appearance of sanctioning a conference on Vietnam in order to avoid the risk of demoralization within South Vietnam.[90]

Whatever its reasons, the administration's tough line on a negotiated settlement was stated repeatedly by Secretary Rusk in late February and early March. In his February 25 news conference, he referred often to Hanoi's willingness "to stop doing what it is doing" to South Vietnam and Laos as "the missing piece" in the question of negotiations. In effect, the United States was insisting that North Vietnam indicate its readiness to halt its direction and support of the guerrilla wars as a precondition for a negotiated settlement. Under questioning, the secretary declined to specify what the United States would regard as evidence of this readiness, saying that "we would find it out very shortly on the ground, as well as through any diplomatic channel." On March 4, he repeated these affirmations in a public address in New York, including the earlier statement that "a negotiation aimed at the acceptance or the confirmation of aggression is not possible." Mr. Rusk emphasized these same points again, on March 7, over CBS television. He declined, however, to make the United States demands specific. When asked if the United States position meant that the North Vietnamese would have to stop supplying the Viet Cong before the United States would begin talks, he stated:

> I am not getting into the details of what are called preconditions, because we are not at that point — we are not at that point. Almost every postwar negotiation that has managed to settle in some fashion some difficult and dangerous question has been preceded by some private indication behind the scenes that such a negotiation might be possible. That is missing here — that is missing here.[91]

The administration's position included more than the view that its own participation in negotiations did not seem useful at the time. It also attempted to discourage certain other governments from pushing the issue and, particularly, from holding out to the Communist powers hope of obtaining concessions through a negotiated settlement. On February 20, after three days of broad-ranging discussions in Washington, administration officials were reported as rebuffing an offer from French Foreign Minister Couve de Murville to attempt an accommodation of United States and Chinese differences on negotiations. During his stay, the French minister attempted to persuade United States officials that

they could gain advantages from accepting a peaceful neutralization settlement before the conflict in Southeast Asia intensified.[92]
On March 6, Secretary Rusk urged that the members of NATO
support current efforts to defeat Communist aggression in Southeast Asia. "Above all," he cautioned, "they should do nothing to
encourage aggressors to believe that aggression will be allowed to
succeed on the ground or to reap a reward at the conference
table." [93]

In mid-March, top-level administration officials met in seclusion
at Camp David to review their policy position. Washington observers speculated that their main purpose was to evaluate the
effectiveness of the various pressures being exerted on North Vietnam and whether or not the bombing attacks should be intensified. No details of the meeting were announced, but on the
following day officials were reported to have judged that neither
the Communist governments nor many United States allies had
yet come to fully understand the United States commitment and
purposes in Vietnam. Even many Americans were thought to be
unclear as to their government's current objectives. Accordingly,
the account continued, the officials were persuaded that more "intensified but still measured military action against North Vietnam
and more energetic but still guarded public and private explanations of the [supporting] rationale" were needed.[94]

As if to bear out the authenticity of the reports, the next few
days were marked by an increased air effort against targets in
North Vietnam. On March 15, over 100 United States Air Force
and Navy aircraft struck an ammunition depot at Phu Qui, only
about 100 miles south of Hanoi. Four days later, over 120 aircraft
struck ammunition and supply depots about 130 miles south of
Hanoi. On the 14th and 21st, United States Air Force aircraft
escorted the more range-limited Vietnamese aircraft on missions
against communications and infiltration bases closer to the South
Vietnamese border. Following the first attack in this series, official
statements said only that the raids were carried out because of
"continued acts of aggression" against South Vietnam. However,
close White House observers were apparently able to learn more
about their intended purposes. For example, Max Frankel reported
that, by their size and their choice of targets farther north, the
raids were designed to indicate that North Vietnam would suffer
increasingly serious punishment if it persisted in aiding the Viet
Cong insurgency. Further, they were intended to demonstrate

that the United States government was prepared to commit its air forces against Hanoi's jet interceptors, within whose range the targets were located, and that neither North Vietnam's defenses nor its Communist allies could prevent the United States from damaging Hanoi's assets at will.[95]

Thus, during a period covering roughly a month's time, an attempt was made to pressure the North Vietnamese government into backing away from its efforts to overthrow the government of South Vietnam by force and, at the same time, to motivate the Soviet Union into playing a constructive role vis-à-vis Hanoi in this respect. By combining gradually increased military pressures, a diplomatic position that professed no interest in early negotiations, and a public campaign to highlight Hanoi's responsibility for the level of the military conflict in Southeast Asia, the United States administration attempted to create sufficient leverage to force the DRV off its chosen course. In addition to its intensified, "unprovoked" bombing attacks on North Vietnam, it continued air operations in the south. Moreover, although as yet symbolic only of an intention to persevere, it had deployed to South Vietnam two battalions of United States Marines to set up perimeter defenses and to establish security patrols around Da Nang Air Base.[96]

Administration officials were apparently aware, however, that its public posture was not altogether unambiguous. They were concerned that the message that continued Communist infiltration would bring even more intensive United States bombing was not getting through to Hanoi.[97] Yet, rather than indicating explicitly its intention to subject North Vietnam to increasing punishment, the administration preferred to signal the threat subtly. This it attempted by the pattern of its successive attacks and through policy background briefings to selected reporters.

Moreover, Washington's rejection of negotiations was not without tacit qualification. For example, in those same statements in which Secretary Rusk decried "the missing piece" from Hanoi, he also hinted that the United States anticipated a negotiated settlement at some future date. He stated that channels for exploring the "possibilities of a peaceful solution" were being kept open and that direct talks had been held with every signatory to the Geneva agreements except the government in Hanoi. Moreover, some of the strength of Secretary Rusk's initial rebuff of negotiations may have been eroded by his appearing to respond to an unintended slur by U Thant. On the previous day, in a press statement urging a peaceful settlement of the conflict, the secretary general implied that the American people did not know "the true facts" regarding developments in South Vietnam.[98] *

Of course, Hanoi did not depend solely on public statements for its perceptions of United States policy. The administration's position was presented to the Soviet Union, both directly and through the British government, and according to Mr. Rusk's admission, also to Communist China.[99] Presumably, it was transmitted by these Communist governments to Hanoi, doubtless colored by their impressions of United States intent and by their own policy preferences. Then, too, some of the potential impact of the administration's new position may have been lost because it could not launch its initial policy statement, its documented case against Hanoi, and its bombing program simultaneously. Thus, the signals received by the North Vietnamese government may not have been strong enough or clear enough to lend credence to the threat communicated by the air strikes.

3. Period Three: Shifting the Focus

As later events indicated, the air strikes of mid-March were largely to assume the role of exemplary attacks. During the two weeks that followed, all air missions into North Vietnam remained below the 19th Parallel. In all of March, only the United States raids of the 15th and 19th moved north of this limit. Beginning on March 21, United States and Vietnamese aircraft flew a series of almost daily missions against fixed targets south of the 19th Parallel that included North Vietnamese radar sites. In addition, they embarked on an armed reconnaissance program along Route 1, attacking military targets of opportunity along this important coastal artery as far north as Vinh.

Viewed from an operational perspective, the pattern of these strikes could be regarded as preparation for the heavier blows that were delivered early in April. On April 3, highway and railway

* Mr. Thant's comment came in the context of a plea for informal discussions to establish a stable, representative government in South Vietnam, based on his conviction that military conflict could not resolve the situation effectively. If the American people knew "the true facts," he said, they would "agree with me that further bloodshed is unnecessary. The political and diplomatic method of discussions and negotiations alone can create conditions which will enable the United States to withdraw gracefully from that part of the world."

bridges were struck for the first time in the war. Two were attacked by more than 100 United States Navy and Air Force aircraft at locations just 65 and 72 miles south of Hanoi. On April 4, one of the targets was restruck, and a thermal power plant nearby was also attacked. However, this operation against a purely industrial target proved to be an isolated instance. Surely, the shift to radar targets in the final week of February could have been intended to clear the way for the deeper penetrations and larger strikes that followed.

One Interpretation. This argument is compatible with a view that the new pattern of attacks was intended by the administration, at least in part, to put greater pressure on the DRV and force concessions that it had been unwilling to make heretofore. Two actions of the government lend support to this view. First, during the strikes against bridge targets near Hanoi an official statement from the Department of Defense announced the bombing in considerably more detail than any raid since March 2. It stressed that it had taken seven years for the Vietnamese to rebuild one of these bridges and that "the present regime has taken great pride in its restoration." [100] This statement suggests a kind of rationale accepted by at least some officials that since the bombing was now directed at facilities believed to be of great value to Hanoi, North Vietnamese calculations might be more sensitive to the threat of further attacks and, hence, their leaders more willing to consider alternatives to their present course. Second, the administration chose this occasion to indicate its willingness to negotiate an end to the conflict. Selecting this particular time to offer Hanoi a tacit invitation to hold discussions suggests the operation of a similar rationale.

Of the two, the more compelling piece of evidence for the "greater pressure" interpretation was the public acknowledgment of United States interest in negotiating a settlement. Explicit statement of the new policy came on April 7, in the president's speech at the Johns Hopkins University, but a change in the administration's public position on negotiations had been revealed even earlier, soon after the new bombing pattern went into effect. On March 25, President Johnson emphasized that the United States would "never be second in seeking a settlement in Vietnam" and spoke of "our principles for honorable negotiation." He also spoke of United States interest in helping to support programs of "economic and social cooperation" in Southeast Asia that would be "wider and bolder" once the war ended. Reporters termed the proposal a "carrot" and "an olive branch" to accompany the bombing "stick," and one characterized it as a hint of aid to Hanoi if it ceased its aggression.[101] On April 4, the president's special assistant for national security affairs told newsmen that the United States would insist on "no specific preconditions" for an honorable settlement, a feature that would figure prominently in the president's announcement three days later.[102]

At Johns Hopkins, the president asserted the administration's readiness for "unconditional discussions" and acknowledged his willingness to consider even large-scale negotiations like those at Geneva. In addition, he repeated in even more explicit terms than those used on March 25 his offer to Hanoi of an incentive if it would agree to resolve the conflict peacefully. Cautioning that North Vietnam could provide for the needs of its people "far more readily in peaceful association with others than in the endless course of battle," the president pledged that the United States would assist in a "greatly expanded cooperative effort for economic development" of Southeast Asia, in which "we would hope that North Vietnam would take its place." No doubt intending, in part, to exert added pressure on the DRV, the president invited "other industrialized countries, including the Soviet Union," to join in helping the nations of Southeast Asia in this effort to improve the region. As if to highlight the DRV's alternatives, particularly in the wake of the recent attacks on bridges, he prefaced his proposal with the following warning:

> We have no desire to see thousands die in battle — Asians or Americans. We have no desire to devastate that which the people of North Vietnam have built with toil and sacrifice. We will use our power with restraint and with all the wisdom that we can command. But we *will* use it.[103]

Although conveying a threat of greater destruction, President Johnson specified neither the nature of the punishment to be inflicted nor a time limit by which a favorable reply was expected. However, it is evident that he and others were hopeful that the new "carrot and stick" signals would induce Hanoi to agree to work out a peaceful solution to the political future of South Vietnam. A few hours in advance of the president's speech, McGeorge Bundy, Undersecretary of State George Ball, and Secretary McNamara provided reporters with an unusual preview of the substance and rationale for his message. They emphasized the full literal meaning of the United States acceptance of unconditional diplomatic discussions with the Communists and explained how this and the offer of economic development, when considered by Hanoi as an alternative to suffering alone in further conflict, might move the situation forward toward an effective solution.[104] Buoyed a few days later by well-publicized expressions of approval of his speech from most Western and many non-aligned governments, the president expressed great personal pride in his proposals and characterized them repeatedly as a "war against war itself." [105]

Communist rejections of the idea produced real disappointment. Although officials did not expect early negotiations, they apparently thought that the idea of peaceful settlement might strike a responsive chord, thus providing the basis for gradual movement toward a solution.[106] While Peking's hostile reaction was predictable, the harshness of the Soviet reply of April 10, ridiculing the Johnson proposals as "noisy propaganda," was particularly depressing. Evidently the administration hoped that its "carrot and stick" approach would be effective enough at least to activate the Soviet Union to start influencing Hanoi in the desired direction. Western diplomats in Moscow said that this public stance by the Soviets offered little hope that the Kremlin would attempt to influence Hanoi privately to soften its position on negotiations.[107] After Hanoi's public rejection, in its official newspaper *Nhan Dan*, George Ball refused to "say that North Vietnam has flatly rejected anything" and held out the administration's hope that the North Vietnamese even yet might be moved to display some interest in negotiations.[108] However, the firmness of Hanoi's negative position soon became clear. On April 12, the DRV formally rejected a request for an official "fact-finding" visit by a representative of the British government; on the 13th, it distributed a four-point formula as a basis for international negotiation, in effect rejecting the United States call for unconditional discussions. These events led President Johnson, in what reporters called "somber" tones, to express great disappointment at Communist resistance to the attempts at opening "a window to peace." He stated:

> They want no talk with us, no talk with a distinguished Briton, no talk with the United Nations. They want no talk at all so far. But our offer stands. We mean every word of it.[109]

These expressions of hope and, later, of disappointment, may have reflected belief within the administration that its military-diplomatic initiative at the beginning of April could activate Soviet "cooperation" and also erode some of North Vietnam's intransigence. In view of the government's earlier recognition of its poor bargaining position, we can reasonably interpret its new negotiating posture as relating to results it expected to achieve through the intensified bombing and its regional development proposals.

Willingness to Negotiate. On the other hand, aspects of the president's announcement of the new negotiating policy suggest that he intended to convey a number of quite different messages and to address audiences other than North Vietnam. For example, several foreign governments had joined in the public criticism of earlier United States policy whose actions encouraged some sort of official United States response. On April 1, Washington, along with eight other capitals and the United Nations secretary general, received a plea from seventeen non-aligned nations for immediate negotiations, "without any preconditions," to end the war in Vietnam. A reply in words quite similar to those in his Johns Hopkins speech was sent to these governments on the morning following the speech.[110] On the same day that the seventeen-nation appeal was reported Prime Minister Pearson of Canada — while on an official visit to the United States and *prior* to his initially scheduled meeting with President Johnson — made a public appeal in the United States for a bombing pause. He argued that this could afford Hanoi an opportunity to relax its inflexible resistance to a diplomatic solution without the appearance of acting under duress.[111] Visibly irritated by Pearson's gratuitous and ill-timed remarks, the president may have felt impelled to take some initiative to demonstrate to foreign observers that the United States really favored a negotiated solution.

Pressure for United States efforts on behalf of a peaceful settlement of the Vietnam conflict was also building up within the United States. Since early March, a number of university campuses had become the sites of "teach-in" sessions — largely critical of United States involvement in Vietnam — which were increasingly giving vent to public sentiment in favor of a negotiated settlement. Columnist Walter Lippmann, characterizing the administration's policy as "all stick and no carrot," led a growing chorus of news analysts and editors who urged more effort in the direction of a diplomatic solution.[112] On March 25, following public confirmation of the Soviet refusal to engage in efforts to end the fighting through discussions, new pressures to spell out United States interest in negotiations arose in the Senate. From the Republican side came proposals that United States military measures against North Vietnam be accompanied by a clear statement of a goal of "honorable negotiations." [113] It is indicative of President Johnson's sensitivity to these pressures that he took pains to give private previews of his Baltimore speech to several of his critics, including Walter Lippmann and leaders of the liberal Americans for Democratic Action. Before the latter group, which was attending the organization's national convention in Washington on April 2, he gave special emphasis and intonation to the sections on "unconditional discussions" and on the regional development proposal.[114]

Still, the president's adoption of a stance welcoming negotiations without preconditions was apparently based on more than a mere desire to placate his critics. In the first place, he claimed even before this time to have been "the ringleader of a political settlement." [115] But an even more compelling motivation was revealed in one of the major themes of his Johns Hopkins speech and in other statements by his advisors — namely, that the administration had determined that a long, sustained effort by United States forces might be required. Clearly, it would be easier to build and hold public support for such a commitment if the government were on record as aiming for a reasonable political settlement.

That the president and his advisors were aware of the potentiality of a protracted conflict is evident from what they said in public. On April 4, McGeorge Bundy suggested to a television panel of newsmen that the policy of bombing North Vietnam might have to be sustained for a long time to produce political and diplomatic changes desired by the United States. In Baltimore, three days later, Mr. Johnson reemphasized the intention of the United States to preserve a free and independent South Vietnam, even if a long-term United States investment proved to be necessary: "We will do everything necessary to reach that objective. . . . We will not be defeated. We will not grow tired. We will not withdraw, either openly or under the cloak of a meaningless agreement." He then elaborated in a manner indicating that the administration was prepared to incur substantial costs over time in pursuing its goal:

> We hope that peace will come swiftly. But that is in the hands of others besides ourselves. And we must be prepared for a long continued conflict. It will require patience as well as bravery — the will to endure as well as the will to resist.
>
> I wish it were possible to convince others with words of what we now find it necessary to say with guns and planes: armed hostility is futile — our resources are equal to any challenge — because we fight for values and we fight for principle, rather than territory or colonies, our patience and our determination are unending.[116]

Another Interpretation. While the president may have hoped that recent United States actions would cause Hanoi to soften its attitude toward a negotiated settlement, he was, by these same actions, laying the necessary groundwork for the eventuality of a long-term United States effort in Southeast Asia. We may thus formulate a different interpretation of the events of late March and early April. Actually, the two interpretations — this one and the one emphasizing an attempt to persuade Hanoi to soften its position — do not necessarily conflict. The administration may well have reasoned that if Hanoi did not react favorably to the apparent escalation, the United States would then proceed to build up a different form of pressure.

That the administration was hedging against the possibility that the war might require more extensive and more prolonged commitment than was hoped earlier in the month is evident in the pattern of military operations that began to unfold in the last week of March. As already described, these began with armed route reconaissance missions and attacks on radar targets and were followed by two days of raids against rail and highway bridges deep in North Vietnamese territory. The administration chose to strike them at this particular time for other reasons than their symbolic value, however. As specified in the Defense Department's press announcement, the bridges were "vital links in the North Vietnamese transportation system supporting Communist guerrilla operations in South Vietnam and Laos," and one was the second longest on the only railroad linking Hanoi with the coastal cities to the south.[117] Further, these bridges were only the first of several to be struck during subsequent weeks. Attacks on bridges and radar stations and armed route reconnaissance against highways and railroads were the principal missions of air operations against North Vietnam conducted almost daily throughout April 1965.

To understand the significance of attacks against transportation targets and lines of communication during April, we must look briefly at some of the military developments that occurred in February and March. In mid-February, the administration was concerned that increased Viet Cong aggressiveness in the vicinity of Route 19 (Qui Nhon-Binh Dinh-Pleiku) might represent an attempt to divide South Vietnam in two. Indeed, the American Embassy in Saigon identified the threat represented by Viet Cong successes and troop concentrations in this region as the reason for using United States jets to furnish supporting fire for embattled South Vietnamese ground forces.[118] Moreover, the need for more South Vietnamese troops to cope with the broader Viet Cong offensive in part precipitated the decisions to raise an additional 100,000 men for ARVN, and to send United States Marines ashore to relieve ARVN forces from base defense tasks. Secretary Rusk explained that the arrival of the Marines at Da Nang would enable the South Vietnamese forces to undertake "pacification operations." [119] The seriousness of the Communist military threat and the probability that it would get worse were dramatized on March 1 by reports that Hanoi was passing the word that any increase of anti-Communist manpower in South Vietnam would be countered by an increase of forces infiltrated from the north. North Vietnamese sources claimed they were capable of infiltrating an additional 2000 men per month.[120]

The seriousness of the military situation in South Vietnam became public during a week-long staff visit of the United States Army Chief of Staff and other high-ranking administration officials in early March. As General Harold K. Johnson's party neared Saigon, United States military officials announced that ARVN casualties during February were the highest of any single month to date.[121] Amid reports from the GVN that the Viet Cong were intensifying their aggression in the northern provinces, visiting United States officials found trends in the war interfering with activities of the Saigon agencies attempting to improve the GVN's relations with the South Vietnamese people. For example, the deteriorating military situation in the countryside prevented information agency officials from traveling among the various provinces to stimulate greater government activity.[122] United States Mission officials were reported as calling attention to the serious need for larger troop reserves in South Vietnam and even considered "a number of manpower plans" to relieve the shortage. One of these plans, reportedly recommended to the Johnson party, was for "the stationing of a U.S. Army division in South Vietnam for defensive security" purposes.[123]

The recommendations that General Johnson made upon his return, on March 15, lent weight to a concern voiced increasingly in Washington. Particularly since the renewal of air strikes against the North in early March, officials were apprehensive lest increased emphasis on bombing detract from the kinds of actions needed to prevent a Communist seizure of power in the South.[124] Speculating whether political and military developments in the South might not have progressed to the point where northern assistance was not really needed to force a collapse, Peter Grose reported doubts among "many observers" that the bombing of North Vietnam could improve the situation as expected. Apparently, they feared that a collapse might occur before the "two or three months of attacks" seen as necessary in "one official estimate" could produce the desired effect. Some observers cautioned against expecting significant effect from the aerial bombing in Vietnam, and General Johnson, on his return, was reported to stress that the air strikes against the North were not sufficient measures in themselves to bring the insurgency under control. Among his recommendations were that more American-manned helicopters and 200 to 300 more United States combat advisers be sent to assist the South Vietnamese Army. The administration promptly approved these recommendations.[125]

As Jack Raymond said, the recommendations of General Johnson's party helped focus administration attention on the primary importance of winning the battle in South Vietnam. Emphasis on the view that "even with the air offensive, the anti-guerrilla operations [there] must be made more effective" meshed well with President Johnson's frequently illustrated predilection to view United States interests and the primary United States objective in terms of bringing about a healthy situation within South Vietnam.

Reports from South Vietnam warning of increasingly ominous military trends gave added urgency to the ground war in the South. On the day following General Johnson's report, the in filtration of three new battalions into the Kontum area created the largest Viet Cong strike force ever assembled in the Central Highlands area. The United States Military Mission in Saigon reported that Communist guerrilla activity during the second week of March had reached "its highest level since last September." [126] On March 22, Ambassador Taylor told a public audience in Saigon that the Viet Cong were apparently beginning an all-out drive for a Communist victory, expending "great effort . . . to cut the country in two from Kontum to Qui Nhon and, at the same time, to threaten the Hué and Da Nang area." Further, he suggested that continued escalation of the war might require the entry of United States ground combat forces into the fighting.[127] Taylor's widely reported comments came two days after the president announced the ambassador's forthcoming return to Washington for a review of United States efforts in the war.

Under these circumstances, then, the shift in the air operations against North Vietnam to emphasize transportation targets — first, armed route reconnaissance and, later, bridges — can be interpreted as a means of supporting various efforts to improve the military situation in South Vietnam as well as an attempt to persuade Hanoi to soften its position. As indicated by the Defense Department announcement following the first bridge attacks, the targeting shift was intended to limit the southward flow of traffic aiding the Viet Cong.*

Decision to Shift the Focus. The shift to transportation targets — as well as the public negotiating initiative — may have been reviewed and confirmed during the strategy sessions attended by Ambassador Taylor from March 29 through April 2, just prior to the first bridge attacks. Reporters had been told that an evaluation of the air strike program would be the chief topic for discussion, and officials had indicated beforehand that new "tactical decisions" might be required.[128]

The meeting with Taylor was announced shortly after it became apparent that the Soviet Union would not attempt to influence Hanoi to reduce its efforts in the South and seek a peaceful solution. President Johnson made the announcement on March 20, the day following Soviet Foreign Minister Gromyko's statement from

---

* Later, the attacks were praised for interrupting the train and truck traffic across "vital links" in the regular North Vietnamese transportation system and for making it more vulnerable to subsequent attack. See Mark Watson, *Baltimore Sun*, April 7, 1965.

London that the United States would have to deal directly with North Vietnam and after reports that his meetings with Prime Minister Wilson and Foreign Secretary Stewart had failed to achieve an agreement between the Geneva co-chairmen to work jointly for discussions to halt the fighting.[129] This development, coupled with the Army Chief of Staff recommendations a few days earlier, would seem to have urged anew those military programs appropriate for a prolonged conflict with a stubborn enemy.

A decision to direct air operations against transportation targets was in line with the announced results of the strategy conference. Government comments on the air campaign stated merely that it would continue and that, if intensified, the raids would carry with them a threat of open intervention by China or North Vietnam. Other decisions were discussed more substantively. Ambassador Taylor told reporters that the Viet Cong continued to expand their areas of control in the South and that improvement of conditions there had received the "greatest attention" during the conference. Specific United States actions to help bring about such improvement were announced after the final session, held in conjunction with a meeting of the National Security Council. These included sending "several thousand" United States troops, in addition to the 27,500 already there, to South Vietnam "in the next few months" to provide greater security for United States bases and to train the South Vietnamese forces; increasing South Vietnam's military, militia, and police forces by 160,000 men; and increasing economic assistance, with emphasis on strengthening the position of the GVN in the rural provinces. Though both the president and Ambassador Taylor took pains to point out that the conference decisions did not represent "far-reaching" or "fundamental" changes in strategy, reporters were quick to recognize that they represented "a still deeper American involvement" in the Vietnam War.[130]

The announced conference decisions were perhaps significant for their lack of dramatic content. Pre-conference speculation gave emphasis to the likelihood of an intensified air campaign against highly valued targets farther north. It included rumors of recommendations for deploying a United States combat division to South Vietnam to participate directly in anti-guerrilla operations. Moreover, conference reporters referred to congressional concern over a supposed contingency plan to commit 350,000 American troops in the event of Chinese intervention.[131] In lieu of any of the rumored spectacular developments, the post-conference announcements dampened expectations of dramatic solutions — perhaps reflecting what one reporter regarded as Washington's viewpoint that "the whole Vietnam situation was . . . stalemated both militarily and politically." [132]

Also significant in the conference decisions was the apparent conclusion that continued air operations would make little sense if they did not contribute materially to a favorable outcome on the ground in South Vietnam. In what was clearly a view with a long-term focus, administration officials regarded future air operations against the North and the efforts to improve conditions in the South as having complementary effects. Specifically, they would confront Hanoi with a continuous military threat while at the same time discouraging its hopes that continued aggression against the South could bring eventual Communist control.[133]

New Priorities — New Strategy. The high-level decisions of early April confirmed a bombing policy oriented primarily to the military issues in South Vietnam, indicated by the subsequent pattern of air attacks against the North. The bridge raids of April 3 and 4 represented the most dramatic and the most psychologically potent of the air strikes carried out during the next several weeks. Not only did they occur within 65 to 80 miles of Hanoi, but their targets were fairly near each other, thus concentrating the attacking and escorting aircraft in an area threateningly close to North Vietnam's industrial and economic centers. For most of the rest of April and the first two weeks of May, the daily attacks employed significantly fewer sorties, allocated among a variety of military targets and armed reconnaissance missions farther south. Only on April 9, 16, and 23 and on May 4 and 8 did the attacks involve total numbers of aircraft as large as or larger than in the first bridge raid. Even on these occasions, the attacks against comparable targets were carried out by smaller groups of aircraft in widely scattered areas. Only rarely did any of the sorties of April and May venture to within 100 miles of the Hanoi-Haiphong complex.[134]

In retrospect, the geographical relationship between the air strikes of April 3 and 4 and those which followed can be readily explained on purely military grounds. If North Vietnam's transportation system and logistical traffic were to be curtailed, good operational sense demanded striking first at the major rail and highway bridges to the north. Then the trucks and particularly the rail equipment that had already passed beyond those spans would be trapped for a time between them and the South Vietnamese border. Subsequent route cuts farther south would confine them to even smaller areas of mobility and enable armed reconnaissance flights to locate and attack them in detail. Thus, while the seemingly less threatening and less concentrated air operations of most of April and May lacked the political and psychological punch of the earlier bridge strikes, they conformed to a highly rational military pattern.

These efforts to reduce the flow of troops and supplies to the South were compatible with the new order of priorities and new strategy that were emerging from the national policy councils.

On April 19, in a speech originally prepared for William Bundy, Deputy Assistant Secretary of State for Far Eastern Affairs Leonard Unger stated an unusually explicit policy theme: "We will take whatever actions are necessary to convince the leaders in North Vietnam that their efforts are self-defeating as well as futile." [135] Although implicit in previous statements, this theme had not been stated so unequivocally and so free from euphemism. Of particular significance on this occasion, the speech stressed the administration's intention to demonstrate the futility of continued aggression at a time when public speculation was mounting over whether United States ground forces would soon enter the conflict. Though Mr. Unger's speech made no reference to this possibility, it perhaps did reflect the administration's new determination to take effective countermeasures against the Communist guerrillas in South Vietnam. Its aim, as reflected in the speech, was to prove to the North Vietnamese leadership that in the long run the war in the South would be a losing one.[136]

During April 1965, when this determination came into being, the administration recognized that its aim would have to be accomplished gradually and only over a considerable period of time. The principal means proposed for its accomplishment, a significant addition to South Vietnam's armed forces, was estimated as requiring at least a year to prepare.[137] In the meantime, the performance of the existing forces was to be improved through increased United States logistical support and an expanded training and advisory program.

A conference of top-level diplomatic, military, and defense

officials was called at Honolulu for April 19 and 20 for the professed purpose, according to Secretary McNamara, of planning such assistance.[138] At its completion, official public statements gave an indication that the conference had dealt with a broader range of actions. Secretary McNamara announced that the conference considered the disruption of infiltration traffic from North Vietnam and made plans to increase the interdiction of infiltration by sea. He stated that the United States would provide more helicopters and tactical aircraft than originally planned and would increase its close air support for South Vietnamese units.[139] United States officials conceded that these increases and the additional advisors and logistical support personnel could realistically be expected to raise the United States troop commitment to at least 40,000 men.[140] Administration sources stressed that the troop increases would remain limited in order not to precipitate enemy reactions that would destroy whatever prospects existed for a diplomatic settlement. Thus, a reporter said military requests for division-level reinforcements had been denied.[141]

Appearing along with the accounts of announced administration decisions were several reports that plans were being made for an even larger United States build-up, for the purpose of assisting directly in ground combat operations against the Viet Cong. Such measures were necessary during the next few months to cope with the increasing infiltration of forces from the North, an anticipated major Viet Cong monsoon offensive, and the poorly defended condition of United States air and logistical bases in the South.[142] Knowledgeable observers have since insisted that President Johnson did not actually decide to send United States forces to South Vietnam for ground combat purposes until a few days before the public announcement of a major United States force build-up there, on July 28.[143] However, some administration officials apparently expected at the time of the Honolulu Conference that combat involvement would occur much earlier. Reporters had learned from authoritative sources in both Washington and Saigon of expectations that more active patrolling by forces deployed to protect United States bases would lead to operations designed to seek out and engage the enemy.[144] From Saigon came detailed accounts of discussions between Ambassador Taylor and the South Vietnamese prime minister to arrange for the introduction into the country of as many as 5000 additional

United States combat forces — probably either Marines or airborne troops.[145] That these reports were reliable was borne out by the events of May and June, when the Marines at Da Nang and the 173rd Airborne Brigade, deployed in early May around Bien Hoa, became involved in a series of progressively more intensive patrolling actions and in offensive thrusts against Viet Cong base areas.

Several observers reported that the administration's new emphasis on measures to improve the effort against the guerrillas in South Vietnam was accompanied by a revision in its expectations regarding the bombing campaign in the North. That campaign would continue despite increasing demands for a bombing pause from the international community, from the academic world, and from such respected congressional figures as Senator Fulbright. However, it would not be intensified beyond the level of the daily raids against North Vietnam's transportation system, initiated in early April. For several reasons administration officials perceived that the bombing campaign was approaching the limits of its utility. First, it had already stirred up strong expressions of opposition to United States policy in Southeast Asia, which probably would increase if the bombing were intensified. Second, intensification would have to take the form of attacks around Hanoi or operations closer to the border of Communist China. These developments would likely entail the unwanted risks of killing larger numbers of civilians and of provoking stronger reactions, and wider conflict, from the Communists. Finally, authorities thought, an intensified air campaign might result in such destruction of targets that nothing of value would be left to threaten in bargaining or negotiations. Thus, while the North Vietnamese appeared willing to live with the kind and quantity of air attacks mounted during April, United States officials believed that the attacks should be continued primarily to inhibit the flow of reinforcements and supplies into South Vietnam.[146]

Toward the end of April, when rumors were rife concerning an impending ground involvement and near the time when additional ground units would actually be deployed to the combat zone, the administration spelled out in public its current bombing rationale. Before a nationwide television audience, Secretary McNamara explained that the current strikes were "designed to impede [the] infiltration of men and materiel, an infiltration which makes the difference between a situation which is manageable and one which is not manageable internally by the Government of South Viet-Nam." He continued:

> The airstrikes have been carefully limited to military targets, primarily to infiltration targets, to transit points, to barracks, to supply depots, to ammunition depots, to routes of communication, all feeding the infiltration lines . . . into South Viet-Nam.

After explaining that primary emphasis had been placed on attacking "the routes south of 20 degrees north" and describing in detail the damage done to bridges along these routes, McNamara concluded with a statement characterizing the expected nature of future air operations:

> These *carefully controlled rail strikes* will continue as necessary to impede the infiltration and to persuade the North Vietnamese leadership that their aggression against the South will not succeed.[147]

For several weeks at least, subsequent air strikes against North Vietnam conformed to this prescription. Even after submitting to public pressures for a pause in the bombing, only to have the North Vietnamese scoff at United States attempts to initiate discussions, the president held to the restrained bombing policy decided upon in April. Following the bombing pause and diplomatic initiative of May 12 to 17, air operations in the North continued to focus on military and transportation targets associated with the flow of Communist military resources into the South. In view of the expected involvement of United States ground forces in combat against the Viet Cong guerrillas, the interdiction of troop and supply movements from North Vietnam was a publicly defensible and sustainable use of United States air capabilities. The interdiction mission was also rationally compatible with the administration's reported conviction that the critical "test of wills" would occur on the ground.[148]

Thus, by May 1965, the United States leadership had settled into a strategy designed for the long pull. It was determined to keep substantial military pressure on Hanoi, but in a manner intended at once to limit North Vietnam's ability to reinforce the Communist forces in South Vietnam, and to avoid precipitating large-scale Communist intervention and an abrupt intensification of the war. While the immediate objective was to avoid defeat in the intensifying military struggle in the South, the administration's purpose was to buy time. During this time, it hoped, the South Vietnamese forces could be rebuilt and so strengthened as to cope effectively with the insurgency. By so doing the government might avoid the need to commit United States ground forces in large numbers to another Asian war. Ultimately, however — and it was conceded that this would probably take at least the rest of 1965 — the strategy was to bring about negotiations by wearing down Hanoi's will to fight. In the South, this would be done by the attrition of the opponent's forces, thereby denying him hope of victory. In the North, this end would be pursued by maintaining direct pressure on Hanoi through continuous selective air attacks. Hence the initial effort to coerce Hanoi failed and gave way to a strategy of attrition.

IV. CONCLUSIONS

To what extent did United States military intervention in Vietnam represent an effort to coerce the government of North Vietnam during the early months of 1965? One conclusion is clear. During none of the periods in question — (1) first three weeks of February, (2) approximately February 20 to March 20, and (3) end of March through July 1965 — were even the minimally coercive actions * employed in an unambiguous and uninhibited manner. Even during the second period, when the coercive objective appeared to be quite prominent, the administration observed important restraints in the nature of the demands it communicated to Hanoi and in the manner in which it documented its public case against Hanoi's aggression. During the preceding and subsequent periods, the coercive actions were less in evidence and less systematically applied, and the coercive objective appeared to occupy an importance secondary to that attached by the administration to other, more immediate objectives.

United States behavior in the first three weeks of February indicated that while the administration desired successful coercion of Hanoi, it was not central to immediate administration intentions. Rather, the central objective during this early period was to demonstrate, for the benefit of several different audiences, that

* See pp. 149–150.

the United States was determined to stand by its commitment to prevent removal of the governments in Southeast Asia by force. Of the minimally coercive actions, neither the progressive intensifying of military operations to suggest a still larger threat nor the public campaign to document Hanoi's complicity in the Viet Cong insurgency was initiated. In fact, whether or not and on what basis to go ahead with systematic pressures against the North were still subjects of intense debate during this period. The administration demanded that Hanoi halt its aggression, but in euphemistic terms. The air strikes were staged as retaliations in kind and implied that further United States actions were not to be feared unless Communist provocations continued. A desire to avoid extreme reactions from Communist governments and the need to assure observers that the United States intended to act responsibly led to restrained and ambiguous behavior. Moreover, the government avoided harsher actions and more explicit statements to preserve its freedom of action at a time when future policy was as yet not fully determined.

As February neared its final days, coercing Hanoi into abandoning its support of the insurgency assumed greater prominence as an element of administration policy. Along with bolstering Saigon's will to resist, and improving the bargaining assets available to the United States and the GVN, the coercive objective was pursued purposefully, though within firm policy constraints. To those actions already a part of its behavior, the administration added the remaining minimally coercive actions along with a tough public stance opposing early negotiations. Through use of the newly released (February 27) State Department White Paper in the United Nations and in foreign capitals, and through its channels to the Soviet government, it attempted to bring diplomatic pressure against the North Vietnamese regime to supplement its military actions. With each successive air raid in March the number of United States bombing sorties increased, and they crept farther north as the month progressed. Moreover, statements released to reporters and press inferences allowed by government officials gave the impression that these steadily rising pressures would continue to whatever extent necessary until Hanoi curtailed its aid to the insurgents.

Yet, the administration steered clear of an explicit link between the pattern of its bombing operations and Communist compliance with its demands. During March, it specifically refrained from describing actions that Hanoi should take to elicit a halting of the bombing or from stating "preconditions" for peaceful settlement of their respective differences. Its motives apparently were a mixture of wanting to avoid the appearance of stating ultimata that might provoke increased Communist hostility and to avoid an appearance of interest in a compromise settlement that might lead to South Vietnamese disillusionment. Moreover, at no time did the United States government explicitly threaten the DRV with increasing punishment or suggest eventual damage to its industrial capability if it did not comply. Neither did it attempt to convey any sense of urgency by indicating a period of time during which compliance would be expected. Whether these messages were inferred in the Communist capitals in spite of United States caution is not known. From the viewpoint in Washington, however, the administration's relations with its Vietnamese ally and its uncertainty with respect to the Soviet role constrained it from pursuing a more explicitly coercive course.

As its diplomatic initiatives and the interdiction efforts of April unfolded, administration behavior varied considerably from the minimally coercive actions pursued earlier. Of these, only the public campaign to bring international pressure on Hanoi remained free from erosion and from ambiguity. With the important exception of one attempt to exploit the effect of shock early in the campaign, United States air operations against the North ceased to describe a pattern of steadily rising pressures designed primarily for their psychological impact. The pattern and intensity of subsequent raids — designed to erode a limited target complex essential to North Vietnam's military effectiveness — gave this one attempt the appearance of an unsuccessful bluff. Moreover, if the administration's statements and actions of late February and March provided evidence of a demand for Hanoi's compliance under coercive pressure, then those of April and May were indicative of something less. Where the United States government had previously implied that talks could occur only after Hanoi indicated that it would stop aiding the insurgents, now it explicitly waived such a condition. In May, by virtue of its unilateral bombing halt, it implied that readiness to negotiate, not necessarily readiness to stop aiding the guerrillas, was the price being demanded for an end to the bombing pressures.

Clearly, therefore, getting Hanoi to abandon its support of the Viet Cong had lost prominence among the objectives of the

United States bombing campaign in North Vietnam. Or, stated another way, the enemy responses which the administration perceived that bombing might bring about were now perceived differently. Of dominant concern in May 1965 was the problem of reversing military trends in South Vietnam. For the next several months, bombing in the North and other forms of pressure were viewed primarily in terms of their contributions to this end.

Variations in the prominence accorded the coercive objective were important, but also significant was that this objective was held in some degree throughout the early months of 1965. In February, for example, official statements, implying a clear threat of further United States actions if Hanoi's aggression continued, indicate that successful coercion was regarded at least as a not too distant hope. In May and June, as early ground force deployments progressed, a new form of pressure was evidently being added to those coercive actions regarded as minimum in our study. This continuous presence suggests — as do the more clearly intentionally coercive actions undertaken in 1966 — that a desire to subject the DRV to harsher pressures may have been present within the administration all along but that it had been suppressed in varying degrees in deference to other overriding policy constraints.*

By the late spring and summer of 1965, however, the relationship between United States military actions and the ultimate United States goal of eliminating armed aggression from Southeast Asia had changed in two significant respects. First, the time required to achieve this goal was now clearly recognized by the administration as considerably more than it had hoped for in February and March. Second, the military pressures that would contribute to the achievement of this goal increasingly incorporated as their central conceptual element United States and GVN ground combat operations against the Communist guerrilla forces. The American portion of this had been hopefully regarded as avoidable in February and March. Thus, having abandoned the short-term attempt to coerce primarily through bombing pressures, the

---

* We can further hypothesize that either the president, himself, desired to subject Hanoi to more severe pressures but felt constrained from doing so early in 1965, or the president admitted minimally coercive elements to administration behavior in early 1965 to accommodate pressures from influential agencies or persons among his advisers in spite of a personal desire to avoid such actions.

United States was now embarked on a long-term process of attrition against what had proven to be a highly motivated, deeply committed opponent. To this task increasingly large contributions from ground, naval, and air forces would be applied.

Significantly, at no time during the periods in question — even by the standard of "minimally coercive actions" — did the coercive objective exist alone. Even from the last week of February to the final week of March, it was pursued together with two other objectives given similar degrees of emphasis.

The existence of multiple objectives, typical of most situations where military intervention is contemplated, leads to two observations, one methodological and the other empirical. First, we could subject a similar record of United States behavior in Vietnam to separate analyses focusing on different objectives, for example, the objective of improving the United States-GVN bargaining position for future negotiations. If this were done, we would subdivide the record into periods relevant to the pursuit of that objective. Moreover, these would probably be quite different periods than those identified here. Second, while different objectives may have equal significance for the national policy, differences are apt to occur in the effectiveness with which they are implemented. Different objectives are likely to be pursued in reaction to the policy advocacy of different government agencies. And, by virtue of its advocate's role and of its specific operational responsibilities, one agency may emphasize the implementation of one objective more strongly than another. In fact, it may not even be aware of the progress, or lack of, being made toward certain other objectives.

These observations account for several ambiguities in the evolution of public policy where military intervention is at issue. Different objectives may be pursued at different rates of time, with different intensities of effort, and with different kinds of effect that are not always reflective of the design or the effort. Yet the political and military actions employed in their pursuit appear as a *Gestalt*, as components of an integrated policy. Even if inconsistent approaches taken to different objectives can be compatibly rationalized from the standpoint of a government's internal relations, their intended meanings may not be readily differentiated by opponents and other outside observers.

In the Vietnam case, some of these ambiguities may have been deliberate — for example, in mid-February 1965 while future

United States policy was being debated and worked out, or in early April when it was apparently hoped that the DRV might react favorably to the initial heavy strikes against northern bridges. On the other hand, some ambiguities may have been unintentional, and would appear to have stemmed from the conflict between crisis management requirements and those of a coercive strategy. For example, the deliberate pace of diplomatic developments imposed by the United States posture toward negotiations during March may have been incompatible with the momentum of the bombing campaign and with the deterioration of the military situation in South Vietnam. It appears in retrospect that Hanoi had already publicly closed the door to negotiating possibilities, allegedly in reaction to the bombing but no doubt also affected by anticipation of larger military gains in the South, before a public United States negotiating initiative had been decided upon.*

The United States experience in Vietnam during the early months of 1965 contains fresh evidence that calculations of the costs and risks of particular actions and the assignment of relative priorities among objectives tend to change in the course of military conflict. The case provides arresting illustrations of the kinds of inherent difficulties incurred when governments intervene militarily in complex political-military situations.

* There is good reason to believe that the Soviet refusal to work with the British to encourage discussions to halt the fighting in Vietnam, in March 1965, was based on a prior rejection of negotiations by Hanoi. A *Nhan Dan* editorial on March 18 declared, "There can be no question of negotiations with the U.S. imperialists when they openly declare and brazenly step up the aggressive war in South Vietnam and extend this war to North Vietnam."

NOTES

[1] Charles Mohr in *New York Times*, February 12, 1965; see also Murrey Marder in *Washington Post*, February 12, 1965, who asked if this did not signify a broader United States challenge to "the basic Communist ideological and actual pursuit of guerrilla warfare, by countering that threat with air strikes against the home territory of the nation directing and supplying the guerrillas."

[2] See Tad Szulc in *New York Times*, February 10, 1965, and John Norris in *Washington Post*, February 11, 1965.

[3] Taylor is quoted from CBS interview in *New York Times*, February 15, 1965. For broader interpretations of air strike strategy, see William Beecher, *Wall Street Journal*, February 12, 1965; Richard Fryklund, *Evening Star* (Washington), February 12, 1965; and John Norris, *Washington Post*, February 13, 1965.

[4] Address before the National Industrial Conference Board at Washington, D.C., White House press release, in *Department of State Bulletin*, March 8, 1965, pp. 332–333.

[5] *Department of State Publication 7839*, February 27, 1965, reprinted *ibid.*, March 22, 1965, and in *Washington Post*, February 28, 1965.

[6] CBS television interview, August 9, 1965, in *Department of State Bulletin*, August 30, 1965, p. 350.

[7] See McNamara's public report on United States policy in Vietnam at the meeting of the National Security Industrial Association, March 26, 1964, in *New York Times*, March 27, 1964. In a list of four policy options presented to the president, he included "initiation of military actions outside South Vietnam, particularly against North Vietnam, in order to supplement the counterinsurgency program in South Vietnam."

[8] See the views attributed to Ambassador Taylor and the Saigon mission by Bernard Gwertzman, *Evening Star* (Washington), November 26, 1964, and by Seymour Topping (from Saigon) in *New York Times*, February 7, 9, and 14, 1965.

[9] On several occasions throughout 1964, journalists reflected views of government officials which stressed Hanoi's pride in its recently acquired economic base and the vulnerability of these resources to air attack. See William Beecher in *Wall Street Journal*, April 13, 1964; Roger Hilsman, "Plea for 'Realism' in Southeast Asia," in *New York Times Magazine*, August 23, 1964; Peter Grose in *New York Times*, September 27, 1964; and Gwertzman, *Evening Star* (Washington), November 26, 1964.

[10] Michael Janeway, "Bill Moyers Talks About LBJ, Power, Poverty, War and the Young," *The Atlantic Monthly*, July 1968, pp. 29–30.

[11] See Elie Abel, *The Missile Crisis* (Philadelphia: J. B. Lippincott Co., 1966). Compare this with the description of the coercive strategy presented in Chapter One.

[12] See Roger Hilsman, *To Move a Nation* (Garden City, N.Y.: Doubleday, 1967), p. 527. The possible influence of such a recommendation is indicated in public warnings by both President Johnson and Secretary Rusk that "those engaged in external direction and supply [of the South Vietnamese insurgency] would do well to be reminded and to remember that this type of aggression is a deeply dangerous game," on February 21 and 25, respectively, *Department of State Bulletin*, March 16, 1964, pp. 394–395, 399.

[13] *Newsweek*, March 9, 1964, p. 16.

[14] See David Halberstam in *New York Times*, November 23 and 24, 1964, and a *New York Times* editorial on November 25, 1964.

202   WILLIAM E. SIMONS

¹⁵ According to the testimony of generals Wheeler and McConnell, the Joint Chiefs of Staff believed that stronger actions would be necessary; other officials may have had similar views. See "Air War Against North Vietnam," *Hearings Before the Preparedness Investigating Subcommittee of the Committee on Armed Services*, United States Senate, 90th Congress, 1st Session, Part 2, August 16, 1967, p. 141, and Part 3, August 22, 1967, pp. 211–212.

¹⁶ See Walt W. Rostow, *View from the Seventh Floor* (New York: Harper & Row, 1964), pp. 118–119; also the statements of William Bundy (to a Japanese audience), September 29, 1964, the White House (following a major strategy conference), December 1, 1964, and Secretary Dean Rusk (before NBC television), January 3, 1965, acknowledging the importance of coping with the problem of the infiltration of men and materiel from North Vietnam. Bundy and White House statements in *Department of State Bulletin*, Vol. 51, pp. 537 and 870, respectively. Rusk statement *ibid.*, Vol. 52, pp. 64–65.

¹⁷ In an interview for *Life* magazine in November 1964, Ambassador Taylor was asked to comment about the possibility of bombing supply routes or major targets in North Vietnam. He answered solely in terms of striking the infiltration routes ("generally by way of Laos") and the training area for infiltrators in North Vietnam, and stressed the value of such operations in reminding the DRV "that it cannot get off unscathed, that indeed they stand to lose far more than they have any likelihood of winning," *Life*, November 27, 1964, p. 51. See also commentary surrounding Taylor's views and his return to Washington for a policy meeting in late November by Bernard Gwertzman, *Evening Star* (Washington), November 26, 1964; David Halberstam, *New York Times*, November 23, 1964; and story filed from Saigon *ibid.*, November 25, 1964.

¹⁸ See accounts by administration insiders during the period: Hilsman, *To Move a Nation*, pp. 526–534, and James C. Thomson, Jr., "How Could Vietnam Happen?" *Atlantic Monthly*, April 1968, pp. 51, 52.

¹⁹ On September 7 and 8 and from November 28 to December 1. On both occasions, Ambassador Taylor returned from Saigon to participate. See *New York Times*, September 8, 9, 10, November 25, 28, and December 2, 4, 1964.

²⁰ See Robert Brunn, *Christian Science Monitor*, September 5, 1964; Tad Szulc, *New York Times*, September 11, 1964; Peter Grose, *ibid.*, September 27, 1964; Hanson Baldwin, *ibid.*, November 29, 1964; *Wall Street Journal*, December 2, 1964; *Christian Science Monitor*, December 12, 1964.

²¹ See the press conference held by Secretary Rusk on December 23, 1964, in *Department of State Bulletin*, January 18, 1965, pp. 38–39, and the speech by William Bundy on January 23 *ibid.*, February 8, 1965, p. 171.

²² This perception was linked with the attitude trends shown in public polls. For example, in June a Gallup poll suggested that little more than a third (37 per cent) of the public showed any interest in Southeast Asia, and that these were divided primarily between those urging United States withdrawal and those urging direct United States action against North Vietnam. Despite a brief surge of concern over United States policy following the incidents in the Tonkin Gulf, this apportionment had not changed appreciably by December. At that time, a Louis Harris survey reported 20 per cent favoring withdrawal and negotiations, 18 per cent for bombing in the North, and the remainder either content to continue supporting the government of South Vietnam (GVN) or undecided. *Washington Post*, December 21, 1964.

²³ See stories filed simultaneously from Saigon and Washington on January 27, 1965, in *New York Times* and *Washington Post*. The estimates compare

favorably with those revealed in an article filed much earlier from Saigon by Peter Grose in *New York Times*, November 2, 1964.

[24] Philip Geyelin, *Lyndon B. Johnson and the World* (New York: Praeger, 1966), p. 193. See also policy commentary in editorial, *St. Louis Post-Dispatch*, November 8, 1964; Max Freedman, *Evening Star* (Washington), November 14, 1964; and Keyes Beech, *St. Louis Post-Dispatch*, January 18, 1965.

[25] *New York Times*, November 8, 1964. See also views reportedly expressed by Ambassador Taylor, *ibid.*, November 25 and 27, 1964, and White House policy decision reported *ibid.*, December 6 and 7, 1964.

[26] Compare John Finney's report of initial reactions, *New York Times*, January 28, 1965, with the editorial and with Seymour Topping's report of "sour" contingency preparations in Saigon *ibid.*, January 31, 1965. See Max Frankel, *ibid.*, February 2, 1965; also the belief in strong South Vietnamese neutralist sentiment recalled by Thomson, "How Could Vietnam Happen?" p. 51, and the impressions of Geyelin, *Johnson and the World*, p. 215.

[27] United States-Soviet conversations occurred between Secretary Rusk and Foreign Minister Gromyko on December 2, 3, and 5, and again on December 9. On the latter occasion, the discussion of Vietnam was described as "lively conversation." Also on December 9, Mr. Gromyko spent more than an hour with President Johnson. See *Washington Post*, December 4 and 10, 1964, and *Christian Science Monitor*, December 11, 1964. Soviet aid was pledged to North Vietnam in a Gromyko letter of December 30, reported in *New York Times*, January 5, 1965. The pledges were reported on January 17 and 22. See *Washington Post*, January 18, 1965, and *New York Times*, January 23, 1965.

[28] President Johnson's message to Congress, requesting enactment of a resolution to resist aggression in Southeast Asia, August 5, 1964, in *Department of State Bulletin*, August 24, 1964, p. 262. For impressions of reactions to the lack of a response to Viet Cong attacks on Bien Hoa and the Brink Hotel, see Geyelin, *Johnson and the World*, pp. 199–201; Edward Weintal and Charles Bartlett, *Facing the Brink* (New York: Charles Scribner's Sons, 1967), pp. 75–76; Townsend Hoopes, *The Limits of Intervention* (New York: David McKay Co., 1969), pp. 27–28; and comments by Robert McNamara in interview with Henry F. Graff, "How Johnson Makes Foreign Policy," *New York Times Magazine*, July 4, 1965.

[29] He made almost identical statements in addresses before the American Bar Association, New York, August 12, 1964; at a political gathering near his ranch in Texas, August 29, 1964; at Eufaula, Oklahoma, September 25, 1964; at Manchester, New Hampshire, September 28, 1964; and at Akron, Ohio, September 30, 1964.

[30] See Hanson Baldwin in *New York Times*, November 29, 1964; Laurence Barrett, *New York Herald Tribune*, November 29, 1964; and John Norris, *Washington Post*, February 11, 1965. See also Geyelin, *Johnson and the World*, p. 215, and Thomson, "How Could Vietnam Happen?" p. 52.

[31] See Rusk interview on NBC, January 3, 1965, *Department of State Bulletin*, p. 64, and Secretary McNamara's testimony before the House Armed Services Committee, February 18, 1965, reported in *Washington Post*, February 19, 1965. Many observers in Western Europe, in Japan, and in India viewed the Vietnamese conflict as a continuation of the Vietnamese revolution and as having little influence on Chinese expansionism if it remained confined to Vietnam and Laos.

[32] Hanson Baldwin, *New York Times*, November 29, 1964, and February 10, 1965; John Norris, *Washington Post*, February 11 and 13, 1965. Cor-

roborated by Wheeler and McConnell testimony, August 16 and 22, 1967, "Air War Against North Vietnam," Part II, p. 141, and Part III, p. 212.

33 Administration concern over the build-up of Communist forces in Laos was reported in *New York Times*, January 23, 1965, and *Evening Star* (Washington), January 24, 1965.

34 See Charles Mohr, *New York Times*, December 2, 1964, and the remarks attributed to Ambassador Taylor *ibid.*, December 4, 1964, and in *Christian Science Monitor*, December 5, 1964. Also the policy position implemented by officials in the Saigon Mission as reported by Takashi Oka, *ibid.*, December 14, 1964.

35 In response to an Associated Press survey of the United States Senate, Republicans Miller (Iowa), Thurmond (S. Carolina), and Tower (Texas) and Democrat Sparkman (Alabama) urged carrying the war to the North as a means of halting deterioration of the effort to counter Communist aggression in South Vietnam, reported in *New York Times*, January 7, 1965. During the mid-January debates on United States air operations in Laos, Senator Long (D., Louisiana) and Representative Ford (R., Michigan) argued that such actions were necessary to the success of our policy and were the kind of actions needed to protect our forces in South Vietnam. See *Washington Post*, January 18, 1965. On January 26, 1965, Richard Nixon proposed United States air and naval operations in North Vietnam and Laos to avoid being "thrown out [of Vietnam] . . . within the year" in *New York Times*, January 27, 1965.

36 Max Frankel, *ibid.*, February 3, 1965.

37 McGeorge Bundy's statement to the GVN in a story filed from Saigon *ibid.*, February 5, 1965; his statements to reporters in Charles Mohr, *ibid.*, February 9, 1965. Bundy's later statements are reported by Tom Wicker, *JFK and LBJ: Influence of Personality Upon Politics* (New York: William Morrow & Co., 1968), pp. 258–259. In 1968 Bundy recalled that "the basic decision of 1965" had as its object "the avoidance of defeat in Southeast Asia," at the DePauw University symposium on "Law, Liberty and Progress," October 12, 1968, reported in *New York Times*, October 13, 1968).

38 Richard Goodwin, *Triumph or Tragedy: Reflections on Vietnam* (New York: Vintage Books, 1966), p. 31. See also Hoopes, *The Limits of Intervention*, p. 29.

39 For descriptions of United States aims and actions in Laos since May 1964, see Seymour Topping, "The Twilight War in Laos," *New York Times*, January 24, 1965. Thai concerns regarding United States policy and its version of the "domino theory" were expressed by Foreign Minister Thanat Khoman in an interview at the United Nations on December 10, and reported in *Washington Post*, December 11, 1964.

40 Tad Szulc, *New York Times*, January 4, 1965.

41 See Jack Raymond, *ibid.*, December 27, 1964, and *Washington Post*, January 4, 1965.

42 E. W. Kenworthy, *New York Times*, January 16, 1965, and *Washington Post*, January 18, 1965. The account of United States air operations in Laos was filed over U.P.I. wire service by correspondent Arthur Dommen on January 14, 1965.

43 Wicker, *JFK and LBJ*, p. 205.

44 *Ibid.*, p. 255; Geyelin, *Johnson and the World*, pp. 218–219, 222; Charles Roberts, *LBJ's Inner Circle* (New York: Delacorte Press, 1965), p. 23. This one element of the Johnson style is well documented by Rowland Evans and Robert Novak in *Lyndon B. Johnson: The Exercise of Power* (New York: The New American Library, 1966).

45 Wicker, *JFK and LBJ*, p. 255; Max Frankel, *New York Times*, February 3, 1965. See also a story filed before the Pleiku attack from Saigon by Seymour Topping *ibid.*, February 7, 1965. In "The Very Expensive Education of McGeorge Bundy," *Harper's Magazine*, July 1969, pp. 34–35, David Halberstam relates how members of the administration had coalesced about the policy position of escalating the war and how Bundy's own views had hardened in support of retaliatory bombing during his visit to South Vietnam.

46 Geyelin, *Johnson and the World*, p. 216.

47 Reprinted in *Department of State Bulletin*, February 22, 1965, p. 238.

48 Ambassador Adlai Stevenson to President of the Security Council Roger Seydoux, February 7, 1965, *ibid.*, pp. 240–241.

49 Secretary McNamara, Pentagon news conference, February 7, 1965, from a Department of Defense news release. Secretary Ball's remarks were made at the same conference.

50 Reported by Max Frankel in *New York Times*, February 8, 1965.

51 McNamara at Pentagon news conference, Department of Defense news release, February 7, 1965.

52 Reprinted in *Department of State Bulletin*, February 22, 1965, p. 238.

53 Stevenson to Seydoux, February 7, 1965, *Department of State Bulletin*, February 22, 1965, pp. 240–241.

54 Reprinted in *Department of State Bulletin*, February 22, 1965, p. 239.

55 Pentagon news conference, February 7, 1965.

56 Reported by Charles Mohr in *New York Times*, February 9, 1965.

57 See Max Frankel, *ibid.*, February 9, 1965.

58 See Tad Szulc, *ibid.*, February 10, 1965.

59 *Ibid.*, February 9, 1965.

60 *Ibid.*, February 10, 1965. See also John Norris, *Washington Post*, February 11, 1965.

61 See James Reston, *New York Times*, February 9, 1965, also Tom Wicker, *ibid.*, February 11, 1965, and Murrey Marder, *Washington Post*, February 11, 1965.

62 White House press release, February 11, 1965, reproduced in *Department of State Bulletin*, March 1, 1965, p. 290.

63 Charles Mohr, *New York Times*, February 12, 1965.

64 See Murrey Marder, *Washington Post*, Richard Fryklund, *Evening Star* (Washington), and William Beecher, *Wall Street Journal*, February 12, 1965; John Norris, *Washington Post*, February 13, 1965; John Finney, *New York Times*, February 14, 1963.

65 Taylor's interviews in Saigon by the Mutual Broadcasting System and the Columbia Broadcasting System were reported in *New York Times*, February 14 and 15, 1965, respectively.

66 Tad Szulc, *ibid.*, February 15, 1965. See also James Reston, *ibid.*, February 12, 1965, and Murrey Marder, *Washington Post*, February 19, 1965.

67 See in particular the columns of James Reston and Walter Lippmann and the editorials of leading newspapers for the period.

68 See James Reston, February 12; John Finney, February 14; Max Frankel and Tad Szulc, February 14 (all in *New York Times*, 1965). Townsend Hoopes, *The Limits of Intervention*, pp. 29–30, attributes the lack of policy clarity to a deliberate effort by President Johnson to make the emerging intervention appear as a mere continuation of existing commitments — to avoid any appearance of consciously increasing the commitments.

69 Max Frankel, *New York Times*, February 24, 1965.

70 Louis Harris, *Washington Post*, February 22, 1965. A Gallup poll completed on February 27 indicated similar results; about two-thirds of those

polled approved specific United States actions in Vietnam and urged a continuation of its present efforts (reported in *New York Herald Tribune*, March 1, 1965).

71 John Finney, *New York Times*, February 22, 1965.

72 Reported from Saigon by Jack Foisie in *Los Angeles Times*, February 24, 1965.

73 Story filed from Saigon in *Baltimore Sun*, February 22, 1965. Details of the capture of this ship and its cargo were included in the State Department White Paper, "Aggression from the North," released on February 27.

74 From a prepared statement issued at Secretary Rusk's news conference, February 25, in *Washington Post*, February 26, 1965.

75 "Aggression from the North — The Record of North Vietnam's Campaign to Conquer South Vietnam," *Department of State Publication 7839*, February 27, 1965.

76 "News of the Week in Review," *New York Times*, February 28, 1965. For the Saigon Embassy's statement of February 24, see *Department of State Bulletin*, March 15, 1965, pp. 371–372.

77 In *New York Times*, March 2, 1965.

78 Max Frankel, *ibid.*, March 3, 1965. See also Chalmers Roberts, *Washington Post*, March 3, 1965.

79 John Norris, *Washington Post*, March 3, 1965.

80 See Chalmers Roberts, *ibid.*; Peter Grose, *New York Times*, March 4, 1965; Robert Kleiman, *ibid.*, March 8, 1965.

81 Jack Raymond, *ibid.*, March 3, 1965. See also Chalmers Roberts, *Washington Post*, March 3, 1965. That this kind of argument was being made by the Joint Chiefs of Staff has been confirmed in the testimony of Generals McConnell and Wheeler before the Senate Committee on Armed Services, August 1967.

82 Robert Kleiman, *New York Times*, March 1, 1965.

83 See Philip Geyelin, *Wall Street Journal*, February 23, 1965; Chalmers Roberts, *Washington Post*, February 26, 1965; "News of the Week in Review," *New York Times*, February 28, 1965.

84 See *Washington Post*, February 18 and 23, 1965.

85 Evans and Novak, *The Exercise of Power*, p. 537.

86 For the former view, see *New York Times* editorials for February 1 and 7, 1965, and the views of some officials reported by Tad Szulc, *ibid.*, February 2, 1965. For the latter view, see Robert Brunn, *Christian Science Monitor*, February 2, 1965, and Z. Brzezinski's letter to the editor (replying to the February 7 editorial), *New York Times*, February 16, 1965.

87 The pro-negotiation view was reported by Stephen Rosenfeld in *Washington Post*, February 18, 1965. For the anti-negotiation view, see Henry Tanner, *New York Times*, February 19, 1965.

88 *Baltimore Sun*, February 19, 1965.

89 Reported by Murrey Marder in *Washington Post*, February 24, 1965. See also the account, from London, of the British exploratory note passed to the Soviet government on February 20, by Anthony Lewis, *New York Times*, March 8, 1965.

90 See Paul Ward, *Baltimore Sun*, February 24, 1965, and Murrey Marder, *The Washington Post*, February 24, 1965.

91 From a transcript of the CBS program, "Face the Nation," March 7, 1965, in *Department of State Bulletin*, March 29, 1965, p. 445. The preceding Rusk references are also found *ibid.*, March 15, pp. 363–364, and March 22, p. 402, respectively.

[92] *New York Times*, February 21, 1965. For more on the French diplomatic visit, see Max Frankel and Jack Raymond, *ibid.*, February 20 and 22, respectively.

[93] At the Cleveland Council on World Affairs, Cleveland, Ohio, reported *ibid.*, March 7, 1965.

[94] See Max Frankel, *ibid.*, March 11 and 12, 1965. The meeting was held on March 10 and was attended by the president, Secretaries McNamara and Rusk, and Presidential Assistant McGeorge Bundy.

[95] Max Frankel, *ibid.*, March 16, 1965.

[96] See *ibid.*, March 4 and 8, 1965. See also Mark Watson, *Baltimore Sun*, March 9, 1965.

[97] Max Frankel, *New York Times*, March 11 and 12, 1965.

[98] Thomas Hamilton, *ibid.*, February 25, 1965.

[99] During a press conference following his major policy speech on February 25, 1965, in *Department of State Bulletin*, March 15, 1965, p. 364.

[100] Tad Szulc, *New York Times*, April 5, 1965.

[101] The president's statement was made in the context of a White House press release following a meeting of the Cabinet. For its full text and reporters' comments, see Murrey Marder, *Washington Post*, March 26, 1965, and Bernard Gwertzman, *Evening Star* (Washington), March 26, 1965.

[102] McGeorge Bundy's statement occurred on NBC's "Meet the Press" broadcast, reported by Tad Szulc in *The New York Times*, April 5, 1965.

[103] From the text of address by President Johnson at the Johns Hopkins University in Baltimore, Maryland, April 1965, reprinted in *Department of State Bulletin*, April 26, 1965, p. 608.

[104] See Max Frankel and Charles Mohr, *New York Times*, April 8, 1965, and the summary account in "News of the Week in Review," *ibid.*, April 11, 1965.

[105] In an address dedicating the Gary Job Corps Center, San Marcos, Texas, April 10, 1965, in *Department of State Bulletin*, May 3, 1965, p. 653.

[106] See Max Frankel, *New York Times*, April 8, 1965.

[107] *Ibid.*, April 11, 1965. The Soviets had taken an uncooperative position as early as March 19.

[108] Dan Kurzman, *Washington Post*, April 12, 1965. See also *New York Times* story, filed from Hong Kong on this same date. Ball insisted that the only reply that would count would be Hanoi's as yet undelivered answer to a formal request from seventeen non-aligned nations that the Vietnam problem be settled through negotiations without preconditions.

[109] To news correspondents at Johnson City, Texas, April 17, 1965, in *New York Times*, April 18, 1965.

[110] News report and text of seventeen-nation appeal in *New York Times*, April 2, 1965. Text of the United States reply in *Department of State Bulletin*, April 26, 1965, pp. 610–611.

[111] At a banquet in Philadelphia, where he received an annual Peace Award from Temple University, reported in *New York Times*, April 3, 1965. For the president's reaction to this event, see Evans and Novak, *The Exercise of Power*, p. 546.

[112] In *New York Herald Tribune*, March 18, 1965. See also *Newsweek*, March 29, 1965.

[113] Soviet disinterest in cease-fire discussions was announced by British Foreign Minister Michael Stewart following discussions with President Johnson, March 23, 1965, and was reported by Max Frankel in *New York Times*,

March 24, 1965. The new Senate proposals were reported in *Washington Post*, March 26, 1965.

114 Evans and Novak, *The Exercise of Power*, pp. 541–542. These authors have placed the timing of the president's decision to make public the proposal for "unconditional discussions" as just prior to April 2, 1965. If their view is accurate, the decision would have been made concurrent with a high-level strategy conference convened in Washington on March 29.

115 Geyelin, *Johnson and the World*, p. 219. See also Evans and Novak, *The Exercise of Power*, p. 546.

116 President Johnson at Johns Hopkins, *Department of State Bulletin*, April 26, 1965, pp. 607–608. Some experienced White House observers viewed this part of the president's speech as indicating a fundamental element in the administration's newly announced policy. Having offered a positive economic inducement to show Hanoi that material advantages could result from a peaceful settlement of the Vietnam problem, he made explicit the American commitment to maintain active military pressure until an acceptable solution was found. See David Lawrence, *New York Herald Tribune*, and William S. White, *Washington Post*, both April 9, 1965; see also Max Frankel, *New York Times*, April 8, 1965.

117 Tad Szulc, *New York Times*, April 5, 1965.

118 *Department of State Bulletin*, March 15, 1965, pp. 371–372. See also Richard Fryklund, *Evening Star* (Washington), February 25, 1965.

119 On "Face the Nation," March 7, from *Department of State Bulletin*, March 29, 1965, p. 442.

120 Reported from London by Seymour Freidin, in *New York Herald Tribune*, March 1, 1965.

121 From Saigon, in *Baltimore Sun*, March 5, 1965.

122 Reported from Saigon by Jack Langguth in *New York Times*, March 8 and 9, 1965.

123 Jack Langguth, *ibid.*, March 13, 1965. For troop deployment rumors reported from Washington, see also Jack Raymond, *ibid.*, March 12, 1965.

124 See Jack Raymond and Peter Grose, *ibid.*, March 3 and 4, 1965, respectively. See also Jack Foisie, *Los Angeles Times*, March 4, 1965.

125 See Jack Raymond, *New York Times*, March 17, 1965.

126 Communist infiltration was reported from Pleiku, South Vietnam, by Seth King, *ibid.*, March 16, 1965. The United States Mission report was cited in *Washington Post*, March 18, 1965.

127 *Evening Star* (Washington), March 22, 1965.

128 See Tad Szulc, *New York Times*, March 29, 1965.

129 President Johnson's announcement was reprinted in *Department of State Bulletin*, April 5, 1965, pp. 488–489. That same source contains a statement by Secretary Rusk on March 19, expressing regret that the Soviet Union had declined to support the Geneva agreements of which it was a signatory. For accounts of the British-Soviet discussions, see *New York Times*, March 17, 1965; David Culhane, *Baltimore Sun*, March 19, 1965; and Paul Ward, *Baltimore Sun*, March 20, 1965.

130 Conference decisions reported by John Finney in *New York Times*, April 3, 1965. See also Tad Szulc, *ibid.*, April 2, 1965, for coverage of presidential comments.

131 For air war speculations see Tad Szulc and Charles Mohr, *ibid.*, March 29 and 30, 1965, respectively. Rumors of United States ground intervention were reported by Marquis Childs in *St. Louis Post-Dispatch*, April 1, 1965, Chalmers Roberts in *Washington Post*, April 2, 1965, and John Finney in *New York Times*, April 3, 1965.

[132] Tad Szulc, *ibid.*, April 2, 1965.

[133] John Finney, *ibid.*, April 3, 1965.

[134] The air attacks on April 9 and 23 and on May 8 involved more than 200 sorties each.

[135] Parts of Mr. Unger's speech to the Detroit Economics Club were quoted in *New York Times*, April 20, 1965. It is reproduced in full in *Department of State Bulletin*, May 10, 1965, pp. 712–719.

[136] See Philip Geyelin, *Wall Street Journal*, April 21, 1965.

[137] *Ibid.*

[138] *Philadelphia Inquirer* and *New York Times*, April 20, 1965.

[139] Reported in *Washington Post*, April 21 (from Honolulu), and April 22 (by Howard Margolis), 1965. See also Tom Wicker, *New York Times*, April 22, 1965.

[140] Reported by Howard Margolis, *Washington Post*, April 23, 1965.

[141] Murrey Marder, *Washington Post*, April 22, 1965.

[142] See Hanson Baldwin, *New York Times*, April 21, 1965; Philip Geyelin, *Wall Street Journal*, April 21, 1965; Howard Margolis, *Washington Post*, April 23, 1965; Jack Foisie, *ibid.*, April 25, 1965; and Chalmers Roberts, *ibid.*, April 26, 1965.

[143] Bill D. Moyers stated that "the President really believed there would be some alternative [to sending large numbers of ground troops] right up to the last minute until July of 1965," in his interview, *Atlantic Monthly* (July 1968), p. 30. For the president's announcement, see *New York Times*, July 29, 1965.

[144] See Hanson Baldwin, *ibid.*, April 21, 1965; Philip Geyelin, *Wall Street Journal*, April 21, 1965, and *Los Angeles Times*, April 21, 1965; also Jack Foisie (from Saigon), *Washington Post*, April 25, 1965.

[145] Foisie, *ibid.*, and Jack Langguth, *New York Times*, April 25, 1965.

[146] Philip Geyelin, *Wall Street Journal*, April 21, 1965; Murrey Marder, *Washington Post*, April 22, 1965; Tom Wicker, *New York Times*, April 22 and 25, 1965.

[147] *Department of State Bulletin*, May 17, 1965, pp. 750–751. Italics added.

[148] See Philip Geyelin, *Wall Street Journal*, April 21, 1965.

BIBLIOGRAPHY

Abel, Elie, *The Missile Crisis* (Philadelphia: J. B. Lippincott Co., 1966).

Baltimore Sun, February–April 1965.

Christian Science Monitor, September 1964, December 1964, February 1965.

Department of Defense news release, February 7, 1965.

Department of State Bulletin.

Department of State Publication 7839, "Aggression from the North — The Record of North Vietnam's Campaign to Conquer South Vietnam," February 27, 1965.

Evans, Rowland, and Robert Novak, *Lyndon B. Johnson: The Exercise of Power* (New York: The New American Library, 1966).

Evening Star (Washington), November 1964, January–March 1965.

Geyelin, Philip, *Lyndon B. Johnson and the World* (New York: Praeger, 1966).

Goodwin, Richard, *Triumph or Tragedy: Reflections on Vietnam* (New York: Vintage Books, 1966).

210   WILLIAM E. SIMONS

Graff, Henry F., "How Johnson Makes Foreign Policy," *New York Times Magazine*, July 4, 1965.
Halberstam, David, "The Very Expensive Education of McGeorge Bundy," *Harper's Magazine*, July 1969.
Hilsman, Roger, "Plea for 'Realism' in Southeast Asia," *New York Times Magazine*, August 23, 1964.
————, *To Move a Nation* (Garden City: Doubleday, 1967).
Hoopes, Townsend, *The Limits of Intervention* (New York: David McKay Co., 1969).
Janeway, Michael, "Bill Moyers Talks About LBJ, Power, Poverty, War and the Young," *Atlantic Monthly*, July 1968.
Life, November 27, 1964.
Los Angeles Times, February–April 1965.
New York Herald Tribune, November 1964, March 1965, April 1965.
New York Times, March 1964, September–December 1964, January–April 1965, July 1965, October 1968.
Newsweek, March 9, 1964, March 29, 1965.
Philadelphia Inquirer, April 20, 1965.
Roberts, Charles, *LBJ's Inner Circle* (New York: Delacorte Press, 1965).
Rostow, Walt W., *View from the Seventh Floor* (New York: Harper & Row, 1964).
St. Louis Post-Dispatch, November 1964, January 1965, April 1965.
Thomson, James C., Jr., "How Could Vietnam Happen?" *Atlantic Monthly*, April 1968.
U.S. Senate, 90th Congress, 1st Session, "Air War Against North Vietnam," *Hearings Before the Preparedness Investigating Subcommittee of the Committee on Armed Services*, Parts II and III.
Wall Street Journal, April 1964, December 1964, February 1965, April 1965.
Washington Post, December 1964, January–April 1965.
Weintal, Edward, and Charles Bartlett, *Facing the Brink* (New York: Charles Scribner's Sons, 1967).
Wicker, Tom, *JFK and LBJ: Influence of Personality upon Politics* (New York: William Morrow and Co., 1968).

5

Alexander L. George
COMPARISONS AND LESSONS

Kennedy's success in employing coercive diplomacy in the Cuban missile crisis may have encouraged members of the Johnson administration to believe in the winter of 1964–65 that some variant of this strategy could be used also against Hanoi. As William Simons suggests, some members of the administration assumed that since American power and resolution had succeeded in forcing the Soviet Union to back down in the Cuban crisis, a similar combination of power and will could surely be brought to bear against an infinitely weaker opponent, Hanoi. The learning experience of the Cuban case was held generally applicable even though the administration recognized that the conflict in Vietnam differed in many respects from the missile crisis. Indeed, the two conflicts bore only the most superficial resemblance to each other. To pass over the differences between them in assessing the feasibility of coercive diplomacy against Hanoi was to ignore the basic fact, stressed in Chapter One, that this strategy, more than any other strategy, is highly context-dependent.

I. LAOS AND VIETNAM

Actually, the kind of situation in Vietnam that faced the Johnson administration in the winter of 1964–65 did have an analogue in recent history. But the analogous situation was the Laos crisis of 1961, not the Cuban missile crisis. Laos and Vietnam were both cases of internal war between rival political forces that were, in turn, receiving limited assistance from outside powers. Both of these internal wars, moreover, had been going extremely badly for the side to which the United States had already committed itself.*

Faced with a losing situation in Laos, we have seen, President Kennedy substantially reduced the objective which the previous administration had been pursuing in that conflict. Kennedy judged that the victory over the Communists that Eisenhower had initially sought in Laos was not important enough to United States interests to warrant more direct military intervention and the substantial additional resources and risks that it would entail. Kennedy reduced the objective, therefore, to neutralization of Laos and sought to prevent the advancing Communist forces from overrunning the key positions of the Royal Lao government. Moreover, it was only after he clearly formulated and communicated this shrunken objective to the opposing side that President Kennedy resorted to coercive diplomacy to induce acceptance of his demand for a cease-fire prior to negotiations.

In the winter of 1964–65 President Johnson was also faced with a losing, indeed desperate situation, this time in Vietnam. In contrast to the way in which Kennedy had handled this dilemma in Laos, Johnson did not reduce the ambitious objective of achieving victory in this internal war. Instead, he proceeded to use coercive diplomacy against Hanoi as part of a major American escalation of the war geared to the continuing objective of winning the war in South Vietnam. This was a much more ambitious use of the strategy of coercive diplomacy than that which Kennedy had made in the earlier Laos crisis. Kennedy had asked the other side merely to stop what it was doing; Johnson demanded, in

* An earlier, highly relevant historical analogue was the Chinese civil war which came to a head after the end of World War II. In that case Truman eventually made the difficult decision to draw the line against direct United States involvement. In attempting to deal with a similar situation in Vietnam, however, neither the Kennedy nor the Johnson administrations took their bearings from the precedent Truman had established in dealing with the Chinese civil war.

effect, that Hanoi undo what it had done and reverse the success it had already achieved.*

Johnson was pressed by his leading national security advisors — mostly holdovers from the Kennedy administration, who had by now developed important political and personal stakes in the United States commitment to South Vietnam — to employ air attacks against North Vietnam as part of a coercive diplomatic strategy against Hanoi. On the face of it, Johnson's demand was merely that Hanoi stop assistance to the Viet Cong. But in reality, since it became clear that Washington was committing itself to increased military involvement in the South on behalf of the Saigon government, Johnson in effect was calling on Hanoi to abandon the National Liberation Front and to stand aside while the United States made still additional efforts to enable Saigon to defeat the Viet Cong forces.

Clearly, Johnson was asking a great deal of Hanoi, for its leaders were on the threshhold of a great and long-awaited victory in the South. But the following paradox existed: on behalf of his exceedingly ambitious objective, Johnson exerted only a relatively weak form of the coercive diplomatic strategy, whereas on behalf of his more modest objective, Kennedy employed a stronger form of the coercive strategy. As David Hall shows, in late March and again in April 1961, Kennedy managed to convey some sense of urgency and a sufficiently credible threat of American intervention should the opponent fail to comply with his demand. But, as William Simons points out, "at no time [in February–April 1965] did the United States government explicitly threaten the DRV with increasing punishment or suggest eventual damage to its industrial capability if it did not comply. Neither did it attempt to convey any sense of urgency by indicating a period of time during which compliance would be expected" (p. 197). In effect, Johnson's attempt at coercive diplomacy did not go much beyond what we have called the try-and-see approach, whereas Kennedy's use of the strategy eventually verged upon a strong ultimatum variant of the strategy.

For a while, as Simons shows, the Johnson administration did try to convey the impression, without saying so, that its initial air

---

* This distinction between the two types of demands that can be made in coercive diplomacy is discussed in Chapter One, pp. 22–23.

attacks against North Vietnam might be gradually expanded to new and more important targets as part of a determined application of graduated escalation. But evidently this threat was not sufficiently credible to Hanoi, or else it did not constitute a sufficiently potent stick to persuade North Vietnam to curtail its help to the Viet Cong. In any case, Washington's bluff about an upward escalation of air attacks against highly valued industrial targets was called in mid-April by both Hanoi and Moscow, and the administration's response was to back away from implementing a strong variant of coercive strategy.

When its effort to use exemplary air attacks as a basis for coercive diplomacy failed, the administration might have been well advised to cease its air attacks against the North and to use air power, as it had before the attacks of February–April, as a means of deterring Hanoi from increasing its assistance to the Viet Cong. This policy alternative seems scarcely to have been considered in mid-April. Instead, as Simons shows (pp. 188–194), the administration's use of force on behalf of multiple and competing objectives provided considerable impetus for continuing the air operations. The air attacks were now reoriented toward a more traditional pattern of air interdiction on behalf of long-range attrition strategy against Hanoi that was substituted for the abortive effort at quick, economical coercion.

A curious paradox in the contrast we have just drawn between the Laos and Vietnam cases requires further discussion. We regard Kennedy's effort in Laos as an example of the strong variant of coercive diplomacy, and Johnson's effort against Hanoi in 1965 as an example of the relatively weak form of the strategy. We judge them to be strong and weak, respectively, even though the military action Kennedy actually undertook in Laos — ordering the United States advisers to put on their uniforms — was far more modest than the air attacks Johnson initiated against North Vietnam. For this reason some readers may object to, or become confused by, our labelling of Johnson's strategy as weak and Kennedy's strong. The paradox is, however, a genuine one. The strong-weak dimension applies to the form of the strategy, not to the magnitude of the action taken. The action taken is only one component of coercive diplomacy. The other components are a threat of additional, imminent action that is credible and potent enough for the task in question. As we noted in Chapter One (p. 28), even a relatively modest initial action, as in the Laos case, can have an unusually strong coercive impact on an opponent if it is coupled with a credible and potent enough threat of additional action to follow in short order if he does not comply with the demand made on him. Conversely, even a relatively strong initial action, as in the Vietnam case, may not have sufficient coercive impact if it is not coupled with this kind of credible and potent threat. This, then, serves to explain the paradox implicit in our designation of the form of coercive diplomacy employed by Kennedy in Laos as strong and that attempted by Johnson as weak. This paradox is but another reflection of the complexity of coercive diplomacy.

II. PRE-CONDITIONS FOR COERCIVE DIPLOMACY

Overlooking the profound differences between the Cuban and Vietnam cases, some critics have tried to argue that a stronger variant of coercive strategy should have been applied in the latter case. The hawks in the controversy over Vietnam policy, by no means confined to members of the military services, have been critical of the way in which Johnson initially used airpower against North Vietnam. They argue that he dissipated its potential coercive impact by engaging in too slow and too weak a form of graduated air escalation in February–April 1965.[1]

The question is: Could Johnson have employed air power as part of the stronger variant of coercive diplomacy? The hawks assume this was a viable option and that the administration is to be blamed for not resorting to it. This assumption is quite dubious. The strong form of coercive diplomacy cannot be considered to have been a real alternative because the pre-conditions for its adoption and success were lacking in this case. This emerges more clearly if we compare the situation surrounding Johnson's effort to coerce Hanoi with the contexts of the earlier Laos and Cuban cases.

Before proceeding with the comparison, it will be useful to state the major conclusion we will draw: *Only seldom — only when a special set of conditions is present, as in the Laos and Cuban cases — is it feasible for United States leaders to undertake and to succeed with the strong variant of coercive strategy,* what has been called the ultimatum approach.

What, then, are these special conditions? They emerge from comparative analysis of these three cases and of two other historical cases that we have not examined in as much detail.* We have identified eight conditions which seem to have causal importance. To the extent that these conditions are present in a crisis — and *all eight were present in the Cuban and Laos crises* — they favor adoption and successful implementation of the strong tacit-ultimatum form of coercive diplomacy. On the other hand, to the extent that the eight conditions are absent — and perhaps as many as six of them were missing in 1965 when Johnson attempted to coerce Hanoi, or were present in relatively weak form — then it is difficult and imprudent for American leaders to adopt the strong form of coercive diplomacy. If, nonetheless, they try to employ this strategy, as Johnson did in Vietnam, they risk having their bluff called or having to settle for the weak try-and-see form of the strategy, which may not suffice for the purpose and which may then degenerate into an attrition strategy.

Let us consider now each of these conditions and attempt to judge the extent to which they appear to have been present in each of the three crises. These judgments are admittedly impressionistic. However, they enable us to explore further the difficult problems inherent in attempts to make confident use of the strategy of coercive diplomacy.† The eight conditions are:

1. Strength of United States motivation
2. Asymmetry of motivation favoring the United States
3. Clarity of American objectives
4. Sense of urgency to achieve the American objective
5. Adequate domestic political support
6. Usable military options
7. Opponent's fear of unacceptable escalation
8. Clarity concerning the precise terms of settlement

1. Strength of United States Motivation

Obviously American leaders must be sufficiently motivated by what is at stake in a crisis to act at all and to accept the perceived

---

* The U.S. response to the North Korean attack against South Korea in June 1950 and to the Chinese artillery shelling of Quemoy in 1958. (See below, pp. 246–249.) Some of these conditions are also recognizable in Thomas C. Schelling's discussion of "compellance" in his *Arms and Influence* (New Haven: Yale University Press, 1966).

† Several simplifying procedures have had to be introduced into the analysis of these conditions. See *Appendix*, "Note on Theory and Methodology."

costs and risks of the action they decided upon. We are tempted to add that the stronger their motivation, the more likely it is that American leaders will resort to the strong variant of coercive diplomacy. That may be generally true, but the considerations affecting the president's choice between the try-and-see and ultimatum approaches are likely to be complex; they cannot be reduced to the single variable of national interest and motivation. United States leaders are more likely to resort to an ultimatum, as Kennedy finally did in the Cuban missile crisis, when truly vital national interests are perceived to be at stake. But it is not certain that a president will do so even when much is at stake. We have seen how difficult it was for Kennedy to bring himself to give Khrushchev an ultimatum in the Cuban missile case.

Nor can we say that the strong variant of coercive diplomacy will be adopted only when the national interest and motivation is so strong. Lesser motivation may suffice for the adoption of a strong coercive strategy, as in the Laos case in 1961, if other circumstances favor it. In other words, we must keep in mind not only that coercive diplomacy is highly context-dependent but that various interactions may occur among the pre-conditions for it.

Kennedy's motivation in Laos was not at all comparable with the much stronger motivation he experienced in the Cuban missile crisis. He was not sufficiently motivated to continue to pursue the overly ambitious objective of driving Communist influence out of Laos that the Eisenhower administration had set for itself. Kennedy became motivated strongly enough to exert coercive pressure only by reducing his objective to the aim of preventing, if possible, the complete defeat of the Royal Lao forces that was then taking place. Even the extent of his motivation on behalf of this lesser objective was not entirely clear. As Hall points out in his study of this case, there is some question as to what Kennedy would have done had the opponent not accepted his demand. Available materials do not exclude the possibility that Kennedy's strategy of coercive diplomacy in this instance rested in some, or even in considerable, measure upon bluff.

In the Cuban missile crisis, Kennedy was much more powerfully motivated; the stakes were higher both for the country and for himself personally. Moreover, as we have noted in our case study, his motivation grew even stronger when the U-2 was shot down over Cuba and it appeared that the crisis was getting out of hand. Then, out of a desperate desire to try to end the crisis before it erupted into war, Kennedy converted the try-and-see approach he had been following into an ultimatum to Khrushchev.

Turning to the Vietnam case, it is true that in early 1965 the Johnson administration was strongly motivated to avoid defeat in South Vietnam, a prospect which appeared to be imminent if the United States did not increase its military involvement. But Hanoi's assistance to the Viet Cong was not as important as the administration's inflated claims made it out to be, and the cessation of Hanoi's assistance would not immediately have reversed the trend of the war in the South. True, if Johnson could persuade or coerce Hanoi to write off the Viet Cong, the task of assisting Saigon to win the civil war in the South would become appreciably easier, but a considerable increase in American military participation in the South would still be required. This became clear particularly in March when alarming reports of the deterioration of the ground war in South Vietnam reached Washington. Thus, whether or not Hanoi withdrew its aid, the prospect was for a prolonged struggle in South Vietnam.

The administration's strong motivation in this crisis, therefore, was not focused entirely on the one objective of forcing Hanoi to stop assistance to the Viet Cong — as Kennedy had focused in the Cuban case on the dominant strategic objective of getting the missiles out. Moreover, despite the administration's rhetoric, vital American interests were not really at stake. The only reliable measurement of one's estimate of what is at stake in such crises is the costs and risks one is prepared to accept. There were costs and risks to giving Hanoi an ultimatum or employing strong forms of pressure against it that Johnson, quite understandably, was not prepared to accept.

We conclude that this first condition — strong United States motivation — was present in some sense in all three cases. While necessary, therefore, strong motivation is far from sufficient to ensure successful coercion of one's opponent.

2. Asymmetry of Motivation Favoring the United States

This condition is listed separately in order to highlight the fact that motivation is a two-sided matter. The theory of coercive diplomacy outlined in Chapter One and the individual case studies have already stressed the importance of the relative motivation of the two sides. The likelihood of successful coercion is greater if one side is more strongly motivated by what is at stake than its opponent, and, particularly, if its opponent is aware of this.

In some cases the relative motivation of the two sides tends to be fixed by the nature of the conflict and may not be subject to much manipulation by means of coercive diplomacy. In other crises, however, the side that engages in coercive diplomacy may be able to create an asymmetry of motivation in its own favor that leads to successful application of this strategy. As we emphasized in Chapter One (pp. 24–26), two levers are available to the coercing power for this purpose: (1) the choice of the demand made on the opponent and (2) the choice of the carrot offered him. In both the Laos and Cuban missile crises Kennedy made use of these levers in order to create an asymmetry of motivation in his own favor. The success of his coercive threats in these two cases cannot be properly understood without taking this into account.

In contrast, the Vietnam conflict did not provide Johnson with an asymmetry of motivation in his favor. Nor was what little he did to manipulate the levers adequate to alter the asymmetry of motivation more to his advantage. His efforts in this direction were not helped by what appears to have been an initial under-estimation of the extent to which Hanoi was motivated by what was at stake in South Vietnam. Some members of the administration were disposed to believe that Hanoi was not so strongly motivated to secure a Viet Cong victory in the South as to place at risk to American airpower its new industrial plant, its economy, and its military forces. Given this initial miscalculation, American policy-makers did not see the need to limit at the outset what they demanded of Hanoi or to offer a substantial and credible quid pro quo.

Besides, the very nature of the conflict in Vietnam, in contrast to Laos and the Cuban missile crisis, was such as to encourage both sides to perceive it as virtually a zero-sum conflict, one that either one or the other would have to win and one not easily susceptible to a compromise settlement. The basic question was who was going to govern South Vietnam, and given the internal instability in the South there appeared to be no half-way solutions between an anti-Communist and a Communist government. To the extent that both sides perceived the conflict in these terms it severely limited the opportunity available to the Johnson administration for manipulating the levers in order to create a favorable asymmetry of motivation. The structure of the situation seemed to drastically reduce the number of possible inducements that John-son could offer Hanoi that might suffice to persuade it to cut off its aid to the Viet Cong.

In the Laos crisis, we recall, Kennedy was able to neutralize the asymmetry of motivation that was operating in favor of the op-ponent by substantially shrinking his objective and making a rela-tively modest demand. In the Cuban missile crisis the asymmetry of motivation latent in the situation favored Kennedy, but he had to convince Khrushchev that he would act, if necessary, to prevent the expected damage to American interests arising from the de-ployment of missiles into Cuba. Kennedy's initial task in the crisis, therefore, was to alter Khrushchev's image of his determi-nation, which implementation of the blockade finally enabled him to do. Once having accomplished this tactical psychological objec-tive, Kennedy was then able to generate credible threats to give coercive impact to the ultimatum he finally gave Khrushchev.

In Vietnam it turned out, contrary to Washington's expecta-tions, that the asymmetry of motivation operated in Hanoi's favor. In Cuba Khrushchev did not test Kennedy further once the president gave him an ultimatum. In Vietnam, however, not only did Johnson's threats fall clearly short of an ultimatum, but the administration's bluff to engage in a sharp escalation of air attacks was called by Hanoi, and the administration responded with air attacks concentrated on scattered military targets in what was at most a slow step up in pressure. Having bluffed unsuccessfully that it was applying a strong variant of coercive diplomacy, the admin-istration then settled for a long-term attrition strategy.

We conclude that this second condition was sufficiently pres-ent in the Laos and Cuban cases, but clearly absent in the Viet-nam case.

3. Clarity of American Objectives

When a crisis occurs it will generally be difficult for policy-makers to decide how much and what kind of force to use unless they can first decide what objective they will pursue. Clarity as to the objec-tive, while perhaps not always essential, may be necessary in some situations if limited force is to be applied effectively on behalf of the strategy of coercive diplomacy.

In the Cuban case, Kennedy and his advisors found it difficult to choose among the various options under consideration until the president decided that the objective would be to secure the removal of the missiles, no more and no less. Other objectives were considered and discarded. The work of the Executive Committee in weighing alternative diplomatic-military moves was greatly facilitated because Kennedy's objective remained clear and consistent throughout the crisis.

In the Laos case, too, Hall finds that the clarity and consistency with which Kennedy was able to communicate his broad political objective, neutralization of Laos, contributed importantly to the eventual success of the effort at coercive persuasion.

In the Vietnam case, on the other hand, there was persistent opaqueness, and seeming inconsistency as to what Washington's objectives really were. Indeed, several different objectives were being pursued at once, and as Simons demonstrates, their nature and relative strengths changed from period to period. Efforts to convey a more modest, reasonable objective were not convincing to important and increasingly larger sectors of the American and Allied publics or, evidently, to Hanoi.

We conclude, therefore, that this third condition was satisfied in the Laos and Cuban cases but not in the case of Johnson's effort to coerce Hanoi.

4. Sense of Urgency to Achieve the American Objective

The presence of this condition is particularly important for motivating American leaders to adopt the strong ultimatum approach rather than the weaker try-and-see variant of the strategy.* And the opponent's perception of this sense of urgency is a critical factor in motivating him to credit American coercive threats with credibility and potency.

In the Laos crisis, Kennedy did experience some sense of urgency which he finally managed to convey to the other side even though he did not clearly define it. This was because the president's sense of urgency was of a special kind, one that was geared to events under the opponent's control rather than to some fixed calendar deadline. Kennedy cloaked his intentions with a measure of deliberate opaqueness as to just where he would draw the line against the advancing enemy forces. His objective was to prevent a total

---

* This is not to say that the absence of a sense of urgency excludes resort to the strong form of coercive diplomacy. For example, it would appear that on occasion Hitler resorted to ultimata even in the absence of a real, as against a manufactured, sense of urgency.

defeat and collapse of the Royal Lao forces and regime, but he refused to make public the exact geographical line or point of advance of the enemy forces that would trigger his decision to intervene. His reluctance to do so was motivated partly by a desire to conceal the extent of losses he was prepared to tolerate, partly by a hope that the resulting uncertainty would complicate the opponent's calculations and make him more cautious, and partly because he did not want to be explicitly committed to intervene if a clear line he had drawn was then violated. Nonetheless, he managed to convey some sense of urgency, evidently sufficient for the purpose, first to the Russians and then later, with their help, to the other members of the opposition as well. And this Kennedy did without having to give the opponent an explicit and short deadline as he had to do in the Cuban missile crisis.

In the Cuban crisis Kennedy's sense of urgency was motivated by his desire to secure the removal of the missiles before they became operational. Once again, therefore, his sense of urgency was geared to events under the opponent's control. In this situation, however, Khrushchev was not satisfied merely to continue work on the missile sites; he ordered the preparations speeded up, thus adding to rather than moderating the sense of urgency Kennedy was experiencing. Additional urgency for Kennedy, probably decisive in motivating him to resort to the ultimatum, was generated by the shooting down of a U-2 over Cuba and by other events on Saturday, October 27. These events confronted the president with the feeling that the possibility of managing the crisis without war was fast running out. The ultimatum, therefore, was a desperate effort to try to bring the crisis to a close, before the momentum of events unleashed war.

In Vietnam, as we have noted, the Johnson administration pursued multiple objectives that shifted somewhat over time. During most of February 1965 the administration's keenest sense of urgency was aroused by objectives other than coercing Hanoi. Basically it was not urgent from the American standpoint that Hanoi cease its aid to the Viet Cong immediately. However, particularly in March and early April, although to some extent also in February, Johnson did try to give Hanoi the impression that air operations would be gradually or perhaps not so gradually expanded to new targets as part of a strong, determined application of graduated escalation. But no time limit and at most only a moderate sense of urgency was conveyed, which the slow pace of air operations itself further weakened by giving the impression of creeping escalation. (We shall consider later some of the reasons for the administration's failure, or perhaps unwillingness, to create a sense of urgency at all comparable to that in the Laos and Cuban crises.)

It is important that in both Laos and Cuba, Kennedy was able to manufacture events that conveyed to the opponent the urgency of the situation. He employed a set of highly coordinated diplomatic maneuvers for this purpose. In regard to Laos, he used SEATO meetings; talks with Nehru, MacMillan, Gromyko; Soviet-British talks. In regard to Cuba he used OAS meetings and resolutions; activity in the United Nations; personal envoys to European leaders. These moves undoubtedly reinforced for Soviet leaders the seriousness and urgency of the problem at hand. In contrast, there appears to have been a total neglect of such moves at the commencement of the bombing of North Vietnam, and in fact the administration spurned diplomatic channels.[2]

We find, once again, that this condition favoring the adoption and successful implementation of strong coercive diplomacy was present to a sufficient degree in the Laos and Cuban crises but not in Johnson's action against Hanoi.

5. Adequate Domestic Political Support

A certain level of political support at home is needed for whatever objective American leaders choose to pursue in a crisis and for the military-diplomatic measures they decide to employ on its behalf. However, the subjective aspect of this requirement is particularly important since what counts is how the president perceives public support and chooses to be guided by it. If he perceives political support to be inadequate, he may feel constrained to pursue only the minimal objective of hanging on to avoid defeat; further, inadequate public support may severely constrain him in his choice of military means to achieve even those minimum objectives.

The requirements for domestic support in a democracy are particularly stringent for the kind of strong coercive strategy, with its attendant risks, that Kennedy applied in the Cuban missile crisis. Obviously public opinion strongly supported the president during this tense but short crisis. (Whether Kennedy would have continued to enjoy strong domestic support had the Cuban crisis been prolonged, which could easily have happened had Khrushchev suspended work on the missile sites, is another matter. This would have removed the basis for the sense of urgency necessary to Kennedy's coercive strategy and, at the same time, allowed the Soviet leader to engage in prolonged, hard bargaining to make Kennedy pay a bigger price for the removal of the missiles.)

We have not looked closely at the nature and magnitude of public support for Kennedy's handling of the Laos crisis. It appears, as Hall suggests, to have been adequate for Kennedy's purposes. Certainly the president's dramatic TV presentation of March 23, regarding the dimensions of the Laos crisis and the possible need for United States action, did not boomerang so far as American public opinion is concerned. Moreover, there is little indication that lack of domestic support was considered worrisome by the president or served to constrain him in applying his strategy. On the other hand, possibly the crisis was prolonged because some members of the opposing alliance believed that Kennedy lacked sufficient support at home to put into effect his threatened intervention. Whatever the limitations of domestic public support, however, they would appear to have been compensated for by more favorable factors present in the situation.

As for Vietnam, Johnson was concerned from the beginning that he lacked sufficient domestic support to engage in air escalation against Hanoi and to enter into a substantial commitment of American forces to South Vietnam. Certainly he attempted to develop further support and to maintain it.* It is entirely possible that he decided upon a slow, step-by-step escalation of the American involvement for this reason, although there were also other, perhaps more important considerations for doing so.

We conclude, once again, that this condition was present in the Laos and Cuban crises but not in Vietnam.

6. Usable Military Options

We include this condition in order to call attention to the fact that special kinds of military capabilities are often needed for coercive diplomacy. We distinguished in Chapter One between gross military capabilities and usable options. That distinction is relevant here. The United States possesses ample gross military capabilities to do various kinds of damage to a variety of targets. The requirements for usable options, however, are more stringent than this and often difficult to satisfy in practice. For military

---

* For an indication of Johnson's close attention to public opinion at the outset of this escalation see Chapter Four, pp. 151, 154–155, 160–162, 168–169.

capabilities to be usable in a crisis which the president wishes to manage carefully, he must be satisfied that they will do the job in the way he thinks appropriate or necessary — i.e., in a controlled, discriminating manner.

In all three crises we have studied, the president and his advisers applied special political and military criteria for developing and selecting military options. Usable options were available, at least initially, in all three crises. Kennedy was reluctant in Laos, and again in the Cuban crisis, to use up his last remaining controlled, discrete options. And in both cases, particularly with respect to the blockade option in the Cuban missile crisis, he and his advisers were ingenious in creating a larger number of smaller options out of a large one. In Vietnam, too, one might say, the Johnson administration created additional options by deliberately spacing out in smaller steps over a longer period of time the coercive air campaign against Hanoi.

Since usable options were available in all three cases, this condition does not serve to account for the variance in the nature and outcome of the coercive strategy employed by Kennedy and Johnson.

7. Opponent's Fear of Unacceptable Escalation

Coercive diplomacy is enhanced if the initial small steps taken against the opponent begin to arouse his fear of unacceptable levels of warfare. This happened, certainly, in both the Laos and Cuban crises. In the Laos case, American military maneuvers of March 23, 1961, evidently stirred considerable anxiety in the Russian leaders and further motivated them to play the broker's role that was all-important for the success of Kennedy's strategy. Later, at a critical juncture in the developing Laos situation Kennedy ordered the three hundred American civilian advisors in Laos to put on their uniforms and to accompany the Royal Lao Army to the combat zones. This move appears to have made a significant impression on Peking and Hanoi as constituting a signal of Washington's resolution and as the first step in what might prove to be large-scale American military intervention. Within a matter of days Peking and Hanoi finally agreed to negotiate.

In the Cuban case, it may have been the United States Navy's harassment of Soviet submarines escorting vessels bound for Cuba that impressed Soviet leaders with Kennedy's determination and with the danger of escalation should the Soviet government attempt to force the blockade by refusing to submit to boarding and inspection procedures. Later in the crisis, Kennedy's threat of an air strike or invasion was regarded as credible by Soviet leaders, and hence their fear of unacceptable escalation became influential.

In the Vietnam case, the initial American air attacks against the North created concern and hesitation, particularly on the part of the Soviets who displayed interest for a while in arranging negotiations. As for Hanoi, it is true that these initial attacks aroused considerable apprehension as to the danger of further escalation. However, this did not suffice to persuade the North Vietnam government to enter into negotiations, let alone call off its assistance to the Viet Cong, because Hanoi was so strongly motivated by what was at stake. In addition, it would seem that Hanoi did not believe that Washington would engage in unlimited air attacks or follow them with a ground invasion, if necessary. For these reasons, we surmise, American actions and words did not arouse fear of unacceptable escalation.

This condition, then, was satisfied in the Laos and Cuban cases but not in the action against Hanoi.

8. Clarity Concerning the Precise Terms of Settlement

Clarity regarding the political objective being pursued (condition 3) may not suffice. In addition, it may be necessary in some, though not all, cases to formulate rather specific demands on the opponent and to accompany them at some point with detailed terms of compliance. Specificity and clarity of demands may facilitate coercive diplomacy from two different standpoints. First, as Thomas Schelling has emphasized, specificity may increase the coercive impact of a demand, somewhat paradoxically, by assuring the opponent as to what is not being required of him.[3] Second, specificity is useful insofar as it pins down the precise obligations the opponent agrees to undertake if he accepts the demand made on him.

In Laos, Kennedy made clear his terms of compliance, an effective and verified cessation of hostilities prior to an international conference, and this appears to have been influential in the achievement of a negotiated settlement. Kennedy was also able in the Cuban missile case — more so than Johnson, who was faced with a far more intricate situation in Vietnam — to formulate not only specific demands and an explicit quid pro quo, but also explicit and verifiable terms for compliance with his demand for removal of the missiles. The latter helped to assure that he actually got what he wanted from Khrushchev by reducing the opportunity for Khrushchev to agree in principal but to renege by disagreeing later on the all-important details.

This condition, therefore, was satisfied in the Laos and Cuban crises but not in the Vietnam case. The judgments made in the preceding pages as to whether the eight conditions were present or absent in the three cases are summarized in Table 1.

TABLE 1. *Presence of Conditions Favoring Successful Outcome of Coercive Diplomacy in Three Crises*

	Laos 1961	Cuba 1962	Vietnam 1965
1. Strength of United States motivation	+	+	+
2. Asymmetry of motivation favoring United States	+	+	
3. Clarity of American objectives	+	+	
4. Sense of urgency to achieve American objective	+	+	
5. Adequate domestic political support	+	+	
6. Usable military options	+	+	+
7. Opponent's fear of unacceptable escalation	+	+	
8. Clarity concerning the precise terms of settlement	+	+	

Not all of these conditions would appear to be equally important for coercive diplomacy. Three seem particularly significant in affecting the outcome: asymmetry of motivation favoring the United States; a sense of urgency behind the demand made on the opponent; and the opponent's fear that unacceptable escalation may take place. The perceptions of these three variables, particularly by the opponent, appear to be critical in shaping the success or failure of coercive diplomacy. The possibility of misperception by either or both sides is present and can affect the outcome in either direction. Thus, American leaders may misperceive the asymmetry of motivation as operating in their favor. While an erroneous perception that this condition is satisfied would favor adoption of coercive diplomacy, the fact that the opponent's motivation was really stronger relative to that of American leaders would increase the likelihood that coercive diplomacy would fail.

Misperception of a condition could operate in the opposite direction. Thus, the opponent might attribute to American leaders a stronger sense of urgency to achieve their objective in the crisis than was, in fact, the case. Such a misperception of this variable could affect the opponent's behavior in such a way as to contribute to the success of the United States effort at coercing him.

Thus, while American leaders' perceptions of the presence of these three conditions are most directly relevant in accounting for the adoption of the strategy, the opponent's perceptions of them become more important in determining the success or failure of the effort at coercive diplomacy. The numerous possibilities for misperception in coercive diplomacy enormously complicate the task for both the policy-maker and the investigator.

Thus far in our analysis we have identified and discussed eight conditions whose presence in a situation favors the adoption and success of the strategy of coercive diplomacy. But by no means does the presence of these conditions guarantee success. Other requirements, having to do with additional variables, must also be met. We turn to these in the next section.

III. PROBLEMS OF OPERATIONALIZING COERCIVE DIPLOMACY

We emphasized in Chapter One the limited utility for policy-making of even a well-formulated theory of coercive diplomacy. Any theory is necessarily stated in somewhat abstract, generalized terms. A theoretical, text-book model of coercive diplomacy such as we outlined in Chapter One is useful up to a point. It identifies critical variables and factors and depicts the general relationships among them. But it does not and cannot say very much about the feasibility of applying the text-book model in particular cases. The limitations of a theoretical model are particularly severe in the case of coercive diplomacy. For, more so than any other strategy for using force as an instrument of diplomacy, the strategy of coercive diplomacy is highly context-dependent. The meaning and full implications of this fact require discussion.

No theory, of course, can provide blueprints either to ensure good judgment in deciding whether coercive diplomacy is a viable strategy in any particular situation or to ensure skillful implementation of the strategy in the variety of complex situations where it seems applicable. Being highly context-dependent, coercive diplomacy must be tailored in a rather exacting manner to fit the unique configuration of each individual situation. Tailoring force to diplomacy is a difficult enough skill to begin with; it is also a skill that is not easily acquired. Even if that skill is available within the presidential circle and even if it survives the clash that typically occurs among competing viewpoints and judgments within the policy-making group, the skill of tailoring the strategy of coercive diplomacy to a given situation cannot be exercised successfully unless the special configuration of that situation is clearly understood.

But it is precisely the special configuration of the crisis situation — the values of the various critical variables identified in the theory — that is seldom clearly visible to the policy-maker. As a result, the policy-maker must tailor somewhat in the dark, guessing at some of the dimensions that must be fitted by the strategy being developed, hoping for but not certain of having opportunities for correcting one's initial errors and first approximations by successive fittings and alterations — all the while with an uncooperative subject who quite rightly regards what is being tailored for him as a straitjacket rather than an attractive suit of clothes.

For these reasons, again more so than with other strategies, the effort to devise and employ coercive diplomacy rests heavily upon the skill at improvisation. It is extremely difficult — and dangerous — to pre-plan coercive diplomacy as if it were a standardized military campaign. There was, as our case studies indicate, a large and necessary element of improvisation by the president in all three crises. So far as we can judge from available materials, there was very little pre-crisis planning for Kennedy's handling of the Laos and Cuban missile crises. The important planning for the response to the Soviet missile deployment to Cuba took place on a crash basis during the six days following discovery of the missiles. Earlier contingency plans were evidently confined to military options such as invasion; the possibility of responding to a hypothetical Soviet missile deployment by means of coercive diplomacy apparently did not enter into pre-crisis military planning.

The Vietnam crisis, on the other hand, developed much more slowly and offered plenty of time for a variety of contingency planning. As contemporary newspaper accounts throughout 1964 make clear, much of the year preceding Johnson's decision to use air power against Hanoi was taken up with studies within the government of alternative strategies for coping with the gradually deteriorating political and military situations in South Vietnam. Not merely military planning of the traditional kind, but also various plans for using air power on behalf of coercive diplomacy were developed. While contemporary newspaper accounts and subsequent disclosures do not clarify the details, nonetheless major disagreements evidently were present among the members of the Johnson administration regarding the feasibility of coercive diplomacy against Hanoi and the way in which this strategy could be best tailored to increase the likelihood of its success, while controlling some of the major risks to which it would give rise.* In the end, however, it appears that Johnson did not follow closely any of the various available plans for using air power in a coercive mode which were laid before him. Rather, he felt it necessary to improvise the implementation of his coercive objective, just as Kennedy had done in the earlier two crises we have studied. In fact, as Simons shows, the administration felt obliged to pursue a number of different objectives when it began to escalate, and this encouraged improvisations at variance with the strategy for coercion. If the Joint Chiefs of Staff could, as it did, express criticism that its advice for stronger military escalation had not been followed by the president, others in the administration could be critical on the opposite grounds that the president had made too crude and open an effort to intimidate Hanoi, one that was bound to boomerang and strengthen Hanoi's motivation to resist.[4]

We have stressed that coercive diplomacy requires skill in tailoring the strategy to the special configuration of a particular situation. We must add, however, that skill can contribute to the successful application of the strategy only if the conditions that favor it are present in that situation. Skillful tactics can only capitalize on favorable conditions already latent in the situation; skill cannot compensate for the absence of these favorable conditions. This is certainly one of the major lessons and warnings to be drawn from this study.

We have seen that Kennedy was indeed skillful in turning to account those aspects of the Laos and Cuban missile cases that favored coercive diplomacy. But, as we stressed particularly at the end of the Cuban case study, there was no guarantee that Kennedy would be able to capitalize upon the favorable conditions present

---

* Since Simons's case study has a different research focus, it provides only a glimpse of these disagreements. See especially pp. 150, 164–168, 173.

in these two crises. Nor was there any way of predicting that he would tailor the strategy skillfully to the configuration of the situation. It could easily have been otherwise. We saw in Chapter Three how extremely difficult it was for Kennedy to apply coercive diplomacy effectively in the Cuban missile crisis even though he possessed overall strategic and tactical military superiority over his opponent.

On the other hand, when conditions that favor the strategy of coercive diplomacy are lacking in a particular situation it becomes harder than ever, if not impossible, to deal skillfully with the many problems of operationalizing the strategy, of tailoring it to the situation. We saw this vividly in the case of Johnson's effort to coerce Hanoi. Precisely because the administration attempted coercive diplomacy in the absence of favorable conditions, its implementation was marked by considerable ineptness.

To regard skill as the most critical factor on which the success of coercive diplomacy depends, then, would be superficial and misleading. Too sharp a focus on skill in policy implementation encourages a narrow, technocratic approach to strategy, one that emphasizes the importance of techniques of manipulation as if to imply that one can hope to overcome more fundamental contextual disadvantages in a conflict situation by sheer virtuosity of technique in signalling and bargaining. Accordingly, the basic criticism of the Johnson administration's handling of coercive diplomacy against Hanoi concerns not its inept implementation of the strategy but rather its failure to recognize that the situation was intrinsically wrong for it.

For this reason we have thought it particularly important in this concluding chapter to identify more sharply the specific kinds of problems encountered when one attempts to operationalize the strategy of coercive diplomacy, that is, tailor it to the special, always somewhat unique configuration of a particular crisis. We have identified six problems or tasks of this kind that may be expected to arise in every case in which this strategy is employed:

1. Risks of an ultimatum   Will ultimatum be provocative?
2. Conflict between crisis management and coercive diplomacy   Will adherence to requirements of crisis management dilute sense of urgency needed for coercion?

3. Timing of strong coercive threats	Has opponent been sufficiently impressed with your determination to regard coercive threat as credible?
4. Timing of negotiations	Can negotiations be delayed until opponent is sufficiently impressed with your determination?
5. Content of carrot and stick	Are the carrot and stick adequate to overcome opponent's disinclination to accept demand?
6. Timing of carrot and stick	Can the carrot and stick be applied before military actions harden opponent's determination?

1. The Risks of an Ultimatum

The first problem concerns the risks of an explicit ultimatum. As our account of the Cuban missile crisis suggests, a responsible leader such as Kennedy, even when strongly motivated by what is at stake, draws back from the risks of giving an ultimatum to an opponent who is also strongly motivated and commands formidable military capabilities of his own. To be sure, in their early planning sessions Kennedy's advisors did briefly consider a private diplomatic ultimatum to Khrushchev. They quickly abandoned this option, however, for fear that either it would not be credible or might provoke Khrushchev into seizing the initiative himself.

Eventually Kennedy found himself forced to transmit a virtual ultimatum to Khrushchev, but he did so through oral diplomatic channels rather than in a formal written note. In the Laos case, Kennedy's threat of military intervention was in the context of a veiled, indirect ultimatum which remained unspoken. In the Vietnam case, so far as we know, the pressure exerted on the opponent fell far short of even an informal and implicit ultimatum.

2. Conflict Between Crisis Management and Coercive Diplomacy

The second problem — the conflict between the requirements of prudent crisis management and effective coercive diplomacy — was evident in all three crises. Several of the requirements of crisis management listed in Chapter One (pp. 8–11) conflict with the requirements of the ultimatum variant of coercive diplomacy, which requires, above all, that a sense of urgency be created for the opponent's compliance with the demand made on him. Crisis management, on the other hand, requires that the momentum of military actions be slowed down and spaced out, and this may easily conflict with the need to generate a sense of urgency.* Crisis management also requires that the opponent be given enough time to receive and reflect on the signals and communications directed toward him, to reconsider his goals and probable costs, and to set into motion the desired changes. But granting him time for this inevitably risks that he will choose to use it for other purposes — to mount counter-pressure to undermine the strategy of coercive diplomacy directed toward him, to increase his own military preparations, or even to seize the military initiative. Finally, crisis management requires that time be provided for ample communications back and forth and for ad hoc negotiations; but this, too, risks a dilution of the sense of urgency needed to apply and enforce the ultimatum variant of the strategy of coercive diplomacy.

The tension, if not conflict, between some of the requirements for crisis management and those of coercive diplomacy can be seen in the three cases we have examined. In the Laos crisis Kennedy was forced to weaken his tacit ultimatum of March 23 somewhat by being ambiguous with regard to its time limit. This he did in order to give the other side sufficient time to consider and concert its response.

In the Cuban case, the need for prudent crisis management dominated in Kennedy's handling of the crisis in the first three and a half days — so much so that implementation of the blockade verged on the try-and-see approach. The president broke up the blockade option into a series of smaller steps which he applied one by one, jealously safeguarding and hoarding his usable options so as to maintain personal control of the conflict and to prevent it from reaching the dangerous point of no return toward war. For his careful adherence to prudent crisis management principles Kennedy paid a price. Khrushchev used the time given him to rush the missiles already in Cuba to completion and to devise and put

---

* Hence, as stated on p. 223, it is advantageous to generate urgency also through political-diplomatic means and not rely exclusively upon military measures for this purpose. Political-diplomatic moves tend to be less provocative and thus more in line with crisis management.

into effect a counter-strategy for salvaging as many gains as possible from his venture.

The requirements of crisis management can also be seen at work slowing up the pace of air attacks against North Vietnam. This is, indeed, an important part of the explanation for the fact that only a weaker form of coercive strategy was deemed possible by the president in this case.

The requirements for crisis management were in some respects even more complex in the Laos and Vietnam cases because the opponent in these two crises was not a single country — the Soviet Union, as in the Cuban crisis — but several autonomous Communist states. This complicated the effort to influence the calculations of the opponent in the desired direction. Let us consider the differences in this respect between the three crises in greater detail.

The momentum of events must be deliberately slowed up, as we have shown, to give the opponent time to deliberate. This is necessary whether the critical policy decisions in the crisis are made by the top leader on the other side or whether they emerge from the consultations of a larger policy-making group. One of the complexities and uncertainties of crisis management concerns the possibility that those who comprise the policy-making group on the other side will disagree over what the response of their government should be to the actions of the opponent. To the extent possible, the coercing power attempts to act and speak in ways that will strengthen the policy position of those members of the opposing government who are more disposed to accept the demands being made on it and to neutralize or weaken the influence of those who are opposed. At the same time, however, detailed information is usually lacking as to the range of policy views and the relative influence of their advocates within the opposing government. While the assumption that the members of the opposing government do not think alike on the relevant policy considerations may be entirely justified, it is not easy to acquire the detailed information that would enable the coercing power to make the fine adjustments in its own behavior in order to play upon these real or latent differences. At a critical point toward the end of the Cuban crisis, for example, Kennedy and his advisors had great difficulty interpreting an important sequence of seemingly inconsistent Soviet moves. They were not certain whether these moves were part of a well-integrated strategy determined by Khrushchev, whether the apparent inconsistency reflected the vagaries of bargaining and compromise within a badly divided Soviet policy-making group, or even whether Khrushchev had in effect been displaced from control of Soviet policy, which was then being determined by the hawks in the Soviet government. This refers, of course, to the sudden hardening of Soviet behavior and diplomatic position on Saturday, October 27, following the more conciliatory moves of the preceding day.

Difficulties such as Kennedy faced in the Cuban crisis are further compounded when the opponent in a crisis is not a single country but a multi-national opposition of several countries. Both the Laos crisis and the war in Vietnam confronted American policy-makers with this kind of opposition. The task of crisis management, therefore, was distinctly more complicated than it was in the Cuban missile crisis, which was essentially a confrontation between the two superpowers and, therefore, more like the earlier Cold War crises of the bipolar era. In Laos and in Vietnam the opponent was no longer a monolithic Communist world movement, dominated and directed by the Soviet Union. Now three or four independent Communist actors were significant in both of these two crises — the Viet Cong (Pathet Lao), Hanoi, China, and Russia — who simultaneously, but in different ways, were the targets of Washington's coercive diplomatic strategy. The interests of these separate Communist actors in the crisis at hand both overlapped and diverged in intricate ways that were not easily predictable, and certainly not easily manipulated by what the United States was doing or could do.

And yet the success or failure of the coercive diplomatic strategy Kennedy employed in Laos, and Johnson later against Hanoi, depended critically upon the ability to use force and, especially, the threat of additional force as a means of exerting political leverage to manipulate the relations and policies of the several Communist actors. Not only in retrospect, but also at the time — particularly in the Vietnam case — it was clear that Washington was undertaking an enormously complex and difficult assignment. In order to balance responsibly the possible gains and risks of the coercive diplomatic strategy, American policy-makers found it necessary to take a close, continuous reading of the impact of each major move upon the attitudes and interrelationships of the several Communist actors on the other side. Under these circumstances, neither Kennedy nor Johnson felt that he could commit himself in advance to any pre-programmed concept or plan of escalation. In each case the president thought he must proceed cautiously and play it by ear. Both the choice and the timing of the next step in pressure had to be decided after evaluating the effects of previous moves taken on the several members of the opposing line-up.

Kennedy eventually succeeded in orchestrating pressures on the members of the multi-national opposition in Laos so that a convergence of their policies accepting his demands finally emerged. This story is told in Chapter Two. Kennedy's initial increase in coercive pressure as expressed in military movements and in his March 23 news conference sufficed to erode the Soviet Union's disinclination to cooperate in his plan for a settlement. But the Soviet Union's initial efforts to influence the Pathet Lao and the North Vietnamese in this direction were not successful. Only with Kennedy's introduction of United States military advisers to the combat zones on April 19 did his threat of military intervention become sufficiently convincing.

In the Vietnam case the effort to apply coercive diplomacy in a similar manner to manipulate and orchestrate the opposing multi-national forces did not succeed. It is important, nonetheless, that Johnson felt himself compelled — as Kennedy had in Laos — to observe the requirements of crisis management in the intricate strategy directed toward a multi-national opposition. The administration thought the application of force in discrete, controlled doses was essential to permit the president to apply just enough political-diplomatic pressure at one point without pressing too hard at another point — that is, to threaten to "punish" North Vietnam severely enough to make "sitting it out" an unrewarding policy, yet not to damage Hanoi so precipitately that it would be driven into the hands of Communist China.[5] It also feared that China would intervene on a large scale if the pressure on one of its buffer states were too great. The lesson of Korea was not forgotten.

This was an extremely delicate set of balances to achieve, more difficult in Vietnam than it had been in Laos. The major differences are clear. Far more was at stake for Hanoi this time. In the 1961 situation, as Hall describes in Chapter Two, the priority Hanoi placed on furthering its objectives in South Vietnam made it unwilling to risk war with the United States in Laos, particularly as Kennedy was obviously engaged in a limited disengagement from Laos that left Hanoi's essential interests in that country intact. In 1965, on the other hand, Hanoi was on the verge of gaining finally its long-standing national aspirations in South Vietnam.

Moreover, the situation had changed also with respect to the Soviet Union. In 1961 the Soviet Union believed it had no interests in Southeast Asia worth a confrontation with the United States. Following Khrushchev's ouster in October 1964, however, the Soviet Union altered its stance toward Southeast Asia and reasserted a stronger interest in developments there and, as Simons reminds us in Chapter Four, was strengthening its ties and commitments to North Vietnam. As a result, it was far more difficult for Johnson to activate Soviet cooperation to persuade Hanoi to accept his demands than it had been for Kennedy to persuade Khrushchev to play this role in the Laos crisis.

Communist China's position, too, had changed in the intervening four years. In 1960–61, Peking was experiencing economic disaster on a nationwide scale following the collapse of its Great Leap Forward. It was in poor condition to intervene in Laos and refrained from suggesting that it might. By 1964–65 a considerable recovery had taken place and Peking repeatedly expressed its strong interest in the course of events in Vietnam.

Finally, and of considerable importance, as we have emphasized previously, Johnson's demands on Hanoi were much more ambitious than Kennedy's modest objectives in 1961. Kennedy's limited demands reduced the motivation of the members of the opposition to resist his pressure and gave him a chance, with Soviet cooperation, to orchestrate the relationship among them to his own advantage. Johnson's far-reaching objectives and demands, in contrast, maximized the disinclination of the members of multinational opposition to yield, made it far more difficult for the Soviet Union to resolve its ambivalence toward the heightened danger of war in favor of playing the same role it had in 1961, and generally increased to formidable proportions the task of coercive diplomacy. With respect to the Soviet Union, the contrast between Kennedy's strategy in 1961 and Johnson's in 1965 is striking. Johnson gave the Soviets no reasonable basis for trying to persuade Hanoi to negotiate. In the Laos crisis, because Kennedy's demands were more modest, the Russians could point to existing gains which Hanoi and the Pathet Lao would be allowed to keep.

It was not surprising that Johnson failed; it would have been far more surprising had he succeeded. The configuration of the situation this time was only superficially the same as it had been in Laos in 1961. Johnson's task of tailoring coercive diplomacy to the special configuration of the situation in Vietnam was substantially more difficult, if indeed not an impossible one.

One of the most important policy dilemmas revealed by our three case studies, therefore, is that prudent crisis management tends to conflict with the requirements for effective coercive diplomacy. This was true not only in the Vietnam case, in which Johnson could not bring himself to adopt the strong variant of the strategy because of the multiple constraints on his action; it was true also in the Laos and Cuban crises in which, under special circumstances, Kennedy finally converted an initial try-and-see approach to something approaching the ultimatum form of coercive pressure. The requirements of crisis management, it turns out, are much more compatible with the try-and-see approach than a stronger variant of coercive diplomacy.

3. The Timing of Strong Coercive Threats

The strong variant of coercive diplomacy can succeed only if the opponent accepts as credible the threat of punishment for non-compliance with the demands made upon him. Important subjective and contextual dimensions determine credibility, which is created not merely by the opponent's knowledge that the coercing power has the military capabilities to back its threat but even more so by the opponent's perception of the coercing power's willingness to do so.

The timing of coercive threats can be critical to their success in a crisis. If the ultimatum form of coercive diplomacy is tried before the opponent is sufficiently impressed with the determination of the coercing power in the matter at issue, the opponent may fail to regard as credible the coercing power's threat of punishment for non-compliance, creating a dangerous situation in which the opponent regards as bluff what is in fact a serious threat. The coercing power may then be faced with the need to carry out its threat or some portion of it. War may needlessly result from a miscalculation of this kind, whereas the coercive diplomatic strategy, more skillfully applied, might have succeeded in achieving an acceptable outcome without a costly escalation. Therefore, it is very much in the interest of the power attempting coercive diplomacy to establish whether the ground has been adequately prepared to ensure that the opponent will credit its coercive threat as being sufficiently credible as well as sufficiently potent.

The timing of coercive threats does not appear to have been as much a problem in the Laos case as in the other two crises. Nonetheless it is interesting that Kennedy made his dramatic TV presentation on the situation in Laos (March 23) a full day after the United States troop movements commenced. He did so, presumably, on the assumption that this prior action would reinforce the credibility of his statement. The problem of timing coercive threats was more critical in the Cuban missile crisis and, indeed, Kennedy recognized this. As we pointed out in Chapter Three, Kennedy saw that his only chance of getting the missiles out of Cuba without war lay in finding a way of impressing Khrushchev with his determination as never before since he had entered the presidency. Kennedy was attracted to the blockade option because it offered at least a possibility of correcting Khrushchev's misjudgment of his determination by means short of more dangerous, irreversible military actions against Cuba.

What helped the strategy of coercive diplomacy eventually succeed in this crisis was Kennedy's initial success in using the blockade to impress Soviet leaders with his determination. Kennedy's demonstrated willingness to impose the blockade, against the backdrop of the increasingly menacing American military build-up, very much strengthened the Soviet leaders' disposition to regard as credible the coercive threats Kennedy made several days later when he passed on a virtual ultimatum to Khrushchev.

But the initial actions one takes in a crisis — on which, in addition, one hopes to build the foundation for strong coercive threats later — may not always signal strong enough determination to the opponent. Rather, these initial actions may inadvertently signal timidity and irresolution; or they may be perceived as signalling a level of determination that falls short of the stronger resolution of the opponent who is, of course, attempting to judge how far the coercing power is really prepared to go should its demands be rejected.

Something of this kind happened in the Vietnam case. As Simons reveals, in early 1965 the political-psychological context was not at all favorable to an attempt to employ the strategy of coercive diplomacy against Hanoi. Having retaliated against North Vietnam in the preceding summer in response to the naval encounters in Tonkin Bay, Johnson dissipated the image of resolution he had thereby conveyed when he decided not to retaliate for the strong Viet Cong attack on the United States air base at Bien Hoa on October 31, 1964. The president once more decided against reprisal action after the Viet Cong attack on the American officers' billet in Saigon on December 24, 1964. Both of these attacks were on a large scale and were highly effective. In many ways they were much more flagrant provocations than the activity of the North Vietnamese vessels in the Tonkin Bay, and were in effect Hanoi's answer to United States retaliation at the time. Having tacitly announced the principle of retaliation at the time of Tonkin Bay, the president's failure to retaliate to the two attacks on important American installations in South Vietnam created an apparent inconsistency between his words and his actions. This generated doubts regarding the administration's resolve to take action to prevent the further deterioration of the political and military situation in South Vietnam, which was proceeding at a steady pace during the winter. No doubt the impression of United States irresolution was not lost on Hanoi, and it may have contributed to Hanoi's decision to step up pressure in the South in order to topple the Saigon regime altogether and force an American withdrawal.[6] Reestablishment of credibility "would be essential," Simons points out in his description of the attitude of Johnson's advisors in early 1965, "if the administration expected to use threats of further punishment to get Hanoi to alter its policies toward South Vietnam."

This was the policy background when the Viet Cong struck again in early February, this time at the important United States base at Pleiku. The retaliatory air raids against North Vietnam which quickly followed were an attempt to erase the image of United States irresolution and lack of determination. While the circumstances were quite different, the Johnson administration now faced the same kind of problem Kennedy had faced at the outset of the Cuban missile crisis: how to impress the opponent with his strong determination so that subsequent coercive threats would be regarded as sufficiently credible. The difficulties of accomplishing this initial tactical-psychological objective in the Vietnam context are suggested in Chapter Four. The initial American retaliatory attacks of early February were evidently judged within the administration to have been insufficient for this purpose. Additional air attacks took place in early March, but after weighing their effects in mid-March the administration concluded that it had not yet succeeded in conveying adequately its determination to the other side and stepped up the air attacks. At the same time, however, the reported deterioration of the ground war in South Vietnam was beginning to change the context of the air operations against the North.

This paved the way for the strong coercive pressure which the administration was to exert in early April when it directed the air attacks for the first time to bridges and other facilities, believing these targets to be of such great value to Hanoi as to make it vulnerable to coercive threats. Within a few days, however, Moscow and Hanoi both made clear their rejection of United States demands. In effect they called the bluff latent in the administration's effort to threaten worse damage for non-compliance. At this point, as we discussed earlier, the administration backed away from its strategy of coercive diplomacy and moved quickly toward a prolonged attrition strategy against Hanoi.* Thus, the administration had tried, over a period of two months (February–April) to create the image of great determination that would presumably lend credibility and persuasiveness to the stronger threats of early April. But the effort failed, and perhaps it was never regarded as more than a low-confidence strategy within the administration. In retrospect as well as at the time, it is obvious that the administration's multiple objectives and the many constraints imbedded in the situation made it extremely difficult if not virtually impossible for the president to deal effectively with this and other problems of operationalizing the strategy of coercive diplomacy.

4. The Timing of Negotiations

The effectiveness of coercive diplomacy may depend upon controlling the timing of negotiations. The coercing power may incur serious disadvantages if it is forced to enter into negotiations before it has demonstrated its determination and developed other needed bargaining assets. This possibility arose in the Cuban missile and Vietnam crises. In other circumstances, disadvantages may arise from a delay of negotiations. Thus, caught in a losing situation in Laos, Kennedy wanted an early cease-fire and negotiations in order to salvage as much as possible. His opponents would not cooperate, however; by continuing to advance on the battlefield they were improving both their political and bargaining position. Kennedy had to exert coercive pressure, in which he threatened

---

* Additional bridges and other facilities of value were attacked later on, eventually including electrical power plants, dams, petroleum facilities, etc., but this escalation was gradual and part of a try-and-see approach.

American intervention, in order to bring about a cease-fire and an agreement to negotiate.

In the Cuban missile crisis, on the other hand, Kennedy perceived that it was distinctly to his advantage to put off serious bargaining until he had succeeded in impressing Khrushchev with his determination to get the missiles out. Kennedy succeeded in delaying any bargaining over a quid pro quo until he had forced Khrushchev to back down over the blockade and had accumulated other important bargaining assets. Kennedy achieved this, moreover, without having to pay a high price in unfavorable domestic and international reactions to his delaying of negotiations. An interesting side-light to this is that Kennedy did not himself determine when the time had come for negotiations. Khrushchev helped Kennedy deal with this problem by initiating feelers for a quid pro quo settlement of the crisis.

In Vietnam, the administration lacked bargaining assets at the outset and had not conveyed its determination; accordingly, in February and March it sought to achieve a position of strength before beginning negotiations. Domestic and international pressures for negotiations intensified, however, and the administration paid an important political and diplomatic price for its quite obvious reluctance to enter into negotiations. On February 23 the Soviet government had publicly declared its support for seeking a negotiated settlement through reconvening the Geneva conference on Indochina — a possibility already advocated by de Gaulle. The administration, however, repeatedly took a tough line on a negotiated settlement in late February and early March.

At the same time it became evident that the administration was sticking to its ambitious war objectives and was demanding in effect Hanoi's withdrawal from the war, even though this was not specifically stated. This did not, it may be assumed, encourage the Soviet Union to continue to identify itself as an intermediary. In fact, as we noted earlier, it had the opposite effect, one highly damaging to Johnson's effort to play his cards in such a way as to activate the Soviet Union to play the same kind of helpful role it had done in the Laos crisis of 1961. By March 19 Moscow had reversed its earlier stand, making it clear now that it would not attempt to influence Hanoi to reduce its efforts in the South and seek a peaceful solution.

It was only in early April, after air attacks were escalated against high-value targets in North Vietnam, reaching thereby a new peak in coercive pressure, that the administration indicated a willingness to enter into unconditional negotiations. The administration had succeeded in delaying negotiations until it had improved somewhat its bargaining position. But the other side was not interested now. For, Johnson's offer of unconditional negotiations notwithstanding, there was little indication that the administration had really modified its objective of seeking a victory in the war in the South or reduced its demand for Hanoi's withdrawal.

5. The Content of the Carrot and Stick

In formulating the theory of coercive diplomacy in Chapter One we emphasized that the task of employing this strategy successfully can be relatively easy or quite formidable, depending on what one demands of the opponent and how strongly disinclined he is to do what is asked of him. To employ coercive diplomacy successfully, therefore, one must find a combination of carrot and stick that will suffice to overcome the opponent's disinclination to grant what is being asked of him.

In Laos Kennedy formulated a carrot and stick that was able to cope with the multi-national opposition's view of what was at stake. The president, as we have seen, relied largely upon a carrot — the substantial reduction of the United States objective in Laos — to create receptivity to what he asked. His threat of overt military intervention, presumably on a relatively small scale, sufficed to induce compliance with his demand.

There was greater emphasis on the stick in Kennedy's approach to his adversary in the Cuban missile crisis. But in this case, too, the carrot — Kennedy's willingness to give a no-invasion pledge regarding Cuba — played an essential role. In fact, as we have seen, Khrushchev himself suggested this as part of a quid pro quo by means of which the crisis might be ended.

In other circumstances and in other crises, however, the opponent who is the target of coercive diplomacy may not be so cooperative in helping to formulate the carrot that will contribute to an acceptable quid pro quo. In that event, as with respect to Hanoi in the first few months of 1965, the United States may have great difficulty in formulating a combined carrot and stick inducement that suffices to overcome the opponent's strong reluctance to do what is demanded of him. Johnson's formulation of the carrot and stick, when it finally emerged in early April, suffered from ambiguities as well as insufficient persuasive power. Not only was his attempt to step up pressure relatively mild, stopping well short of an ultimatum, but the positive inducement the administration offered, an offer of economic development for all of Southeast Asia, including North Vietnam, lacked precision, commitment, and perhaps credibility as well. Moreover, it smacked of a public bribe to Hanoi for abandoning the Viet Cong to their fate.

6. The Timing of the Carrot and Stick

Still another problem that may be critical in applying this strategy effectively concerns the timing of the carrot and stick. Assuming that the content of the combined carrot and stick is adequate in principle to overcome the opponent's disinclination to accept what is demanded, its effect may be spoiled if it comes too late, that is, after military operations have further hardened the opponent's determination and engaged his prestige, making it more difficult for him to accept what is asked of him.

As with so many other problems of tailoring the strategy of coercive diplomacy to a particular situation that we have already discussed, it is by no means easy for policy-makers to recognize when the moment is propitious to introduce the different elements of the carrot and stick. Hindsight in these matters can easily obscure the great uncertainties and misinformation with which the policy-makers may have to operate at the time.

Thus it turned out, contrary to Kennedy's pessimistic expectation, that his timing of the carrot and stick in the Cuban missile crisis was just right, neither too soon nor too late. The same cannot be said of Johnson's belated, as well as ambiguous, quid pro quo offers to Hanoi. Even were one to assume what is highly dubious — that the combined carrot and stick of early April was sufficient to neutralize Hanoi's strong disinclination to accept the ambiguous demands being made on it — Johnson's timing of it came after the American military actions probably had made it more difficult for Hanoi to back down or enter into negotiations. As Thomas Schelling has said, "The manner of threatened compliance must not entail costs in prestige, reputation, or self-respect that outweigh the threat. . . . Skill is required to devise a compellant action that does not have this self-defeating quality." [7]

IV. OTHER EXAMPLES OF AMERICAN EFFORTS TO USE FORCE AS AN INSTRUMENT OF DIPLOMACY

We can see the important limits and risks of the strategy of coercive diplomacy even more clearly if we enlarge the sample of historical cases beyond the three that we have considered.

1. The United States Effort to Coerce Japan in 1941 [8]

The most extreme risk that the strategy of coercive diplomacy may encounter is that of provoking the opponent to attack — the first problem in operationalizing this strategy. The leading example of this risk is the sequence of events leading to the Japanese attack on Pearl Harbor. This case is usually regarded, somewhat too narrowly, as a failure of deterrence; and various lessons have been drawn from the failure of United States intelligence analysts and policy-makers to evaluate properly the available indications of Japanese intentions.

What is often overlooked, however, is the broader context within which deterrence failed in this case. The United States government had been engaged for some months in a concerted, persistent effort at coercive diplomacy. Its aim was to persuade the Japanese government not merely to stop its imperialist expansion in Asia but also to give up the more ambitious objectives associated with this policy and some of the gains it had already made. In the language that became fashionable later in describing American objectives in the Cold War against the Soviet Union, the Roosevelt administration was pursuing the objectives of both containment and liberation vis-à-vis the Imperialist Japanese government. The line had been drawn, more or less clearly, against further Japanese advances in Southeast Asia. True, the Roosevelt administration was employing economic sanctions rather than threats of military force to secure compliance with its demands, but the economic pressure was extremely effective. The embargo on oil that the United States and its allies imposed on Japan, whose military forces were highly dependent upon petroleum imports, had the effect of creating the sense of urgency for compliance with American demands that is a critical part of the strong variant of coercive diplomacy. The United States gave no formal or even tacit ultimatum per se, but the oil embargo created the equivalent of a deadline. The Japanese government was confronted with a fundamental choice — whether to back down and retreat or to go to war — and it had to decide within a matter of months.

We shall not attempt a detailed analysis [9] of the various problems the strategy of coercive diplomacy encountered in this case, as we have done for the Laos, Cuban, and Vietnam crises. It is clear in retrospect, as it had become increasingly clear to Roosevelt and his advisors prior to the Japanese attack, that the administration had failed to formulate a carrot and stick that sufficed to overcome the strong unwillingness of the Japanese government to accept demands to curtail its aggressive activities in Asia. Nonetheless, Roosevelt refused to moderate his demands or to offer a larger carrot, even though evidence mounted that the Japanese government was going to act in Southeast Asia in such a way as to challenge the deterrence effort being made by Britain and the United States on behalf of weaker allies, and that such Japanese moves would trigger a military response, and war, with the Anglo-American powers. Hence, Roosevelt perceived and accepted the growing risk of war with Japan. In the days before Pearl Harbor, the high probability and imminence of war was evident; the surprise lay only in not expecting that the Japanese attack would come at Pearl Harbor.

Deterrence failed in the end — resulting in the surprise attack on Pearl Harbor — because Roosevelt's effort at coercive diplomacy completely boomeranged. The ambitious objectives which he pursued by means of this strategy backed the Japanese government into a corner without leaving open an acceptable way out. Caught in this trap, with its highest national-imperialist aspirations at stake, a desperate Japanese government chose the desperate, low-confidence strategy of war with the United States, for it perceived the only alternative permitted it as even less acceptable.

2. The Korean War

The North Korean attack on South Korea in late June 1950 took American leaders by surprise. The North Koreans attacked in full force, hoping to secure a quick military seizure of South Korea before the United States had an opportunity to reconsider its earlier policy of limited commitment to defense of its ally. When confronted by an opponent's resort to the quick, decisive strategy that is designed to create a fait accompli, it is particularly difficult for the protecting power — the United States in this case — to stop or reverse the action taking place quickly except by a strong variant of coercive diplomacy. In Korea, contrary to Soviet and North Korean expectations, the Truman administration did react almost immediately to the attack, reversing the many indications it had given in the preceding months that it had disengaged from its commitment to help defend South Korea against attack. In the first week of the war Truman gradually increased the level and scope of American military operations. But these escalations (a term that has come into use only more recently) had inconsequential military effects on the powerful North Korean forces that were brushing aside the South Korean forces and overrunning the country. Moreover, the piecemeal United States intervention had no discernible political effect on the willingness of the North Korean and Soviet governments to continue military operations against South Korea.

Truman and his advisers gave little or no consideration to employing strong coercive diplomacy in an effort to persuade the North Korean government to halt or pull back its forces. Washington expressed a hope, not a demand, that the North Koreans would call off or halt their aggression, particularly when they encountered token United States combat forces on the battlefield. Washington did not attempt to place the other side under immediate, urgent pressure to call off its action or to limit its scope and objectives. At the most, Truman limited himself to a cautious application of what we have called the try-and-see approach. In fact, a full-fledged American commitment to defend South Korea developed only gradually, in stages, during the first week of the war. Without attempting a fuller explanation here, we can state that crisis management considerations played a role in Truman's caution. The basic assumptions of American foreign policy vis-à-vis the Soviet Union were sharply challenged by the North Korean attack, which came as a distinct surprise and shock. In the first few days of the crisis the administration feared that the North Korean attack meant that the Soviet Union was ready, contrary to Washington's expectations, to risk World War III. Truman's commitment to South Korea developed slowly in part because he and his advisors were initially concerned about the risk of Soviet involvement in the war and the possibility that American intervention would provoke the Soviets and lead to world war. It was only the mild, reassuring Soviet reply on the fifth day of the crisis to an American diplomatic note probing Soviet intentions that relieved the administration of this fear.[10]

3. The Quemoy Crisis of 1958 [11]

Eisenhower was forced to respond to an opponent's move that differed altogether from the kind of challenge the North Korean attack had posed for Truman. The Chinese Communists limited themselves to heavy artillery fire against the large Nationalist garrison on the island of Quemoy, only a few miles from the mainland. This was a limited, carefully controlled military-political probe, rather than the kind of all-out fait accompli that the North Koreans had attempted against South Korea. The Chinese artillery fire was shrewdly designed to clarify United States intentions in the first instance rather than to test Chinese Nationalist and American capabilities for defending the offshore islands. In principle, a limited probe of this kind should be easier to reverse by means of a coercive diplomacy than an all-out fait accompli. But, interestingly enough, the Eisenhower administration did not respond by means of coercive diplomacy. In fact, this strategy was given little if any consideration in the administration's deliberations as to how to respond. Operating under severe constraints on his freedom of action, Eisenhower chose the make-shift strategy of attempting to cope with the situation pretty much within the framework established by the opponent's action without either escalating to a more favorable set of ground rules or threatening to do so as part of an effort to coerce the Chinese Communists to stop the artillery shelling.

The Eisenhower administration was not confronted with the immediate necessity of providing a high confidence defense of Quemoy. So long as the Chinese Communists limited themselves to artillery shelling and attempted no invasion, the defensive task would be limited to resupplying and maintaining the large Chinese Nationalist garrison under fire on Quemoy. But first, the administration had to answer the question of United States intentions implicit in the Chinese Communists' limited probe. Eisenhower's task, given his judgment that too much was at stake to allow Quemoy to fall, was to signal his intention to help defend it and to do so clearly, convincingly, and early enough in the crisis to forestall a possible miscalculation by the other side that might lead to an increase of Communist actions and thereby risk an expansion of the conflict. This, in fact, the administration did, conveying its commitment to prevent the loss of Quemoy.

But while Eisenhower's response disappointed any hopes the Chinese Communists might have had that he would be willing to see Quemoy fall or that he would urge Chiang Kai-shek to give it up in the interests of peace, the administration's response also inevitably conveyed that its commitment was quite limited and that it was inclined to give the Chinese Nationalists only indirect military assistance to ensure resupply of Quemoy. It was amply clear, because Eisenhower wished to make it so in order to cope with strong apprehensions and criticism both at home and abroad, that the administration wished to and would try to avoid the political-military costs associated with a stronger response. In the absence of any real pressure or coercive threats to cease the artillery shelling, the Chinese Communists decided to continue it. They could well afford to wait and see whether the Nationalist Navy, with quite limited, but in the end decisive, American assistance, would be able to resupply Quemoy. In the meantime, the Chinese Communists could and did attempt to exploit the situation politically and diplomatically.

What is important is that Eisenhower was willing to employ this make-shift strategy even though it was considered distinctly unpromising. His advisors were uncertain and pessimistic at first that resupply operations would be successful. Nonetheless, Eisenhower was willing to try because he thought the alternative strategies either infeasible or too risky. Given the limited American commitment and the initial uncertainty that measures to resupply Quemoy would succeed, there remained a question as to what Eisenhower would do should the resupply operation fail. Such a contingency would have faced the administration with a need to step up United States participation. Direct American naval and air operations to ensure resupply were possible. The options for this existed; the question is whether the president would have used them. Faced with the risks of escalation, would Eisenhower and Dulles have weakened in their adherence to their announced objective and sought a compromise solution that would have also compromised the status of Quemoy? We cannot be certain, but this possibility can by no means be excluded.

Both the Korean War and the Quemoy crises — other examples could also be found — are cases in which the strategy of strong coercive diplomacy did not recommend itself to American policy-makers. Without attempting a more detailed explanation here, we can state that many of the eight conditions identified above that favor adoption and implementation of the strong variant of coercive diplomacy were not present in these two cases.

V. THE LIMITS OF POWER AND WILL

Coercive diplomacy is understandably attractive when compared to the alternative strategies that were discussed in Chapter One. It offers the leaders of a country an opportunity to achieve their objectives in a crisis with much greater economy than strategies that rely more directly and exclusively on use of force. If the coercive strategy can be made to work successfully, it is a less costly, less risky way of achieving one's objectives than traditional military strategy.

But the attractiveness of coercive diplomacy must not be allowed to prejudge the question of its feasibility in any particular situation. The beguiling character of the strategy may easily distort the judgment of policy-makers who are confronted by a difficult crisis that poses damage to national interests they would like to avoid. The problems of operationalizing the strategy of coercive diplomacy, as we have discussed, are many. Skill is certainly necessary to deal with these problems adequately, but even an unusually skillful policy-maker can accomplish little when the basic pre-conditions favoring this strategy are lacking. Adding to the risks is the fact that it is often not self-evident whether these basic conditions are present in a crisis situation; the policy-maker can easily err in assuming that the fundamental configuration of the situation is more favorable to coercive diplomacy than is in fact the case. Further, the informational requirements of the strategy are complex and also difficult to meet. A particularly good knowledge of the opponent is necessary in order to estimate properly his motivation and his cost-benefit calculations on the basis of the fragmentary and equivocal information typically available on these matters.

For all these reasons, there will be few crises in which coercive diplomacy — and particularly the strong variant of it that attempts to meet all three components of a classical ultimatum — will constitute a feasible and useful strategy. The reasons for this conclusion, we have emphasized, are many and complex. One can disagree as to the relative importance of the various constraints on the strategy that we have mentioned; and one can also quarrel with the role we have assigned to some of these factors in trying to account for the success or failure of this strategy in the crises we have examined. It is too soon to write definitive histories of every aspect of these crises; indeed that may never be possible. At the same time, it is urgent to learn the lessons that recent history holds for policy-making. We have attempted, therefore, to draw such lessons from plausible interpretations of the historical cases. Whatever the scope of scholarly disagreement in this respect, it surely excludes the simple-minded proposition that to coerce an opponent successfully is, as some imply, merely a matter of the president exercising our national resolution or guts to threaten, and use if need be, the ample military capabilities at our disposal.

So much has been usefully said in recent years about the limits of military power as an instrument of foreign policy that we can hardly hope this book has done more than to reinforce this message by clarifying in some detail why this is so. The prudent statesman knows, or should know, that power does not create national will, beyond a certain limited point. The availability of ample power does not enable him to forgo a sober calculation of the extent to which important national interests are really at stake in a Third World conflict, and what level of costs and risks the public can be reasonably expected to accept. The degree of national motivation available to him is not open-ended; it is manipulable only within sharp limits.

The distinguished historian of the Renaissance, Jacob Burckhardt, made the wry remark that the true use of history is not to make men more clever for the next time but to make them wiser forever. One such lesson emerges from the Vietnam tragedy that is not particularly novel but is easily forgotten. Military power is of greater value to diplomacy when it is not used too often. When it is used, it should not be relied upon to accomplish difficult and complex objectives. The wise statesman of a powerful country knows the value of restraint in both the objectives and means of foreign policy. He will try to avoid actual use of military power on behalf of his objectives. When he feels it necessary to threaten use of force on behalf of what he asks of others he would be wise to threaten only on behalf of the most important of his country's interests and to make modest, not far-reaching demands on others. It is prudent as well as moral that the strong should respect the vital interests of the weak.

NOTES

1 These arguments were drawn together and forcefully stated in "Gradualism — Fuel of Wars," prepared by the Task Force on National Security, for the Republican National Committee, March 1968.

2 I am indebted to David Hall for the observations in this paragraph.

3 Thomas C. Schelling, *Arms and Influence* (New Haven: Yale University Press, 1966), pp. 74f.

4 See, for example, the article by Robert Kleiman, *New York Times*, March 1, 1965. Both types of criticism are briefly summarized in Simons's study, pp. 164–168, 173.

5 Several newspaper accounts at the time observed and discussed this problem. See, for example, the articles by Max Frankel, *New York Times*, March 5 and 7, 1965. I am also indebted to Arnold Horelick's observations on this point.

6 Philip Geyelin argues this thesis in *Lyndon B. Johnson and the World* (New York: Praeger, 1966), pp. 200–202.

7 Schelling, *Arms and Influence*, pp. 84, 89.

8 I am indebted to Professor Nobutaka Ike for comments on this section.

9 See, for example, Robert Butow, *Tojo and the Coming of the War* (Princeton: Princeton University Press, 1961); Nobutaka Ike, tr. and ed., *Japan's Decision for War* (Stanford: Stanford University Press, 1967); James Herzog, "Influence of the United States Navy in the Embargo of Oil to Japan, 1940–1941," *Pacific Historical Review*, XXXV (August 1966); Chihiro Hosoya, "Miscalculations in Deterrent Policy: Japanese-U.S. Relations, 1938–1941," *Journal of Peace Research*, II (1968).

10 Harry S Truman, *Memoirs; Years of Trial and Hope*, II (Garden City, N.Y.: Doubleday, 1956), pp. 331–348. The most detailed account of American policy-making in response to the North Korean attack is Glenn D. Paige, *The Korea Decision* (New York: Free Press, 1968). See also Alexander George, "American Policy-making and the North Korean Aggression," *World Politics*, VII (January 1955).

11 No single authoritative study of United States policy during this crisis exists. Eisenhower's *Waging Peace* (New York: Doubleday, 1965) contains useful materials as do other memoirs of his administration. Various aspects of the crisis are dealt with in publications by scholars such as Tang Tsou, Alice L. Hsieh, Morton H. Halperin, Robert W. Barnet, Thomas C. Schelling, Donald Zagoria.

BIBLIOGRAPHY

Butow, Robert, *Tojo and the Coming of the War* (Princeton: Princeton University Press, 1961).
Eisenhower, Dwight David, *Waging Peace* (New York: Doubleday, 1965).
Frankel, Max, *New York Times*, March 3, 5, 1965.

George, Alexander, "American Policy-making and the North Korean Aggression," *World Politics*, VII (January 1955).

Geyelin, Philip, *Lyndon B. Johnson and the World* (New York: Praeger, 1966).

Herzog, James, "Influence of the United States Navy on the Embargo of Oil to Japan, 1940–1941," *Pacific Historical Review*, XXXV (August 1966).

Hosoya, Chihiro, "Miscalculation in Deterrent Policy: Japanese-U.S. Relations, 1938–1941," *Journal of Peace Research*, II (1968).

Ike, Nobutaka, tr. and ed., *Japan's Decision for War* (Stanford: Stanford University Press, 1967).

Kleiman, Robert, *New York Times*, March 1, 1965.

Paige, Glenn D., *The Korea Decision* (New York: Free Press, 1968).

Schelling, Thomas C., *Arms and Influence* (New Haven: Yale University Press, 1966).

Task Force on National Security, "Gradualism — Fuel of Wars," for Republican National Committee, March 1968.

Truman, Harry S, *Memoirs; Years of Trial and Hope*, II (Garden City, N.Y.: Doubleday, 1956).

APPENDIX: NOTE ON
THEORY AND METHODOLOGY*

As indicated in Chapter 1, coercive diplomacy is one of four strategies available to the policy-maker when an opponent encroaches on his interests. Since we examined only the coercive diplomatic strategy in this study, our research objective was confined to identifying the conditions under which this strategy is likely to be a viable one. That is, we could not compare systematically the relative utility of the four strategies in a variety of contingencies, but we did attempt to formulate a partial, rational-choice model geared to the following question: When is it reasonable for the policy-maker to choose the strategy of coercive diplomacy or to entertain it seriously? We attempted to clarify this issue by identifying the conditions or factors that affected the outcome of the conflict when this strategy was employed in three historical cases, two in which the strategy succeeded, one in which it failed.

From the comparative analysis of the outcomes of these cases in Chapter 5 we identified eight "conditions" that favor success with the strategy. These conditions were present in the two cases in which choice of the strategy led to a successful outcome; most of them were absent or present in a weak form in the case in which an attempt to use the strategy resulted in failure. We suggest, therefore, that a rational, sophisticated policy-maker should not give serious consideration to adopting this strategy if he believes that these eight conditions are weakly or uncertainly present in that situation and cannot be strength-

---

* This Appendix was prepared by Alexander George.

255

ened by means at his disposal. He should not do so because, according to our empirically derived theory, the probability of achieving a successful outcome will be low in the absence of those conditions.

This, however, does not suffice for a rational-choice model. While these eight conditions "favor" the probability of a successful outcome, by no means do they guarantee it. For, clearly, the outcome obtained from the strategy will be dependent upon additional variables, some of which we identified in section III of Chapter 5 when we discussed the six difficult problems policy-makers have encountered in trying to implement the strategy by tailoring it to the specific configuration of a given situation. Therefore, we emphasize that a prudent policy-maker should not choose this strategy merely on the basis of having ascertained as best he can that the eight favoring conditions are present. Before selecting coercive diplomacy as his strategy, he should also consider whether he would be able to deal adequately with the six difficult problems that may arise in any attempt to implement it.

More simply, the policy-maker must choose not merely on the basis of what is the "correct" or "best" strategy in principle, since even the "best" strategy will result in success only if it is skillfully implemented. A novel feature of our theory of rational choice is that it subjects "skill," usually treated by theorists as an elusive residual category, to detailed empirical analysis and codification.

The distinction we have observed here between the policy-maker's choice of a strategy (or, as it is often called, the "decisional output") and policy "outcome" is a standard and useful one in the study of public policy.* It is possible to use the empirical findings drawn from our comparative case analysis for purposes other than constructing a rational-choice model. As already suggested, our theory has some value also for explaining and predicting outcomes. Finally, we should recognize that neither for policy prescription, explanation, nor prediction have we the data needed for constructing more rigorous models. We have only considered three historical cases, and we have had to introduce seven simplications and approximations into our formulation and analysis of the eight "favoring" conditions.

First, our analysis of the relation of the eight conditions to the outcomes of crises in which coercive diplomacy was attempted is, in effect, a selective summary of what we believe have been the critical elements in the estimates and expectations of the two sides.† (The conditions are

---

* See, for example, Austin Ranney, ed., *Political Science and Public Policy* (Chicago: Markham, 1968), p. 8.

† The eight conditions do not exhaust all possibly relevant variables. A ninth condition, for example, might be the need for international support from allies and neutrals.

a shorthand way of referring to these perceptions, estimates, calculations.) The question arises whether each condition would have to be present in the perceptions of both the coercing power and its opponent in order for coercive diplomacy to succeed. Such a shared perception would undoubtedly increase the likelihood of success, but coercive diplomacy may succeed under other circumstances. As noted on pages 227–8, the three perceptions *by the opponent* that appear to be particularly important in this respect are: that he believe there is an asymmetry of motivation in the situation that favors the United States; that he experience an acute sense of urgency for compliance with the United States' demand; that he fear unacceptable escalation. While it is not likely that the opponent will perceive these three "conditions" to be present in the situation unless there is some basis in reality for his perception, it is important to recognize that the opponent's behavior is determined by his perceptions of these three factors, correct or incorrect, and that his perceptions may not coincide with those of American leaders. Thus, for example, American leaders may experience a greater or lesser sense of urgency for achieving their objective than the opponent perceives; or they may feel they have conveyed a threat of imminent escalation that reflects their true intentions while the opponent has not recognized the threat. The opportunities for misperception and miscalculation are numerous.

It would be desirable to state the various causal configurations associated with the success or failure of the strategy more precisely, but we have not attempted it in view of the difficulty of the task. In any case, the more loosely stated analysis of favoring conditions presented in Chapter 5 is not without value for explanatory and predictive purposes and can be useful to the policy-maker as well as the investigator.

Second, we have considered these conditions in qualitative terms; that is, we have asked merely whether each was present or absent in the historical case examined. Of course, some of these conditions are subject in principle to quantitative measurement. Were it possible to do so, it would be desirable for some purposes to measure more precisely the strength of the condition or variable in each historical case. At the same time, however, variables of this kind tend to be dealt with by the decision-maker in rather gross, qualitative terms, and precise measures of the variables, therefore, should not be confused with the nature of the subjective perception of them operative in the decision-maker's mind. The value of precise measurement lies in other directions, for example, in the possibility of correlating or calibrating independent precise measures with the cruder, qualitative evaluations that enter into the decision-maker's calculus.

Third, judgments regarding the presence or absence of a condition were sometimes difficult to make with complete confidence. Historical materials available on the calculations and estimates of American leaders often permitted quite plausible inferences, but to make judgments it was necessary not only to interpret available clues but also, particularly in the case of the opponent's calculations, to make post-facto reconstructions of the kind the historian often makes. While this is not entirely satisfactory, it is the best that we could do. Moreover, not only the investigator who later studies these historical cases but also the policy-maker at the time has difficulty in deciding whether a condition is really present. In some respects, only the actions taken during the crisis by the policy-maker and the outcome itself can clarify whether some of the conditions assumed to favor coercive diplomacy were indeed sufficiently present in the situation. This is true particularly with respect to the three perceptions by the opponent that appear critical to the success of the strategy.

Fourth, the presence or absence of a condition, of course, does not establish its causal importance. The small number of historical case studies available for analysis meant that assessment of causal importance by means of statistical analysis was not possible here. The causal importance attributed to these conditions, therefore, rests upon use of the historian's method of causal imputation in explaining a single case. Confidence in the imputation of causal status to these conditions was reinforced by describing and comparing the role they played in the three cases examined — two of them examples of successful outcomes, the third a case of failure.

Fifth, it was also difficult to clarify the relative contribution that each type of condition made to the outcome of any given historical case. We would have liked to be able to determine the precise causal importance of each condition in each case and to assign "weights" to each. Once again, however, what is possible in principle was difficult in this case to achieve in practice. (This task is further complicated by the fact that not all of these conditions are independent of each other.*)

Sixth, we have avoided attempting to ascertain which of these conditions are "necessary" for the choice of the coercive diplomacy strategy and for its successful employment. While we believe that some conditions (asymmetry of motivation, sense of urgency, opponent's fear of unacceptable escalation) are more important than others (e.g. strength of United States motivation, availability of usable options), we do not wish to go so far as to assert that even these are "necessary" conditions. Rather, we are content to settle for a different

---

* The fact that causal variables are not independent of one another complicates construction of a model and may require the use of complex statistical methods. See, for example, Hayward Alker, "The Long Road to International Relations Theory: Problems of Statistical Nonadditivity," World Politics, XVIII (July 1966), pp. 623–655.

(and easier) formulation of the presumed causal importance of all these conditions. Hence, we have suggested that the presence of these conditions "favors" the adoption of the strategy and its successful implementation. Admittedly, this avoids the more useful, but also more difficult, task of ascertaining whether some of them are "necessary" and "sufficient" conditions.

Seventh, in this connection, we called attention to the likelihood that the same causal pattern will not be found in all cases of successful coercive diplomacy. That is, we must expect that *different weighted combinations* of the conditions will result in the choice and successful outcome of coercive diplomacy. In one crisis the unusual strength of some of the conditions (e.g. opponent's fear of unacceptable escalation, sense of urgency) may compensate for the weaker strength or absence of other conditions (e.g. adequate domestic support). In another crisis, the strength of other conditions (e.g. relative asymmetry of motivation) may compensate for the weaker strength of other conditions (e.g. sense of urgency, usable military options).

As these remarks suggest, there is much about the conditions and circumstances governing the success of coercive diplomacy that we simply cannot state precisely and reliably enough at this time for predictive purposes. We can offer only a partial and provisional theory, one that does not overstate what is known. Its limitations notwithstanding, it does have some prescriptive, explanatory, and predictive value. At the very least, the theory provides a useful, if not indispensable, check-list of relevant conditions that must be taken into account both for purposes of policy-making and for analysis of policy performance. For the policy-maker such a checklist, backed as it is by the three historical cases examined here, provides useful cautions against proceeding on the basis of possibly unwarranted assumptions.

INDEX

Abel, Elie, 112n, 127
Acheson, Dean, 87, 129
Adequate domestic political support:
in Cuba, 223–224
in Laos, 50–51, 224
as a precondition for coercive diplomacy, 216, 223–224, 227
in Vietnam, 151–152, 155–156, 224
Africa, 43
Air strikes in North Vietnam (see also Johnson administration and Vietnam coercion):
as a means of coercion, 144–146, 156–157, 164–165, 171–172, 177, 180
in reprisal for Viet Cong attacks, 144–145, 162, 166
shifting rationale for, 193–195, 197–198, 214
as a signal to: American public, 160–161; Communist China, 158–159, 163; North Vietnam, 158–159, 163, 178; South Vietnam, 159–160, 163; Southeast Asian allies, 160, 163; Soviet Union, 159, 163
Alsop, Joseph, 60, 62
Arab-Israeli War (1967), 17

Army of the Republic of Vietnam (ARVN), 154, 171, 186
Asymmetry of motivation favoring U.S. (see also Motivation of the opponent):
in Cuba, 136, 219–220
as a function of demands, 26
as a function of positive inducements, 25–26
in Laos, 75, 219–222
as a precondition for coercive diplomacy, 216, 218–220, 227
in Vietnam, 219–220
Attrition strategy, 19–20
in Vietnam, 195, 198–199
Australia, 37, 50

Baldwin, Hanson, 166
Ball, George, 112n, 162, 165, 181–182
Bay of Pigs, 90, 98
impact on Kennedy's Laos policy, 67, 70–71
Berlin, 6, 48, 92, 98, 130
Berlin blockade (1948), 20–21
Bohlen, Charles, 60, 63
Boun Oum, Prince, 40
Brown, Seyom, 56
Bucharest, 110

261

Johnson administration (*Cont.*)
  meet provocations, 153–154,
    159
  differences within, over Vietnam
    strategy, 167–168, 173
  lack of interest in negotiations,
    172–177
  military options available to, 154,
    156
  military planning for Vietnam
    War, 166, 188–189, 191–192,
    229–230
  perception of China's role in Viet-
    nam, 151; of international opin-
    ion on Vietnam, 155–156; of
    North Vietnam, 147; of South
    Vietnam, 152; of Russia's role
    in Vietnam, 152; of U.S. opin-
    ion on Vietnam, 151, 155
  renewed interest in negotiations,
    180–184
Joint Chiefs of Staff (JCS), 59, 155
  advice on Vietnam air strikes, 145,
    150, 156, 166, 173
  press for Cuban air strike, 127
  advice on Laos intervention, 49,
    69–70
Jupiter missiles:
  importance of, 123, 124
  as a positive inducement in Cuban
    crisis, 101–102
  Soviet bargaining over, 122–123,
    123n, 124n

Keating, Kenneth, 91
Kennedy, John F.:
  ability to keep options open in
    Laos, 78–79
  anxiety over continued Soviet mis-
    sile construction, 116–117
  correspondence with Khrushchev
    during Cuban crisis, 105, 108,
    120
  and the domino theory, 46–47,
    47n
  image of Khrushchev, 88, 99–100,
    106–107
  objectives in Cuban crisis, 94
  objectives in Laos crisis, 52, 61,
    71, 78
  options in Laos, 54–55
  personal stakes in Cuban crisis,
    89–91

Kennedy, John F. (*Cont.*)
  press conference on Laos, 59–60,
    60n, 61n
  and public opinion during Laos
    crisis, 50–51
  reaction to advisers' recommenda-
    tions on Laos, 49–50, 69–71,
    73
  reluctance to convey ultimatum in
    Cuban crisis, 117, 133
  talks with Khrushchev on Laos, 73
Kennedy, Robert F., 88, 102–103,
    112–113, 128
  meetings with Dobrynin, 108–109,
    125
Kennedy administration (*see also*
    Cuban missile crisis *and* Laos
    crisis):
  actions to dampen repercussions of
    Laos crisis, 71–72
  doctrine of flexible, controlled re-
    sponse, 5–8, 15–16, 147–148
  evaluation of Chinese attitude on
    Laos by, 44–45; of North Viet-
    namese objectives in Laos by,
    44; of Sino-Soviet split by, 44,
    44n; of Soviet objectives in Laos
    by, 43–44, 66; of U.S. interests
    in Cuba by, 89–94; of U.S.
    interests in Laos by, 45, 54–55
  warnings to Soviet Union prior to
    Cuban crisis, 91, 91n
Khanh, General Nguyen, 152, 161–
    162
Khrushchev, Nikita, 57, 62, 73, 89,
    94, 132 (*see also* Soviet Union)
  behavior toward new Kennedy ad-
    ministration, 42–43
  on decision to withdraw missiles
    from Cuba, 125–126
  initiates bargaining during Cuban
    crisis, 118–120
  reaction to American-Chinese de-
    mands on Laos, 63–65
Kleiman, Robert, 172
Kong Le, Captain, 39, 41
Korean War, 1–2, 4
  coercive diplomacy during, 246–
    248
  influence on U.S. strategy in Laos,
    42, 45, 49
  threat of Chinese intervention in,
    11–14